102

Twelve Who Cared

OTHER BOOKS BY
DOROTHY CLARKE WILSON

DR. IDA

PALACE OF HEALING

TAKE MY HANDS

TEN FINGERS FOR GOD

GRANNY BRAND, Her Story

LONE WOMAN

BRIGHT EYES

STRANGER AND TRAVELER

THE BIG-LITTLE WORLD OF DOC PRITHAM

HANDICAP RACE

HILARY

Dorothy Clarke WILSON

Twelve Who Cared

my adventures with Christian courage

HODDER & STOUGHTON
LONDON SYDNEY AUCKLAND TORONTO

Acknowledgment is made for permission to reprint selections from the following books by Dorothy Clarke Wilson:

Used by permission of Little, Brown and Co.: *Lone Woman*: The Story of Elizabeth Blackwell—The First Woman Doctor © 1970 by Dorothy Clarke Wilson; *Stranger and Traveler:* The Story of Dorothea Dix, American Reformer © 1975 by Dorothy Clarke Wilson.

Used by permission of McGraw-Hill Book Company: *The Big-Little World of Doc Pritham* © 1971 by Dorothy Clarke Wilson; *Bright Eyes:* The Story of Susette La Flesche, an Omaha Indian © 1974 by Dorothy Clarke Wilson. Used by permission of Hodder and Stoughton: *Dr. Ida:* The Story of Dr. Ida Scudder of Vellore © 1959 by Dorothy Clarke Wilson; *Handicap Race:* The Inspiring Story of Roger Arnett © 1967 by Dorothy Clarke Wilson; *Hilary:* The Brave World of Hilary Pole © 1973 by Dorothy Clarke Wilson; *Palace of Healing:* The Story of Dr. Clara Swain, First Woman Missionary Doctor, and the Hospital She Founded © 1968 by Dorothy Clarke Wilson; *Take My Hands*: The Remarkable Story of Dr. Mary Verghese © 1963 by Dorothy Clarke Wilson; *Ten Fingers for God* © 1965 by Dorothy Clarke Wilson.

British Library Cataloguing in Publication Data

Wilson, Dorothy Clarke
   Twelve who cared.
   1. Wilson, Dorothy Clarke – Biography
   2. Authors, American – 20th century – Biography
   I. Title
   818'.5'409   PS3545. 1623574/

ISBN 0 340 23276 5

Contents

Preface

Sometimes it seems that I have lived a dozen lives, not only my own but those of all the people whose thoughts, aspirations and most intimate emotions I have tried to penetrate as their biographer. And since each one of them has plumbed depths of faith and courage and scaled heights of achievement which I could never possibly attain, they have given my own life dimensions of spiritual fulfillment for which I must be forever grateful.

As I look back over the half century and more of my literary career—stories, plays, novels, biographies—I am amazed and humbled by the way one phase, even one book, has led inevitably into another. As a writer I have been a little like the chambered nautilus, leaving each compartment for the next, yet dragging the whole behind me. Not that I have "built more stately mansions as the swift seasons roll" or that each one has been "nobler than the last," but at least I have found each one vastly more interesting than the one before. And all the years preceding the writing of biography seem to have been preparation for this to me most fascinating adventure in literary creation.

Here then is a little of the story of those twelve who cared and my adventures in writing about them and learning from them. And to make the story complete, I should probably start with those years of preparation.

1
MYSELF

I was born in a parsonage. At that time sterile delivery rooms were not considered prerequisites for a normal life. On that Monday morning soon after midnight my father rushed to a neighboring town with horse and buggy to fetch a practical nurse, and delivery was by the family doctor.

I was lucky to be born at all, for my parents, married in their thirties, had feared the hazards of childbirth. My father, Lewis Herbert Clarke, one of ten children born on a pioneer farm in Minnesota (his parents having emigrated there from Maine in the 1850s) had put himself through law school late in life, and in the mid-1890s he came to Maine to collect back bills for a law firm. Attending a Baptist church one Sunday evening, he saw my mother, Flora Cross, directing a choir and apparently fell in love on the spot. She persuaded him to give up his law career and enter the ministry. After his three years at Newton Theological Institution they were married in 1899—secretly, because her father was so opposed to losing either of his two daughters. When I was born in 1904 he had been pastor of the First Baptist Church in Gardiner, Maine, for two years. I was definitely an accident.

The church next door, dominating our lives, was symbolic of my life to come. Most of my early memories are connected with it—sitting with my mother in the loft where she directed the choir (my father insisted that I sit there with her, to the displeasure, I was to learn later, of the somewhat rigidly

11

conventional congregation); going to innumerable "mission circles" in various homes, in one of which there was a child's chair in which I loved to sit; attending a beginners' class in Sunday School when my behavior, usually fairly circumspect, went sadly berserk and I joined a companion in consuming a bag of gumdrops, eliciting grieved rebuke from the shocked teacher and getting licorice stains on my favorite pink dress with black velvet trimmings. (Funny how clothes remain more vivid in detail than other things—or is that an early indication of character weakness?) But my most vivid memories of early years are the Bible stories my mother constantly told me, the characters becoming far more real than my few playmates. In fact, I remember no playmates at all. But Joseph, Daniel, Isaac, Rachel and a dozen others, especially of course Jesus, were childhood companions. Even then the fabric of my future career as a biblical writer was being woven.

When I was five life changed. My father, brought up on that farm in Minnesota, had a yearning for the land, and we moved to a 200-acre farm three miles out of Gardiner. It did not mean giving up the ministry. For two more years he continued to hold the pastorate in Gardiner. Then for many more years he preached each Sunday at two country churches several miles away. But the farm was his great joy, and it was to remain in his possession until he was ninety, six years from the end of his life.

I remember the move well. I can see myself sitting on the floor in the dining room while the flowered carpet was being tacked down and marveling at the new gadget, a telephone, attached to the wall. Most of the rooms had carpets with big flowered patterns. Damp sawdust was sprinkled over them to lay the dust when they were swept, and each spring they were put over a line and beaten. There were no vacuum cleaners, no electricity. Light was from kerosene lamps, their wicks trimmed and chimneys wiped out with newspapers and washed each day. There was no bathroom, only a seat at the end of the shed opening off the kitchen.

Though the house burned when I was nine, I remember its layout and furnishings—the "sitting room" with a closet where I kept my innumerable toys (because I was an only child and had few playmates I was badly spoiled); the music room where my Aunt Minnie, who came to live with us, started giving me piano lessons at the age of seven; the parlor with its horsehair furniture and sofa covered with red plush. Here were big portraits of my Grandmother and Grandfather Cross, the work of my mother, who had been a crayon portrait painter before her marriage (I was inexplicably afraid of them because their eyes, looking straight ahead, seemed to follow me); the kitchen with its big wood stove. One of my happiest memories is sitting in my nightgown in front of the open oven door and reading, the magic of books just opening to me. Over and over I read the first sentence of a beloved story about "Mr. Fitz-Herbert Bunnykins Bunny." Though I did not go to school until I was eight, since travel must be by trolley car and my parents were protective, my mother taught me at home, and reading became my greatest joy, books my most precious possessions.

Those fears of mine! They were terrible and profound, largely associated with death. Perhaps they began when I was six and my grandmother died. I went into the parlor, forgetting that her casket was there, and began playing on the floor. Looking up, I was paralyzed with fright. Did my fear of the portraits start then? I don't know.

I must have been a nervous little tyke. Witness my habit of stammering. My first recollection of it is at age seven, when we were visiting some cousins in Boston. Somehow I got into the wrong apartment and tried to explain to a strange woman. "I-I-" The words stumbled out. But the habit had not begun then. It was deep seated. Why? I was certainly not repressed, or changed from left-handed to right. Of course there was no speech therapy in those days. But it was to become a thorn in my flesh for many years.

In spite of such fears and drawbacks, plus the loneliness of being an only child, I had a happy childhood. My mother was a wonderful playmate. She could weave fascinating stories about live dolls and fairies, beloved figments of my overactive imagination. And life on the farm was vigorous and interesting. I knew the cows intimately, all named after flowers—Daisy, Buttercup, Lily, Pansy and so on. I played in the hay in the great haymows. I watched the milk being strained and separated in the front room of the cowshed. Sometimes I rode into town with my father on the high seat of his covered milk wagon, blazoned with the words: "Sun Soil Farm, L. H. Clarke, Proprietor." Each Sunday we went into Gardiner on the streetcar to church. I used to wander into the little cemetery across the street and pick checkerberry leaves and wild strawberries, my fear of the dead somehow not extending to those mute stones, some of them tipsy and blackened and moss-grown, with their fascinating inscriptions.

At age eight I started school, going each day on the streetcar passing our house and beginning work at about third grade level. It was a one-room school, ungraded, with classes ranging from beginners to high school entrance. The room was heated in winter by a big wood stove with a long pipe. Desks were double, but there were not enough pupils to necessitate putting two together. Of course this opened a new world. I had intimate friends, Evelyn, a freckled redhead, and Frances, a cheerful blonde extrovert whose home, more relaxed than mine, I enjoyed visiting. We three, all about the same age, were together constantly, often quarreling. Each recess we would go up to Archie Cole's little store near the school and buy candy, colored wafers, licorice whistles, penny peppermint sticks circled by finger rings. There were boys, of course, and when I criticize children today for starting to date too early, I recall those days. From age eight I was passionately interested in Everett, who lived up the road—until a new boy, Harold, moved into the neighborhood! Of course there was no dating, only much teasing and gossiping.

It was on the fifteenth of February, 1913, a Sunday, that our house burned. How well I remember every detail! The snow was four feet deep around the house, no roads plowed for several days after a big storm, no streetcars running. Though we had a furnace, we were using wood stoves that winter to save money. All at once I looked up at the little register above the stove in the dining room and saw flames playing around it.

"Oh—look!" I cried out to Dad.

He sprang up, fetched a fire extinguisher and sprayed it on the flames. Then he rushed upstairs. The bed in the room above was so charred that it fell down at his touch. Fire had smoldered for hours between the floors, and in no time smoke and flames filled the house. We rushed about trying to save a few things with that strange distortion of values which accompanies such a crisis. From a drawer in the dining room sideboard I salvaged a red soap dish containing forty-five pennies I had saved, forgetting that a five dollar bill lay next to it. My mother thoughtfully threw one of my dolls out a window, a "Campbell Kid" which I kept for years. Men clearing the roads saw the blaze from across the fields and came running, but

14

there was little they could do except relay pails of water from the well to my father, who, standing on the shed roof, managed to save the outbuildings.

I can still see my mother standing in the window of a neighbor's house calmly watching the destruction of a lifetime's dearest possessions. I can see my father coming to join us after the holocaust, blackened, clothes frozen stiff; I can hear him tell us, first of all, to get down on our knees while he thanked God that we were all safe. No lamenting over material loss, no word of complaint, only thanksgiving that, in spite of the gaping cellar with its two stark skeletons of chimneys, life's fundamental values remained intact. That day, I believe, I learned the true meaning of the Christian family.

And in the days that followed I had my first experience of wider Christian fellowship. Church friends opened their doors. They showered us with gifts—food, furniture, books, clothes, money. A new home rose phoenix-like out of the ashes as my father made over the old cowshed into a comfortable dwelling, covering the cement floor with wood, paneling the walls, separating the long building into four rooms arranged tandem, putting a porch on front.

I was living there when at age ten I first felt the urge to write. Going off in a corner one day I scribbled a poem which began:

> "Old Mrs. Witch in her very best gown
> Went sailing away on her broom;
> Away in the air she went whizzing on
> Till she thought she would hit the moon."

My mother helped correct the dubious rhymes. It was sent to a local paper's children's page and published. I kept on writing, mostly poems at first, then stories.

Books continued to be my greatest joy. I assembled many series like "The Bobbsey Twins," "The Motor Maids" and "Ruth Fielding," and read them avidly over and over. But not just these. I began reading Dickens at the age of ten. A collection of Dickens' children's stories had come in the donations, and I know the folks were a bit shocked when I pursued the adventures of Oliver Twist in the original. But I was by no means precocious in most respects. I continued to dote on dolls and fairy stories. The *Lewiston Journal* had a column each night called "Sandman Stories." I cut them out and collected a big shoe box of them. I can see myself running out to get the paper which was tossed off the streetcar each night.

When I was twelve we moved away from the farm. My father wanted to get into full-time religious work and became a traveling missionary for the Maine Baptist Convention, his work visiting churches which needed rehabilitation, a grueling and thankless job. Sometimes he was away for weeks at a time, traveling first with a horse, Old David, and buggy, later with a little Ford car. He suffered intensely being away from home so much, and often he would return with a headache. I can't say enough about the patience, taxing labor and loving concern of my father. The relationship between him and my mother was ideal. I never knew them to exchange a cross word.

Our new home was in Augusta, a rented upstairs flat behind the State House. I became a frequent visitor to the State House, especially the library. (I had no idea then that someday there would be a long array of my books in the State of Maine Authors' Collection!) Education in the old country school had been thorough, and I was able to enter the eighth grade in its A Division. Here stammering became an even greater bugbear and I suffered almost intolerably.

"Who's the little girl who stutters so?" I once overheard a teacher ask.

Recitations were a torture but I was stubborn enough never to be excused from choice. Perhaps because of this handicap I began to develop a yen for scholarship achievement which was to persist all through my school years. My new teacher was a tartar with a tongue razor sharp and very strict discipline but she laid a foundation in English grammar which was to undergird all my writing.

Church continued to be the center of our lives. We attended the Baptist church in Hallowell where my mother and aunt had gone in earlier years. The first January after we moved I was baptized, a memorable experience. The heat was inoperative in the baptistry and though attempts were made to warm the water all the afternoon by lowering into it hods of live coals it still felt like ice when I descended. The mechanics of the experience far outweighed its spiritual values. My father performed the ceremony. Later I went through agonies trying to stammer through a testimony at prayer meetings. Perhaps the

16

prospect of an ice cream cone at Hobbs' drugstore, where we waited for the streetcar after each meeting, helped to relieve the tension.

It was doubtless my attempts to compensate for stammering which explain my pursuit of high rank all through high school, so that I was able to graduate at the head of my class. Though the habit was never obvious in ordinary conversation, recitations continued to be torturing. Sometimes, I felt, I would gladly have changed places with a D student just for the ability to talk! Still I stubbornly refused to be excused from recitations, even speeches in English class, although I found to everybody's amazement that often, when I lost myself emotionally in a subject, I could deliver a speech without a hitch. A habit like this is incomprehensible to anyone not sharing it.

"I can't say 'butter,'" I might remark.

"But—you just *said* it!" would come the bewildering reply.

There were other compensations. I was a good athlete. There was continued piano study. And of course there was writing. All through high school I wrote poetry and stories about things unknown and far away with impossible plots —an American Indian boy who played the violin like a genius without previous experience, twins adopted simultaneously by a man and his wife, each independently of the other! Then, little realizing that I was setting a pattern for almost the next half century, at age fourteen I wrote my first biblical background story. It was called "Zerah's Gift," inspired by another story called "Zerah" but bearing no resemblance to its plot. It was published in a Maine Baptist paper called *Zion's Advocate*.

When I graduated from high school in 1921 it did not occur to me to be excused from delivering the valedictory. The essay was on "American Ideals." A beloved English teacher, Edith Rideout, trained me in its delivery. It was one of those occasions when I could lose myself completely in the subject, and I delivered it before about two thousand people without a sign of stammering. I am sure Edith, who has been my good friend ever since and has rejoiced in my small success as a writer, remembers that evening, not only the speech but the shy prudish child with the big brown eyes who, unlike all her classmates wearing coiffures with high pompadours and prominent "cootie garages" over their ears, graduated from high school with her hair in a braid down her back. The white

17

organdy skirt of my graduation dress which my mother so painstakingly embroidered is still kept in a box along with my wedding dress.

I may have been a mistake originally but as so often happens with an only child I had long since become the axis about which my parents' lives revolved. My father was embarrassingly eloquent in his travels about my small achievements and must have bored his friends to exasperation with readings from my poems and stories. Of course I had understood from the cradle that I must go to college. It was decided that I should go to Bates in Lewiston, Maine, and we moved to Lewiston so I could live at home. Even this taxed the family resources. I was not expected to work. All my time and energy must be devoted to my studies. My father was too proud to ask for a scholarship. He gave up his ministerial work and during my college years engaged in a multitude of activities, all taxing the utmost courage and strength of a man in his mid-sixties—selling stock for a big corporation until he became disillusioned with the management and could not sell it conscientiously, selling and installing furnaces and lightning rods, raising money for a college drive. My mother, always ingenious, eked out extras by baking cakes to sell in Lewiston stores, five cents for each piece. I still have some of the big pans she used. Oh yes, I was incredibly fortunate in having such parents who encouraged, guided without dictating, were as understanding of my failures as they were proud of my achievements. They also were fortunate in that I fitted without protest into their mold of creed, mores and inhibitions with none of the rebellion common to adolescents.

I met my future husband, Elwin Wilson, in my first year of college. He was a mature twenty-three to my volatile seventeen, but only a sophomore, having spent two years in military service in World War I plus a year on his family's farm before deciding to study for the ministry. Symbolically we met in church, a foretaste of our life for the next half century and more. One Sunday night he came to our church on a college deputation team. He was the proverbial "tall, dark, handsome" male, and I succumbed to his charms immediately. The next week I accompanied a group of young people to a Christian Endeavor convention in Portland which he also attended, and I mooned over him secretly throughout the meetings with-

18

out the slightest display of interest in return. On Sunday evening before the last service I saw him sitting in the back seat of the church and decided to make a bold approach.

"This isn't so good if you have a seven-forty class tomorrow morning," I observed.

He said afterward that this was the first intimation he had had that I was a college student. I looked too young. We conversed for a while, then he asked me to go out for a lunch. We ordered ham sandwiches, but I was too excited to eat.

That was how it all began, a romance that was to continue with a few stormy interludes due to my fickleness and immaturity and result in an engagement ring on my twentieth birthday. Its diamond was bright but exceedingly small, for he was working his way through college by mowing lawns, tending furnaces and preaching. Much of our dating was connected with church services, sometimes at his Methodist, sometimes at my Baptist church. That first spring I went with him to a meeting of the Annual Conference of the Methodist Church with Bishop Edwin H. Hughes presiding, little guessing that it was my first of more than fifty such conferences.

Another experience the following summer was portentous of the future. At a missionary conference for young people held at Northfield Seminary in Massachusetts, one of the leaders was a vivacious, blue-eyed, white-haired woman of about fifty who captivated us with her charm and stirred us to dreams of service with the story of her missionary call through "three knocks in the night" and her graphic pictures of the needs of Indian women. Would I have been surprised if I could have foreseen that thirty-five years later I would be flying to India to write the story of Dr. Ida Scudder's life!

I continued to write all through college, taking every English course possible. A literary club to which I was elected in my sophomore year stimulated creative zeal. Other classmates elected with me were Gladys Hasty, destined to become a successful professional writer, and Erwin Canham, long the editor-in-chief of the *Christian Science Monitor*. Gladys and I became intimate friends. She has detailed one semi-humorous episode of our relationship in her book, *To Remember Forever*, when I invited her to my house to avoid the monotony of a college quarantine for scarlet fever, then came down with the disease myself, forcing her to remain incarcerated for a week while all the rest of the college went home! She and her future husband, Herbert Carroll, and Elwin and I had many foursome dates together.

I wrote constantly. Between high school and college I had written a long novelette, another biblical background story called "And Myrrh." It was never published, though my mother sent it the rounds of various publishers with faithful persistance. I used the theme and title later in a play. An essay I wrote in my sophomore year, "Diogenes and the Sphinx," won the prize for composition. A course in creative writing spawned a number of stories with titles such as "Looking Glasses" and "The Tiger and the Tiger Lily." One which won an intercollegiate prize was called "The Peerage of Adam." I am sure they were all heavily philosophical, verbose, and unrealistic, for it was my most vividly imaginative period. For three years I acted as an assistant in the English Department, correcting themes of underclassmen. In my senior year I researched for a prize essay on "Arbitration Instead of War," reading everything I could find on the subject, my first adventure in deep research, and developing a lifelong and passionate concern for world peace.

Was it love of study, an excessive desire to excell or a meticulous urge toward perfectionism which stimulated my desire for high rank? Certainly it was still a means of compensation for that habit of stammering which persisted all through college. But I did get rank, winning prizes for scholarship, Phi Beta Kappa, and the highest honors possible. Not that my interests were solely along scholastic lines. I was active in athletics, especially tennis, and continued to study music, both piano and organ. Once I knew that I was going to marry a minister, in whose work music would be an asset as well as a possible means of income, I did intensive practicing during vacations, often as much as six hours a day. Though the music certainly proved an asset throughout our ministry, its financial benefits were minimal, consisting largely of the exchange of a weekly lesson to a girl in an early parish for her mother's handling of our weekly washing!

During my last year in college Elwin attended Princeton Theological Seminary, persuaded to go there by my mother who felt that its theology was more in harmony with the conservative creed of both our families. That spring he wrote me of a possibility of getting a student preaching charge, so we might be able to get married a year earlier than we had intended. Though I was of age, I would never have thought of taking such a step without my parents' consent. Somewhat to my surprise they made no objection. Possibly they were relieved! I shall never forget my excitement when the telegram arrived:

"CHURCH WANTS ME, DEAREST. SO NOW CAN PLAN DEFINITELY."

We were married in August after my graduation in June. That year we shared an apartment in Princeton with another student couple, Claude and Ruth Thomas, who later became missionaries to China. Elwin had managed to purchase a Ford runabout which we called "Ophelia Bumps," and each week we drove in it to our little Presbyterian church about seventeen miles from Princeton. Our salary, as I recall, was $1060, including a missionary donation from the Presbytery. Fortunately we were frugal by both nature and upbringing, and by purchasing day-old bread for five cents, eating little or no meat, and using the vegetables Elwin had grown the preceding summer on his preaching charge, we not only lived decently but saved money—a rehearsal for the depression years not far ahead. I took more music lessons, practicing on a rattly old piano in our apartment. Ruth was my skilled cooking teacher, for my training had been in English and the classics, not in baking cakes or even boiling eggs. Elwin cooked our first meal, potatoes and summer squash. The next one I cooked, summer squash and potatoes. There were tensions, of course, during the year, as was natural with two newly married couples. Once I became so quarrelsome with my new husband that I lifted one of our landlady's prize antique chairs and managed to break one of its legs, scarcely improving her sentiments toward "those ministers."

The next summer we sold "Ophelia" to our housemates and with our wedding present money plus savings bought a second-hand four-passenger coupe, "Fidelia," which seemed the height of luxury. It could actually travel twenty-seven miles an hour! Our parishoners rented a house for us and loaned us essential furniture. It was a good summer, and we were able to concentrate on the youth work which has always been a central concern of our ministry.

But Elwin was a Methodist, not a Presbyterian. We decided to attend Drew, the Methodist seminary in Madison, New Jersey, that fall. Our parishioners were agreeable, even loaning us the furniture we had been using for the room we had found on the top floor of a house in Madison. We carted it up on the top of our little Chevrolet, getting bogged down on a far worse road than I have ever seen in Maine.

Then one Thursday soon after school started, Elwin received a letter offering him a church in southern Maine with an opportunity to transfer for his last year to Boston University School of Theology. Typically, for we have never been frightened by sudden decisions, we wired acceptance. By Saturday we were ready to leave. Bundling the furniture loaned us back into the car, we set off that afternoon for our church, dreading to break the news of our leaving to our parishioners. One by one that afternoon we visited them, and they registered proper (and we hoped genuine) sorrow. We left the head deacon until the last. When Elwin broke the news to him, we were surprised to see a look of relief cross his face. He had dreaded telling us that we would have to leave! Word had come from the Presbytery that henceforth the church must be served by a Presbyterian student. Leaving his house that night, we looked at each other in wonder. Providence? It certainly seemed so. Not only had a door been opened to us, but we had been kicked through it!

So began our thirty-five and more years of ministry in our native Maine. The first year I lived in the parsonage and boarded the school teacher, who happened to be an old friend, while Elwin spent most of each week in Boston. At first there were few conveniences in the parsonage—no bathroom (a two-seater at the end of the shed), no furnace (only two coal stoves, and education in the classics had not included a course in keeping coal fires!). The front hall was so cold that I recall skating on it after the floor was washed. But we managed that winter. Our next-door neighbor was a saint and constant purveyor of pies, cakes and other delicacies with only the most necessary advice. Weeks passed slowly with Elwin away, and I lived for Friday to come.

We bought a secondhand piano that winter, one of the few things we ever purchased on time. How proud I was of that beautiful instrument with its brand-new mahogany bench! Soon after it came we had company, and a young girl wearing boots with buckles reared one of them and drew it across that smooth, shining surface. I can still hear the scraping sound. The scratch was always there, deep and ineffaceable. But it became for me a symbol of spiritual growth. I wrote a poem about it called "Scars." Here are just a few lines:

"So many, many little scars!
Does one day pass that has not brought
Some rude, despoiling touch that mars? . . .

The little, little scars of life,
That warp the soul and seam the face!
   Dear God, in each day's petty strife,
Let me look upward to your vast untroubled blue,
See love unstained, life whole, unbruised by time and space—
   These things alone are true. . . ."

That first parish, about fifteen miles south of Portland, was one of our happiest. The people were loving and patient with our many mistakes. They cooperated in new programs—vacation schools, youth institutes, union services with other churches. They put a bathroom in the parsonage and built an educational addition to the one-room church. And, we hope, they grew spiritually during our ministry.

It was here that I began my professional writing career. One Christmas we needed a program for our church, and I wrote a play called "The Shepherd of Israel" and produced it. Nothing could have been more natural. The Bible stories from age two, the years in church and Sunday School, the biblical background stories which had been some of my first creative expression— all had led in a plain path to this new development. I enjoyed the writing so much that I was soon writing other plays. One, called "The Lost Church," I sent to a church publication. Never shall I forget the thrill when I went to the post office and found a letter of acceptance with a $25 check. I ran all the way home, doubtless shocking our more staid parishioners. This was in February 1928. I began writing and sending other manuscripts to religious publications, poems, articles, another play called "From Darkness to Dawn," later published under the title "Joseph of Arimathea." It is still in print, having gone through eighteen printings.

Soon short stories began to flow. *Classmate*, a church school publication which syndicated material, was a productive market. A character in one of the short stories, Gay Christopher, burst the bounds of the short story and became the heroine of

23

several serials—as a college student in "Friendship Alley," as a young Doctor's wife in "Friendship Haven" and "The Angel of Friendship Haven," all with a religious emphasis. These were interspersed with more short stories, articles, poems, other serials. Yes, and plays. The expression of my religious faith in drama became my most absorbing professional interest. True, the emphasis of that expression was slowly changing as concepts of religious faith matured. The concern developed during the research on "Arbitration instead of War" was broadening to include all aspects of social justice—racial equality, economic equity, human brotherhood. Though the earlier plays reflected the narrower concepts of religion in which I had been reared, later writings, I hope, have all emphasized this more mature philosophy.

The years of the thirties were prolific in plays, thirty-five of them. Most were published first in church periodicals, notably *The International Journal of Religious Education*, then in pamphlet form by Baker's Plays. One of them, "Smoke," won a prize offered by the New York Council of Churches. We used all the prize money to go to New York to see it produced. Twelve plays were published in a volume, *Twelve Months of Drama for the Average Church*. It is still selling. They were not all what the experts would call "good" plays. Dr. Fred Eastman, the eminent religious playwright and critic, commented with doubtful praise that I "had a flair for drama." To only a few did he give unqualified praise, such as "Peace I Give Unto You," "No Room in the Hotel," "White Christmas." But it was a time when biblical plays were in their heyday, and many of them sold between ten and twenty thousands of copies, some many more. The better ones written in the thirties included: "For He Had Great Possessions," "Simon the Leper," "And Myrrh," "The Whirlwind," "Release," "The Things That Are Caesar's."

During the thirties, the depression years, we served two small city churches, five years in each, and the money I earned through writing enabled us to make both ends meet. I remember once writing to Baker's asking for thirty-five dollars that they owed me, so we could pay up all our bills! We managed to avoid one pitfall into which our marriage might easily have fallen. At first my earnings were all in my name and were used both to eke out my husband's reduced salary and to supply any items of luxury I might choose to dole out. In other words, what I earned was mine, what he earned was ours. It was a bad arrangement. Fortunately we decided, most happily, to pool everything, and so it has been ever since. We have tried also, in a poor way, to live out our creed of stewardship, believing that whatever we have is a trust from God and should be used in the service of humanity.

Those years of the thirties—how to compress a decade into a paragraph or two? It's like trying to distill a river into a capsule. Many of their activities could have been duplicated in any parsonage, the same succession of meetings, problems, successes, failures, forging of lifelong friendships. But for us there were some unique features: the adoption of two children, Harold, a lively blue-eyed boy of eighteen months, and Joan, a sweet, dark-haired little orphan of five years. "She has to be your daughter," someone once remarked, "she looks so much like you!" They were so nearly the same size as to be almost twins. Harold used to take droll satisfaction in announcing to strangers that his sister was two months older than he and watching the puzzlement on their faces . . . and the antagonism of some conservative members of our parish when my husband, never one to compromise on his convictions, expressed himself with vigor on issues involving social justice . . . and going to a new church with problems which our district superintendent hoped we might solve.

This latter might have meant disaster. A supply interim pastor who had proved very popular had been appointed to this church. Not being qualified, he was forced to leave at Conference time. The people there were up in arms, many threatening to leave the church if he was moved. This church had wanted my husband to come there previously, and we had many friends among its members, so we agreed to go, not knowing how we would be received or if we would be paid a living salary. After the appointments were read at Conference we overheard this church's delegate, a good friend of ours, remark, "I won't call home. I told the people I wouldn't call unless the news was good!" Hardly an auspicious beginning for the new minister and his wife! But we were soon accepted with wholehearted support and it proved to be one of our happiest pastorates. I was organist for some time in the church and loved it. The church sanctuary was remodeled while we were there, an interesting and creative experience. I recall one small crisis when a carved wooden decoration for the altar was discovered to have been made by the designer into a bleeding heart, hardly an appropriate feature for a Protestant church! We craftily persuaded him to transform it into a flaming torch.

A stammering minister's wife? It was surely a liability. How well I remember my dismay to find, on moving to that first city church, that the preceding pastor's wife had been superintendent of a large junior department in the church school and that I was expected to take her place! The accepted pattern at that time included a formal worship service for the entire body. I managed to fulfill the duties fairly creditably, but with what mental torture! And how foolish I was! Why try to force myself into a predecessor's mold when there were other things I could do more suited to my abilities? If there is one bit of advice I would give to a timid young minister's wife, it is, "Be yourself!"

I kept on writing plays. In all there have been over seventy of them published, and at least thirty of them are still selling. Some which reflect to an earlier and somewhat outmoded concept of theology I would be glad to see out of print. Others like "The Brother," "The Gifts," "This Night Shall Pass," "No Room in the Hotel," "Peace on Mars," will, I hope, remain in use for many more years. Sales for many of them have gone into the tens of thousands.

Once the editor who had accepted the first play for his church school magazine wrote and asked me to comment on the question, "Why do you write religious plays?" His letter made me think. Why did I? If he had asked, "Why do you write?" it would have been easy. I wrote because I had to. The instinct that sent me off into a corner with a scrap of paper and a pencil at the age of ten was as natural as my appetite for books and apples. If I had never sold anything, I would still be scribbling. But why religious plays? That required some real probing. Because people had come to expect it of me? Because they had become a second-rate substitute for the more popular and lucrative type of writing which I would have liked to do if I had the ability? No. I could honestly say it was because I believed it to be the most effective contribution I could make to the building of Christlike character and a more Christian world.

Drama belongs with religion. It had its birth in the temple and about the altar. In all countries and in all regions it has been at the very heart of religious observance. It was a tragedy when the church during a period of rigid puritanism, drove out this most potent means of ministry. Now, fortunately, drama has been restored to a dignified place in the worship and

26

educational program of the church. A truly religious play, one that has a religious effect on both actors and audience, is worth more, I believe, than a hundred sermons. It involves participation, identification, and action. You don't get far by *telling* people how to live. You have to *show* them. And drama which deals prophetically with the fundamental problems of both audience and actors is the next best thing to actual experience.

To jump ahead a bit in time, any doubt about the high calling of a religious playwright would have been expelled on my first trip to India.

"I want you to come to my room tonight," said a teacher at Isabella Thoburn College in Lucknow, "to meet the girls who took part in your play 'Simon the Leper.' I wish you could know the difference that play has made in some of their lives."

Listening with gratitude and humility, looking at the shining, dedicated faces of these girls, I *did* know. Taking part in the play had been for them a genuine religious experience.

Later, standing in the hall of a mission school in Calcutta, I gazed at a similar array of boys' shining faces—Bengali and Indians of many other backgrounds, Jews, Europeans—all of whom had taken some active part in the adventure of producing my play "And Myrrh" the preceding Christmas.

"The boy who played the part of the colored wise man," the school principal told me, "felt the significance of his role so profoundly that he is seriously thinking of becoming a Christian."

Such are the intangible royalties of the religious playwright. Why, then, did I not continue writing plays for the rest of my life, as I fully expected to do? Certainly not because I tired of drama writing or sought a more lucrative means of expression. Merely because suddenly, unexpectedly, the shell started to grow another chamber.

They say "life begins at forty." A certain phase of mine certainly did, for I was just forty when my first novel was published. I had written a three-act play, "The Brother," into an eight-part serial for *Classmate.* Alfred D. Moore, the editor of that church school publication, was interested in the story and, like my mother long before, began persistently to submit the work to editors. He had better luck than she. Earl Schenck Myers at Westminster Press in Philadelphia gave me three months to turn the serial into a full-length novel. Three months—for a task of mammoth proportions!

At the age of fourteen I had blithely sat down to write my

first biblical background short story with no more mental equipment than the smattering of knowledge obtained in Sunday school, the daily diet of Bible stories fed me from baby days and a large amount of religious zeal and imagination. Between high school and college I had tried to turn out a "novel," using the same stone-age tools. Even when I began writing and selling biblical plays in quantity, I'm afraid my approach was almost as superficial. To illustrate some of the mistakes I must have made, I once received a letter from a kindly biblical authority commenting that I had permitted one of my characters to casually sweep from a bench into a small leather bag an amount of money weighing at least a ton!

Now I discovered the problems with which the writer of biblical fiction is faced if he takes his job seriously. *The Brother* is the story of James, the brother of Jesus. There were so many things I had to know: political, social, and religious conditions in the time of Christ; beliefs and customs, how people dressed, traveled, talked, thought, washed, sat, slept, ate, combed their hair, cooked, prayed, swore, conducted their religious services, celebrated their feasts, made love, went to school, built houses, tended sheep, raised crops, bought, sold, married, died, were buried! I was horrified—and fascinated! Though I did not realize it, the discipline of those three months was to set a pattern for most of my professional activity in the years to come.

This was the summer of 1943. I set myself a formidable stint, writing at least four typed pages a day, when my usual pace was about two. My husband was then Superintendent of the Portland District of the Methodist Church, so my church duties were fortunately minimal. It was wartime, with a dearth of workers in many areas, and we volunteered to spend our vacation working in a YMCA camp where we had led youth institutes for many years. I carried along a huge box of books on New Testament history and Palestinian life and while Elwin counseled, cooked and did odd jobs about the camp I wrote, taking time out only to help with the tables at meals. I finished the manuscript *almost* within the three months.

The book came out the following spring and sold remarkably well—I didn't realize how well until years later when others of my books were far less successful. I have always said facetiously that it rode in on the coattails of *The Robe*, which was a current best-seller. At least biblical novels were popular at the time. While I wrote some plays after that, it was the beginning
28

of a new era in my writing career, another appendage to that chambered nautilus. Westminster asked me to do another novel, this time on the prophet Amos. I knew I would like nothing better, for was not Amos one of the first proponents of social justice? I spent months in intensive research before starting to write, using dozens of books sent me by theological libraries and recommended to me by Dr. Elmer Leslie, the eminent Old Testament professor at Boston University. This time I wrote three pages a day instead of four. I can still see myself taking time out to think while mounted on the radiator in the district parsonage dining room, warmth being a wartime luxury. I enjoyed writing this book more than any other I have written. The idea was fresh. I had an abundance of material. It was an expression of my most mature and profound religious philosophy. And it is still my favorite among all the twenty and more books I have written. Passages from it, telling of Amos' discovery of the Hebrew Yahweh as the one universal God and the source of human justice, have been included in anthologies. When I was asked some years ago by *Christian Herald* to pick my favorite passage from the books I have written, it was the closing paragraphs from *The Herdsman* that I chose, in which Amos, in prison and condemned to death for his battle against injustice, makes his greatest discovery. His young brother Reuel, who had been weak and sinful, has come to the tiny window to bid him good-bye.

"Amos continued to stroke the beloved, familiar features, to run his fingers through the thick, unruly mop of curly hair. How blind . . . he had been! Believing that love like his could be destroyed simply because the loved one had been unworthy! . . . He could no more forget his love for him than Yahweh—than Yahweh . . .

Amos lifted his face. Though night had already fallen in the little room, he was no longer groping in the dark. For his spirit had already sighted another landmark. . . . He knew suddenly that Yahweh did not punish people when they reaped the natural harvest of their mistakes. He suffered with them.

Yahweh—the Eternal—was more than Justice! He was Love! . . .

'Wait!' he called out in sudden panic. 'I have something to tell you—something important. Tell Hosea—'

The words died on his lips as he suddenly remembered

others that his friend had spoken. 'Sometimes I wonder if I don't love Gomer the way—the way Yahweh must love—'

'What is it? Did you—did you want something?' The boy was crying so he could hardly speak.

'No. Nothing.'

Alone again, Amos stood, his face still lifted, and watched the small barred window slowly darken. There was nothing that he needed to tell Hosea. For the slight figure with the clear eyes had already visioned the higher, more luminous landmark. . . . And after Hosea there would be others, seekers of truth like himself, men unafraid of loneliness, climbing higher and higher, forever unsatisfied . . .

Until perhaps there would come One who would follow the thorny road upward to some far sunlit height, giving to man his first clear vision of the Eternal."

The Herdsman came out in the fall of 1946, with the publishers giving it quite a fanfare, and it had an excellent sale. Research had been thorough, and there were few criticisms of its historical substance . . . but there should have been! When I first saw it and read on the jacket the blurb that I myself had written, I was horrified. I had inadvertently located Amos at seventeen hundred years ago instead of twenty-seven hundred! I had also spelled Thomas Paine with a "y." Unfortunately jacket materials had not been included in the proofs. I called my editor post haste to see if something could be done. Something couldn't. The first printing had been 25,000 copies, and a change would have cost hundreds of dollars. The expert copy editors had not caught the mistakes. Would you believe that nobody ever commented on them? It is usually the petty mistakes that critics pounce on. Someone did write in a review that I had made tents out of camel's hair instead of goat's hair, and headlined the fact.

This book was to change my life, opening the way not only to vistas of far places which I had never dreamed of penetrating but eventually to those other "lives" I was destined to live. The next year, 1947, at our Maine Annual Conference Dr. Diffendorfer, the secretary of the Methodist Board of Missions, greeted me with a copy of *The Herdsman* held aloft in his hand.

"You're going to India!" he announced without preamble.

I regarded him with frank disbelief. "Oh, yeah?" I responded silently. But he really meant it. He had been much impressed by the book and wanted the Board to send me to India to gather material for a novel on missions. I was gratified by his interest but thought no more about it. Church boards do not usually spend money on enterprises like that. And I was already embarked on a new subject. Interest in the origins of social justice had led me further back into biblical history, and I was determined to write a novel on Moses, with whom, I felt, the concept had started. Already I was reading avidly everything I could find on Egypt and the Palestinian backgrounds of that era, once more fortified by a bibliography, advice and encouragement from Dr. Leslie. The theological library in Boston was sending me five or six books at a time, and my files were getting filled with three-by-five cards. I must have read in all a hundred books on Egypt—histories, archaeological reports, novels.

I tried to be meticulous in research in spite of the agony it sometimes caused. After months of amassing material in accordance with the chronology earlier accepted by most Old Testament authorities, including Dr. Leslie, I found that new discoveries had caused them to redate the supposed time of the Exodus about seventy years, 1295 B.C. instead of 1225. A vast amount of material down the drain! But I was getting used to such readjustments, and I shifted my attention to the previous century. Accuracy was the important thing. The reward came later when an eminent Egyptologist told me that he had found no detail in the book relating to Egyptian life and history which he could dispute.

This was a year of change, for in the summer of 1947 we moved to the church in Orono, Maine, site of the state university, cutting short Elwin's term as district superintendent because of our interest in Christian education. The Orono church was the center for the Wesley Foundation, the official work of the denomination with students at the university. Some of our preacher peers thought we were stupid. Instead of waiting until Conference and the probability of a big, high-paying city church, going to a small-town, low-salaried parish; exchanging a newly refurbished district parsonage for one with obvious drawbacks—an iron stove in the kitchen, a coal furnace in the basement, and makeshift furnishings! But these were minor defects, soon remedied. And we have never been sorry for the

31

move. The children returned from their summer jobs to finish their last year in high school in a smaller institution which proved more stimulating than their previous big city school. We were soon playing trios for school and church as we had done in the Portland area, Harold with violin, Joan with cello, I at the piano. With the opening of college we began work with students which, with its Sunday night suppers in our two living rooms and discussions around the fireplace, was supremely rewarding. And, though we didn't know it at the time, that small-town church, growing amazingly through the years, was to be the center of our most intimate friendships, our most devoted church loyalties and activities, for the rest of our lives.

Surprisingly, the India trip was not a passing pipe dream. The missions secretary had been serious! In Cleveland the following December, at a big convocation of Methodist youth for which I had written a theme pageant called "The Mighty Dream," I met Dr. James Mathews, the missions secretary for India, who confirmed the plan and began suggesting a possible itinerary. I was really going to India! And, most remarkable of all, I would have a free hand in developing the project. There were no strings on what I might write. My husband could go with me and take an interim pastorate in an English speaking church. As months passed plans took more definite shape, and of course I began reading all the literature I could find on India.

Meanwhile through most of 1948 I was writing the book on Moses. Much of it was done in the parsonage dining room by a window that looked out on the little Stillwater River. While washing dishes in the kitchen I used to gaze out windows with the same view and sing the song we had often used at youth camps—"Peace I ask of thee, O river." A good theme song for a restless and overactive temperament! Somewhere during the writing I discovered that my publishers were giving an annual award for the best religious novel submitted, and I decided to enter the manuscript. The deadline was in the late fall, and by furious concentration, complicated by a major operation which for some weeks kept me alternating between bed and typewriter, I managed to finish it in time. The following May I received a special delivery letter saying that the book had won the Westminster Award of $7500.

Mine was not a conventional Moses, like Sholem Asch's, which came out almost on the heels of mine, not the bearded patriarch who was later to serve his outcast people in the wilderness, but Moses the young man, a "prince of Egypt," a nobleman reared in the palaces and academies of an empire at the height of its power yet renouncing a woman's love and the double throne of the Pharoahs to deliver his people from oppression. It is the story of a man's tormenting search after a God who is relevant to human need and to his own developing concept of social justice, a man living in a world where God's natural law was as immutable as it is today. As I look over the many reviews in my scrapbook, I find that one in the Virginia Kirkus *Bulletin* seems to express the substance of all I was trying to articulate. Some of the reviews, of course, were not so favorable. A few deplored the slowness of action, the multiplicity of details, the weakness of character portrayal.

"The rich tapestry of the background," stated the *Bulletin*, "makes a compelling demand on the reader's imagination, widening one's sense of understanding ancient history. . . . The interpretation of Moses, the elaboration of the sketchily known facts of his life prior to the rescue of the Hebrews from the hands of the Egyptians, may be contested by those who are conventional and dogmatic. . . . For most readers, however, a rereading of that part of the Old Testament which deals with the Egyptian captivity takes on fresh significance, the 'miracles' which had seemed cruelty (though in a just cause) are credible, the transition from the Moses found as a baby in the bulrushes, to the adult, taking on his shoulders the tragedy, the drama of his people, is here filled in with those years as a prince, ignorant of his parentage, his destiny—a questioner, who cannot accept wholly the many gods of the Egyptian hierarchy, the searching for truth, the final acceptance of the role of a Hebrew, suffering as his people are suffering, under worse than slavery."

Publication day was October 31. Following that a whole week of ceremonies had been planned by the publishers, starting with a luncheon at the Boston City Club. From there we came to Portland, to Augusta, to Orono for more autographing parties. I suppose this book, *Prince of Egypt*, is the best known of any of my writings. Thanks to the publicity attending the award, it remained on the best seller lists for many weeks and later was used as background and plot material for the Egyptian section of the film "The Ten Commandments." It was republished in a paperback edition, which sold about half a million copies. All of this fanfare was a once-in-a-lifetime experience. Nothing like it would ever happen to me again. Many of my books would merely sink into comparative oblivion with a faint plop!

But there was far greater excitement ahead, for almost immediately after this week of activity I left for India. The way had been cleared remarkably. Our daughter had recently married. Our son was in Springfield College preparing for his future career as a psychiatric social worker. Though my husband chose not to go with me, a young couple agreed to live in the parsonage, manage the house, and assist with the student work. And here a word of humble and thankful tribute is due my husband, who with patient resignation if not cheerfulness has seen me off on dozens of such research expeditions to near and far places, ever sympathetic with the creative idealism activating each new project. Without his constant support and cooperation I could never have lived any of these dozen lives. How well I remember the farewell talk we had as we faced this six months of separation!

"It's for India," he reassured me, knowing how deeply I had become involved in this tormented country just emerging out of bloody travail into independence and sharing all my concern.

I loved flying, though in 1949 this first medium was no smooth jet, just a lumbering old-style craft which developed an oil leak over Europe (I first detected the black ooze snaking along the wing and called the stewardess), necessitating an unscheduled detour to Rome and a four-hour delay in arrival in Delhi. But to me it was Adventure and Inspiration in capitals. All the way over I wrote poetry, some humorous, some deeply religious. One poem began, "For the first time in my life I am above the clouds . . ." and continued in rapturous apostrophe to the Creator of it all.

This is not the place to detail in full those five months in India and the month following in Palestine and Egypt. They are all preserved in dozens of articles, hundreds of colored slides, a published condensation of my diary titled *Fly With Me to India*. But since this was so important a preface to all my other lives I must include a brief outline.

Making my headquarters in Delhi with Bishop and Mrs. J. Waskom Pickett, I traveled all over the country, about 14,000 miles in all, usually alone, in every sort of conveyance from airplane to bullock cart, exploring temples and mud huts and palaces, making hundreds of friends of many-hued skins, tak-
34

ing copious notes on the thousands of three-by-five pieces of heavy paper which have proved lighter to carry on airplane trips than index cards. There were many high points: lunch at Nehru's home with his daughter Indira as hostess; attendance at the inauguration of India's first president; a dinner in Vellore with Dr. Ida Scudder, white-haired, blue-eyed, vibrantly energetic at age eighty; a trip to the amazing Ellora and Ajanta Caves; and of course the Taj Mahal cameoed under the full moon.

But most of my time was spent researching India village life in the north, for I had decided early that my book must feature a villager, living in the area of India's greatest need and challenge. I studied for a month in Lucknow with Dr. and Mrs. William Wiser, Presbyterian missionaries who had lived intimately with villagers and were considered authorities on village life. Then for two weeks I lived in their India Village Service Center in a little town called Marehra, occupying what had once been the harem quarters in an old Muslim house.

"I admit," I wrote in my diary, "I was a bit disconcerted when I saw my new quarters, although they were really very elegant. Entering the big outer door of the house you come into a large courtyard behind which is a veranda. This opens on one big room, brick paved, which the Wisers use for a living room when they are here. At the rear of another court is one big, long room with a single window. Did I think I would be comfortable here?

" 'Why, yes, this will be fine.' I managed a note of somewhat dubious gaiety.

"Hiding my dismay, I contemplated the hard-packed earth floor, the tiny, curtainless barred window, the long shadowy space containing not a stick of furniture. But, thanks to the services of a smiling young Indian, the room soon became habitable. A *charpoy* was moved in, a bamboo arm chair, a straight chair and a table for my typewriter and research materials. A bamboo stand and low platform lifted my suitcase and bedding bag to safe distances from the earth floor. A few rolls of straw matting relieve the chilly bareness of the floor, and, last but by no means least, a makeshift curtain of cheesecloth protects the window."

Here, except for the chattering monkeys which roamed the walls of the outer courtyard, and a huge rat which interrupted my privacy one memorable night, I lived alone for two weeks

35

among the ghosts of the Muslim mothers and little wives who had once peopled the place. They were the most exciting, the most fascinating, the most depressing and certainly the most valuable two weeks of my five months in India.

Each day I went into the villages with one or more of the three women in the seven-member team of India Village Service. Myrtle, a social worker and graduate of Isabella Thoburn College, a charming young woman with shining dark eyes, satin-smooth hair worn in long braids and a winning smile, was usually my guide. "Come," she would say, and I would follow always with a sense of impending adventure—through thin slits in what looked like impenetrable mud walls, along dusty lanes lined with gaping doorways, stepping over open drains and picking my way gingerly past the black hairy flanks and swishing tails of buffalo cows, into sun-baked courtyards, earth-walled, open to the sky and teeming with human and animal and insect life—in short, into a new world.

Sometimes we would go in an *ekka*, a two-wheeled, horse-drawn vehicle consisting of a high wooden platform covered by a small awning, all four of us crowding together, all but me sitting crosslegged. Later, after the Wisers joined us, we would travel in the "Zipper," a well worn jeep. Soon the villages ceased to be vague brown clusters of earth houses, assumed names and character, became persons—incredibly poor, often sick, most of them illiterate, almost invariably cheerful and courageous, always friendly. I watched Myrtle and the other women workers teach girls to read, women to sew, show "jet" pictures illustrating cleanliness and child care and avoidance of disease and better ways of cooking, saw the men of the team demonstrate the bore-hole latrine, the smokeless *chulha* and more productive methods of farming.

One day I stood with Myrtle in a small courtyard containing the usual minimum of possessions—baskets, shining brass vessels, a few tools and cooking utensils, clay pots and storing jars, and the only article of furniture, a *charpoy* or string cot. On it lay what looked like a pile of rags, beside it an old sandal, a rusty knife and a tiny monkey's skull. "To keep away the evil spirits," whispered Myrtle. A smiling young woman proudly pushed back a corner of the rags, disclosing a wee scrap of humanity.

There, I knew suddenly, was my story, It would begin right here with this newborn child, the symbols of age-old fears and superstitions all about him. He would grow up in a village like this, with its earth houses, its little lanes and shops, its pool, its tiny shrine, its mango grove. But he would not be satisfied with the old ways, the narrow horizons. He would always be asking questions, venturing into new and strange paths, a son of tomorrow rather than yesterday, like the new democratic nation that was struggling to be born.

The month in Palestine and Egypt was rewarding. It was wonderful to see the places I had read and written about so long—Jerusalem, Bethel, Bethlehem, Hebron, the ruins of Jericho. It was spring and the country was clothed in that brief vesture of green which so soon turns brown and sere. One day I stood on the Mount of Olives with my back against an old stone wall and the spring rain washing my face and wondered if that was the place where He had stood and wept over the city. Its outlines had changed, of course, but there were the same stone houses, the same stony eminence where the temple once stood, the same storm clouds as on that other April. But as I watched, the storm clouds broke, the sun emerged. And I knew that the old dream of a new Jerusalem was not dead.

Already I had a new biblical novel in mind, *Jezebel*, and I insisted on taking a trip to old Samaria, where I wandered among the ruins of Ahab's ancient palace and looked down on the plain along which Elijah had run before the King's chariot. In Damascus I traveled along the Street Straight and saw the window from which Paul was let down (perhaps). From Beirut I flew to the outskirts of Petra, and explored that "rose-red city" where Paul is supposed to have spent his years of reflection. It was impossible then to go into Israel and return to an Arab country, so I was unable to fulfill one of my fondest dreams, to stand on the hill above Nazareth where long ago a boy had climbed to dream and stretch his arms high and focus his eyes on far horizons. But certainly no mean climax to the trip was an Easter sunrise service in the Garden Tomb.

In Egypt too I was a bit frustrated, for a week in Cairo gave little opportunity to visit the sites connected with the life of Moses—the old Heliopolis where he had presumably studied, yes, and Saqqara, which he must have known. But it was too hot in April, they told me, to go up the Nile to Karnak and Luxur, the Thebes where much of my story had been laid. Ten years later, in 1960, when I was invited to Alexandria to teach a course in religious drama writing for Lit. Lit. (World Literacy and Christian Literature) I would be able to fulfill that dream—in July!—flying up to Luxor, roaming the great Hypostyle Hall at Karnak which Moses must have known, going across the Nile in the early morning before the heat became too intense, burrowing in the tombs in the Valley of the Kings, especially that of Seti, which I had described in detail in the book.

It was on this first trip to the Middle East, with the evidence of the recent conflict all about me, that my tremendous concern for the plight of Arab refugees was born. Thrust from their rightful homes they were now huddled into caves, tents and other makeshift shelters along the roads we traveled. My concern was to develop into active involvement when in 1960 I visited many refugee camps in Lebanon and Jordan. That visit resulted in many articles, especially one called "Still No Room in Bethlehem." My concern has persisted through the years and still haunts me with its terrible urgency and its burden of injustice.

I returned home in May, 1950, for a challenging new move. As a result of our student work my husband was asked to become the director of the new Maine Christian Association, a ministry to university students in Orono supported by the Protestant churches of Maine. Since it was a new setup, we had to find a place to work. Thanks to the prize money from *Prince of Egypt*, we bought a house which could be used as a student center. An article in a Boston paper called it "The House that Moses Built." So began five of the happiest pastoral years of our lives. The house was full of young people much of the time, and many students made the place their home away from home. Though services were held on campus each Sunday, other work was conducted in the house and its basement, which we had made over into a student center. Every Friday night we put on a supper for twenty-five cents (That was a quarter century ago!). A committee of students would help but of course most of the work fell on us. I still have the recipe book we compiled for those suppers. The work was frustrating. Try as we would, only a tiny percentage of the 5,000 students could be reached. But the small group we did reach offered a wonderful and rewarding opportunity for sharing. Some of the bonuses were national conferences for student workers, many in the Midwest, making possible visits with our son, a psychiatric social worker, and his growing family.

38

After this trip to India a strange thing happened to this shy little stutterer. At first my husband gave lectures on India from my diary, and I showed the many slides I had brought back. Then, little by little, I began interpolating details until finally I was giving the lectures myself! "Speech Begins at Forty," I titled one article I wrote for a church publication (though the forty was really nearer fifty.) It wasn't that I was cured of the troublesome habit, but all at once I had something very important to say and I had to say it. A few words still remain difficult and I try to avoid them. But I manage. And, if you can believe it, to date I have given over nine hundred speeches on my books and travels to small and large groups, most of them illustrated with slides. To me this is a miracle.

I wrote the India novel and called it *House of Earth*. It is indeed the story of that mite I saw lying on the *charpoy*, or one like him. I named him Roshan, a word for light, and his mother was Usha, meaning dawn. The Wisers, or their prototypes, appeared in it, pitching their tent, as they had done in real life, in the village mango grove, and *showing*, as well as preaching, the Christian way of life. "Bill Sahib" became Roshan's friend—a big man with a loud voice and a thatch of flaming red hair and an old auto named Cleopatra and the love of God and man in his heart. With his help Roshan grew and questioned and battled to break the bonds of ignorance and idolatry and the rigid caste system, find fulfillment in a sharing marriage, become deeply involved in the struggle for national freedom, return to his village and try to create a more just and enlightened system of living. It is the story, I hope, of a man and a people reborn. It may not have been just what the mission board expected but after all they had given me a free hand and it was a story I felt impelled to write.

After that I embarked on the writing of another biblical novel, a further study into the origins of the concept of social justice—ninth century B.C. this time, *Jezebel*, with Elijah as the exponent of the theme. Jezebel, I believed, was a much maligned character, condemned merely because she was loyal to her own god. I changed publishers, going with McGraw-Hill. The year the book was published, 1955, we made another change. My husband was again made a district superintendent, this time of Maine's northernmost district. We sold "the house that Moses built" to a group that would continue it as a student center and moved to the district parsonage in Bangor.

Change! I have always welcomed it, whether a trip to India or a move to the next town. Convenient trait for a Methodist minister's wife! The new work involved sufficient travel to satisfy even my roving proclivities, for there were over ninety churches in the district spread over an area of perhaps 10,000 square miles. We traveled about 30,000 miles a year. I loved it. I reckoned that in both districts we served I had probably attended more than seven hundred church conferences. Many of the churches held supper before their meetings, and food has always been one of my favorite preoccupations—though, as I titled one article for a church paper, "I Would Rather Read than Eat." Even the consistent menu of baked beans, casseroles, and salads fazed neither zest nor digestion. Once, I recall, in Aroostook County we had six such meals in a single week, all fortified with the cream, hot breads, potatoes, and other luxuries abounding in "The County." I enjoyed meeting people, too, so the job was a constant joy for me.

Even distance from the typewriter was no great deterrent. I learned to write longhand while riding in the car. Soon I was engaged in another project, this time a novel of the boy Jesus based on my play "The Gifts." What had become of those gifts the Magi brought? Of course no one knows. History and tradition are as silent about the gifts as about their givers. Yet because of the very nature of him to whom they were brought, I felt there could be only one answer. They must have been *used* to help people in need. Perhaps also they played a part in the boy's wakening consciousness of his mission to humanity. I like to think so, and the novel that emerged from this theme, *The Gifts*, is one of my most beloved brain children. Later I was to incorporate the same theme into two juveniles, *The Journey* and *The Three Gifts*, published by the Abingdon Press. But before that time, in 1960, while in the Middle East teaching that course in Alexandria, I was able to realize my dream of walking the streets of Nazareth, seeing other children drawing water from its well, climbing that hill behind the town.

"You're not very lucky," the French priest would say as he showed me the path up the hill behind his church. "It's misty, and you can't see very much."

Unlucky? To be standing on that hilltop where the boy had so often gone to think his long thoughts, the same little flowers in the grass at my feet, the same winds on my cheeks, the same vistas of far horizons, glimpsed however dimly through the mists?

40

But this was all still in the future. Now, in the mid-1950s, India, not Palestine, was dominating much of my life. I felt it was my second country, its flamboyant colors, its pitiful drabness, its riches, its grueling poverty, its triumph of independence through non-violence, its colossal problems—all these as much a part of my daily living as my own comfortable world of stout walls and carpeted floors and overflowing garbage pails. What could I do to interpret its needs to my fellow Christians who must somehow be made to understand, to *care* enough to help create a new world? I had shared many of my concerns in the two books, *House of Earth* (Westminster Press) and the excerpts from my diary, *Fly With Me to India*, brought out by Abingdon. I wrote several plays, among them *The Return of Chandra*, which was published with an accompanying television text, and *That Heaven of Freedom*, written for the Friendship Press. I taught the India course in several mission schools, gave many illustrated lectures, and went to Nashville to write a motion picture script for the Board of Missions, "India, Crucible of Freedom." Then even before I had finished *The Gifts*, another India project claimed attention.

The year 1956 marked the hundredth anniversary of the beginning of Methodist work in India, and I was asked to write a pageant celebrating this landmark for the Methodist General Conference, which meets every four years, this time in Minneapolis. I called it "Live for a Hundred Years;" and plans for its production were elaborate. An Indian chorus came to tour the country and participate. The music and speech departments of Hamline University were involved in the music and choral speech. A director in Minneapolis was hired, presumably an expert. Properties, including a charpoy and a litter, were brought from India. Of course I planned to attend, and to our delight my husband was elected for a third time to be a delegate to General Conference so we could go together.

A word of warning to playwrights: Don't go to see your plays produced unless you are prepared for disappointment. It can be a rewarding experience, atoning for all the sweat and agony of creation. It can be sheer misery. This was the latter. My first prescience of disaster came the day of the pageant when it developed that no dress rehearsal of the various sequences was planned! All the segments were to be brought together for the first time without a test of synchronization! That evening the huge convention hall was full. Delegations had come from all over the country. The program was scheduled to start at

41

over the country. The program was scheduled to start at seven. It didn't. Preliminaries lasted until nine! The production was a disappointment from the first. The litter bearing the first missionaries did not come down the aisle. The charpoy never did appear. Microphones failed at inopportune moments. The four Indian bishops, who had never rehearsed their scene, were predictably ineffective. At the time of the grand climax, when a young man representing Saint Thomas was entering with a cross, the chorus missed its cue and interposed a long Indian dance. And it could have been so challenging, with more planning and practice—and fewer preliminaries! I was presented with a beautiful Indian silver tea set for writing the pageant. The first time I used it, the teapot leaked! A bit symbolic of the whole affair.

But already a new room for creativity was being shaped in my chambered nautilus, one that would give far more scope of expression to my deepest concerns for human betterment and Christian service than I had ever dreamed. The playwright or novelist is always limited by the boundaries and vision of his own experience. Not so the biographer. The insights and achievements of the greatest souls of history are his to explore and share. "Live for a hundred years!" they say in India to bless a new-born child with long life and happiness. "Live for hundreds of years" is the invitation to the biographer. "Live the lives of people who have exhibited far more faith and courage, achieved far greater liberation for humanity than you could ever do."

My invitation was on the way. My other "lives" were about to begin.

PASSAGE TO INDIA

2
DR. IDA SCUDDER:
'DR. IDA'

It all began on a day in June, 1957, with a letter from my editor at the McGraw-Hill Book Company. He enclosed a brief sketch prepared by Christian Herald's Family Bookshelf on the life of Dr. Ida Scudder, founder of the international and interdenominational Christian Medical College and Hospital at Vellore, South India. The company was interested in publishing a book about her.

"The problem," the letter continued, "is how to get a writer, the right writer. Frankly, I wish you were in India yourself. You and your husband have no immediate plans to pack your bags and go back to India, do you? Short of that ideal solution, do you know of any American writer in India who might qualify?"

We were riding to some church meeting when I opened the letter and read it aloud. Then, with amazingly selfless understanding, remembering his unhappy six months when I had been away in India seven years before, my husband said, "Why don't you ask him if the company would finance a trip to India for a couple of months, while you did the research?"

It was like dangling a carrot in front of a rabbit's twitching nose. I waited only until we reached the next town before putting through a call to my editor. He was enthusiastic. No, unfortunately the company could not finance such a trip, but they would be glad to advance sufficient royalties to pay the

45

full cost. He doubted, however, if I could get the necessary material in two months. I might get the outline of her story rather easily, but the digging for personal material, the anecdotes, the eye-witness accounts—that was going to take time.

Plans developed with the speed of an express train. Both my editor and I wrote to Dr. Scudder and received replies from her niece and namesake, Dr. Ida B. S. Scudder, who was representing her aunt. Sometime in July, when plans were formulated, I received a cable, terse but satisfying.

"COME. SCUDDER."

There was much to do in preparation—shots for typhoid, paratyphoid, tetanus, cholera, yellow fever; visa, updating of passport; autographing a thousand fly leaves for my new biblical novel, *The Gifts*, which would be published in my absence—but on September 8 I was ready to leave, equipped with clothes for the tropics, my small Swiss typewriter, a fairly new camera, and hundreds of little three-by-five pieces of heavy paper for taking notes.

There is certainly a hoodoo on my travel across the Atlantic. Remember the oil leak in 1949? Now about an hour out of New York en route for Gander the pilot announced that one of the four engines had failed and we had to return to New York. He consoled us with the assurance that the plane could fly on only two if necessary but I think we were all relieved when we put down in Idlewild. After a long delay we started again, this time straight for Shannon. Ardor for flying unabated I exulted in the view from my little monocle of a window.

"We're flying over a moonlit wilderness of clouds," I wrote, "some as big as mountains, and the plane rocks like a ship on heavy waves. Sometimes we go straight through one. It's as if the Alps had become transparent and you flew right into them. Then suddenly you're looking down—down—on a great white plain. It's beautiful—and awful."

Shannon, Paris, Zurich, Milan, Rome, Athens, Basra. The head of the Persian Gulf, blue-green and misty . . . Dhahran, its heat like a furnace. I make friends with a lovely Indian girl with two sweet children, one of whom spent eight months in the Vellore hospital. And at last Bombay, its lights a glittering tiara circling the sable brow of the India Ocean.

As I rode into the city on the airport bus, India came alive for me again—her flamboyant colors, pungent smells, cacophony of sounds, medley of traffic, yes, and her dust, heat, drabness, poverty. I stayed that night in the Taj Mahal Hotel in a palace of a room with marble floors. How much to tip the cohort of servants who superintended my establishment? Not knowing, I tipped them all, becoming extremely popular. After *chota hazri* (tea) in my room the next morning I wandered through the vast corridors to mail a letter and got lost, and I had to inquire a half dozen times before I found my room. The airport bus was late so we had to careen through the maze of traffic. I gasped as we slithered past bullock carts, grazed the heels of darting coolies, barely missed by a hair bicycles, pushcarts, rickshas and ambling cows. But we arrived safely.

On the small lumbering Indian plane to Madras I tried to picture Dr. Ida as I had last seen her in 1950. It had been the year of her jubilee, marking half a century since her return to India on January 1, 1900, with a brand new doctor of medicine degree from Cornell, one of the first ever granted by that institution to a woman. Though almost eighty she had been as swift of motion, as vibrantly energetic as when I had first seen her, a little over fifty, hustling up the steep paths at Northfield, her eyes the same vivid blue, her shoulders still so straight that she had looked much taller than her five feet three, her crown of white hair just as soft and faintly tinged with gold.

Now, descending from the plane into the blinding heat of Madras, I saw her again, long before I had traversed the scorching apron to the distant terminal. She was standing in the portico, one hand on a cane, the other on the arm of her niece, Dr. Ida B. Scudder. Her shoulders were no longer straight. Her steps were slow and painful. But the eyes were the same lively blue, the white hair still faintly aglow with that youthful sheen. This time I gazed at her with more than curiosity, more even than admiration. For I knew I must not only chronicle her incredible achievements but penetrate the deep recesses of her personality, her sources of tremendous energy, her profound religious faith. I must literally relive her life with her.

Already I knew enough about her and her remarkable family to give zest to the adventure. Her grandfather, Dr. John Scudder I, sailing for India in 1819, was the first medical missionary to go out from America to a foreign country. Every one of his seven surviving sons had become missionaries. And out of the three succeeding generations forty-two members of the Scudder family had given a sum total of eleven hundred years to missionary service. The exploits of any one of them would have been enough to whet any author's appetite, and here I had been given carte blanche to delve into the adventures of the most famous of them all.

I knew the extraordinary story of her "call" to be a missionary, had heard her tell much of it herself at Northfield thirty-five years before. After graduating from Northfield Seminary in 1890 because of her mother's ill health Ida Scudder returned to India, the land of her birth, as a short-term missionary. But not to stay. She was determined never, never to become a full-time missionary like "those missionary Scudders." She had too many unpleasant memories connected with the job: the night of pouring rain when, a girl of fourteen, she had seen her mother off to join her father in India and had rushed upstairs in her uncle's Chicago home to weep out her unbearable desolation in her mother's pillow; worse yet, the days of the terrible famine when, a child of five in India, she and her five older brothers had doled food to starving children in the mission compound with never quite enough in the baskets to go around, feeding gruel and milk and bread into open mouths because the clawlike hands were too weak to lift them; when, riding home from church in the pony cart, she had seen two tiny figures lying by the roadside.

"Look at those children!" she had cried excitedly. "What—why—"

"They're dead," her *ayah* had told her with calm bluntness.

No, Ida Scudder, beautiful and in love with life at nineteen, wanted nothing to do with the appalling needs of a country for which so many of her family had sacrificed their lives. She would remain in India for a short time until her mother was recovered, then return to America and go to Wellesley College as she had planned, wed herself to either a rich man or an exciting career and live Life as she had dreamed it, with a capital "L."

But one night as she sat writing letters in the mission bungalow, dust drifting about her head from the forages of white ants in its thatched roof, something happened. Three men came, one after the other, to the veranda outside her door. The first was a Brahmin, highest of all the Hindu castes, the second a Muslim, the third another high caste Hindu. Each came with the same request. His young wife lay dangerously ill in childbirth, with none but the ignorant barber woman, traditional

48

midwife of India, to attend her. Would the young Missy *Ammal* from America come and help?

"But I couldn't help you. It's my father you want," the girl told each one, first eagerly, then hopefully, finally with desperation. "He's the doctor. Let me go and call him."

No. The answer each time was firm, resigned, final. Custom did not permit any man outside the family to even look on the face of his wife. It was *pavum*, a pity. But if the Missy *Ammal* could not help, then his wife must die. It was no doubt the will of Vishnu, Allah, Shiva.

Ida spent a sleepless night. In the morning she sent a servant to inquire about the three young wives. Even before he returned she heard the sound of funeral drums passing the bungalow on the road to the burning place at the river bank. All three of the young wives, the servant told her, were dead. After more long hours of struggle Ida went to her father and mother and announced simply, "I must go to America and study to be a doctor and come back to help the women of India."

Arriving in Vellore, a teeming city of some 140,000 about 80 miles west of Madras, I found the results of that decision all about me: the little ten-by-twelve room in the mission bungalow where Dr. Ida had opened a tiny dispensary in 1900, ministering during the first two years to over 5,000 patients; the little forty-bed hospital for which she herself had raised the money before returning to India, where for years she had been the only doctor; the huge sprawling medical center down in the heart of the city with its over 700 beds, its multiple departments, its staff of nearly a thousand, its efficient school of nursing, its branch hospitals, rural health centers, leprosarium and traveling dispensaries, its annual ministry to over 175,000 patients; the incredibly beautiful medical college four miles south of town, a small city in itself, abounding in stately stone buildings, profuse gardens, mountain vistas and more than three hundred of the most clear-eyed, alert, intelligent students to be found on any campus in the world.

Settled at the college in a comfortable bungalow built by the Methodists and occupied by the family of Dr. Reeve Betts, an eminent thoracic surgeon, I plunged into my research.

The work I faced was staggering. Not only must I steep myself in eighty-seven years of a great woman's life, crammed to the brim with activity and achievement, but I must soak up all the intricate local color of what was for me a strange environment. Most of my previous research on India had been in the north. Here in the south I would encounter new customs, languages, religious ceremonies, racial backgrounds. Besides assembling those eighty-seven years of facts and impressions about my heroine, I must make available for future reference exhaustive data on climate, flowers, trees, birds, animals, stars, food, crops, houses, cooking, building, transportation, dress, jewelry, education, birth, weddings, funerals, superstitions, feasts, worship, temples, gods, money, government, diseases, remedies, hospitals. And I had promised my husband that I would be home in three months!

"This time," I wrote him, "I shall not be doing much traveling. But I don't need to in order to see south India. Vellore has almost everything. Its huge fort contains a Hindu temple where you can find some of the finest stone carvings in all India. You have only to walk or ride along the streets for five minutes and you see a complete cross section of Indian life: palatial houses surrounded by gardens and villages of red mud-brick with thatched roofs; modern European shops and picturesque open-front bazaars; naked holy men and city officials smartly turned out in spotless white coats and trousers; ragged beggar women with scraps of babies at their breasts and beautiful ladies in rainbow saris wearing solid gold chains and earrings and sparkling nose gems; villagers with huge baskets atop their heads and road workers driving tractors; Fords and Plymouths honking their way insistently through a maze of bullock bandies, push carts, bicycles, buses, pedestrians stubborning scorning sidewalks for the center of the street, farmers with huge cartloads and headloads of vegetables, sugar cane, or bamboo, darting children, rickshas and, of course, cows. It is all part of the contrasts which are India."

But I had not come to travel. Equipped with a dozen notebooks, my ream of paper cut into three-by-fives, four ball point pens, four mechanical pencils (three of them soon stolen) and my little typewriter, I set to work. Just so an artist must assemble his palette, paints, and brushes before attempting his picture. It was a portrait I had come to paint but the subject was elusive. My hopes of spending long hours with Dr. Ida while she poured forth with graphic spontaneity the details of her long life had soon evaporated.

"If you had only come two years ago," I was told regretfully, "or even a year! Since she had the stroke Aunt Ida is not the same person. Oh, if you could only have seen her!"

But I did see her, grateful that the vivid, radiant, energetic figure still lived in my memory. However, I realized with dismay, a fleeting memory had little substance. I must depend on others not only for the outlines of the portrait but for all the subtle lines, nuances, shadings of color which would make it a living thing. Meanwhile I could at least fill in the background, for the creations of her tremendous faith and energy were all about me.

"It is now Saturday," I wrote three days after my arrival. "Each day I have said, 'I must start my diary. I must get this down before I forget it.' But there has been no time. Now, however, I must find time, because I am so full of what I have seen this morning. I got up earlier than usual, had breakfast at 6:45 instead of 7:00 and went with Dr. Ida B. to visit the hospital.

"Words can't describe it," I wrote after a visit to the hospital. "If I had had any doubts of the value of this thing I came to India to do, they would all have vanished this morning. The grain of mustard seed planted in the tiny dispensary by Dr. Ida 57 years ago has certainly grown into a mighty tree. Never have I seen so much need and so much being done to relieve it. We saw all the buildings, including a new out-patient section just going up. As soon as you enter the gate you hear the pounding of hammers, see lean bullocks dragging heavy loads of stone and earth and bricks, watch the workers, many of them women, mount the ladders with towering baskets on their heads. You can easily get lost in the maze of corridors. Many of the buildings are built around open courts with flowering trees and gardens and beautiful Northfield Chapel is in the middle of the whole vast complex. Every inch of space seems to be filled with patients, some even in the corridors, under the beds. The young Indian doctors and nurses, both men and women, many trained at the college or here at the school of nursing, are an inspiration just to look at. Their faces seem to shine. And the gleaming white saris of the women doctors and nurses are the most graceful dress in the world.

"One of the most interesting places we visited was the leprosy ward, where amazing things are being done by Dr. Paul Brand who has discovered new methods of transplanting muscles so that useless hands and other members of the body can be made useful. He has just found a way to graft on a new nose

51

by taking tissue from the hip. The man whose nose had been operated on ran after us crying out that we must see what had been done for him. It was a beautiful nose."

(Why, I wonder now, did I pick out this one marvel of all those multiple areas of healing to write home about? Did I have a prescience that one day the man who performed these miracles would become another of my dozen lives?)

There was no dearth of people willing and anxious to help with research. Dr. Ida was a legend not only in Vellore but for hundreds of miles around. Indeed a letter once sent from America with the sole address, "Dr. Ida, India," had promptly reached its destination. Wherever I went, in college, hospital, church, bazaar or bus, people came to me, faces beaming, with bits of information and anecdotes.

"She used to keep four clocks in her room, all five minutes fast, to make sure she would get places on time!"

"Once, when she was examiner in Anatomy for the University of Madras and snowed under with work, she went and sat in a tub of cold water to wake herself up so she could correct all the papers."

"Have you heard the one about Aunt Ida and the tennis tournament? It happened only a few years ago. A young girl champion drew the doctor's name and went home wailing to her mother, 'Oh, dear, I've pulled a granny!' Hearing of the statement, Aunt Ida remarked tartly, 'I'll granny her!' Whereupon she wiped up the court with her young opponent, not letting her take a single game!"

"After she was worn out from operations, she would come home, change her dress, put on a flower and call gaily, 'Let's have some music and fun!'"

"Once a young American sailor came to Madras with only twenty-four hours leave. Somebody had told him he must see the medical center at Vellore. He arrived at two in the morning. Aunt Ida insisted on getting up and, taking a lantern, she showed him the new hospital with as much enthusiasm as if he'd been John D. Rockefeller!"

Oh, yes, everybody was eager to dispense information—except the one person from whom I most needed it.

"Oh, dear," Dr. Ida would worry when I began asking her questions about the past, "I can't remember. How frustrating! My brains are getting slower than my feet."

Frustrating indeed to one who at fifty, with no buildings, no

52

staff, no money, successfully launched a medical college for Indian women; at sixty was engineering the building of one of the most outstanding medical centers in Asia; at seventy-two was starting a four-year trek up and down America campaigning for her third million dollars; at eighty was still playing championship tennis, climbing mountains, giving the hospital nurses a run to keep up with her, racing sightseers ragged; and at eighty-six, less than a year before, was riding an elephant for four hours through the jungles of Mysore state, looking for wild animals! Frustrating also to one who had come halfway around the world to write her story. Before the first week was over I was close to despair.

"Wait," counseled Dr. Ida B. "We will find material. We're going to Hill Top next week."

We did, traveling the 250 miles to Kodaikanal by car—the two Idas, Lizzie (Aunt Ida's capable companion-nurse), the young driver and myself. In spite of the long summer's drought and the blistering heat the country was beautiful, for the monsoons had just broken. Rice fields shimmered in patchwork squares of turquoise and every shade of green from pale lime to bright emerald. The queer upthrusts of rock hills so typical of south India wore their dingy temples like crowns of old ivory. Even the women bending at their back-breaking labor of transplanting rice seedlings struck bright accents of color in their red saris. Fascinated, I watched this unrolling canvas of Dr. Ida's broader world.

Then as we started up the mountain *ghat* the desert cactus gave way to tall savannah grass, coffee plants and banana trees. Instead of palms there were jungles of giant trees craning their necks out of a sheer abyss. The sweltering heat gave way to blessed coolness until at 5,000 feet we had to don our sweaters. A thousand feet higher we caught the mingled fragrance of roses and eucalyptus which Ida B. assured us was a herald of our journey's end.

Hill Top! A big stone house on the tip and summit of the mountain spur. It was evening when we arrived and a fire was glowing in the upstairs living room where Sebastian, Lizzie's husband and Aunt Ida's caretaker of the retreat, had the table laid with a delicious supper. Never shall I forget the thrill of stepping out on the upper terrace and seeing the lights of Periakulam (Big Tank) stabbing through a rift in the clouds from 7,000 feet below.

The place yielded far more than the invigorating coolness and vistas of incredible beauty. Bless Aunt Ida, she was a hoarder! She had kept letters written by her mother back in the 1880s, their neat spidery script as legible as black type. There was a delightfully naive diary of her last half year at Northfield; and, rarest treasure of all, a packet of some of the most tender and poetic love letters ever written by man to woman! Out of the mass of materials emerging from trunks, closets, bureaus, bare outlines of the portrait began to appear. But I could soon see that it was Ida B. whose deft sensitive brush would supply most of the fine lines and shadings. In fact, I was beginning to sense that the book would be Ida B.'s almost as much as mine!

"You should have seen this place in the hot seasons. Tired nurses, doctors, patients convalescing, all invited here by Aunt Ida for a 'nice restful vacation'! For everybody but herself. She used to get up at three in the morning to write necessary letters and work in the bathroom so as not to disturb her guests."

"And her gardens! The summer residents used to come at all hours, and she had to show every plant and shrub and blossom herself. She was so proud of her rare varieties, like her celebrated 'green rose' and the daffodils that were smuggled in in the toe of a returning missionary's shoe. Oh, Aunt Ida must always have a garden . . . and a view! See how the eucalyptus trees are pruned high toward their tops? There must be a view even if the poor climbers had to risk their necks!"

"How she loved to plant trees! And not just *plant* them. A tree to Aunt Ida was a created being, a personality like the rose bush she named 'Mab' because one of her pet dogs was buried under it. 'Sing,' she would tell the gardener gaily as they planted a tender green eucalyptus, 'Let's sing together. Grow, grow, grow, unto the God who made you!'"

As we ate breakfast on the upper terrace, with Aunt Ida feeding choice bits to her beloved golden Labrador retriever, Tanya, I learned of her succession of dogs.

"Always a dog beside her when she ate," chuckled Ida B., "and a cat on her desk when she wrote letters."

Tiny lines, perhaps, in the portrait, but surely significant—this love of life wherever she found it in God's creation, whether in flowers, animals or human beings!

We returned to Vellore with three huge suitcases full of

letters, diaries, newspaper clippings, notebooks, business files, pamphlets, programs, pictures, souvenirs, lecture notes, building plans, engraved invitations, yellowed dust, white ants and silverfish. On the way I stopped in Tindivanum to see the old bungalow where some time between 1890 and 1894 Dr. Ida had heard those "three knocks in the night."

Back in Vellore I moved into Dr. Ida B.'s rooms in the "Big Bungalow," not far from Dr. Ida on the floor below, and plunged into the work of sorting, cataloguing, interviewing, visiting all the places connected with Dr. Ida's life. Ida B. was an invaluable resource person about not only Aunt Ida but everything connected with her beloved India. I pumped her with questions and she taught me about flowers, birds, trees with all their varied blooms, stars, crops, Indian foods, religious customs, sari-draping—even smells.

"Please analyze all the odors," I begged her one warm evening as we walked through the narrow streets around the hospital. She did so—incense, jasmine (as we passed a little temple), cowdung smoke, spices, cooking curry, the open drain in front of the hospital which Dr. Ida worked so many years to get covered up. ("No!" she had protested when the town wanted to erect a monument to her. "Cover up the drain instead!")

"What's that sound?" I asked Ida B. one night as we were getting ready for bed. She listened to the *chuk-chuk-chuk-chuk-r-r-r* and nodded. "It's the call of the night jar." The *tuk . . . tuk* that I heard outside my porch bedroom one morning, she told me, was a coppersmith hammering out his loud call. We studied the stars, as we had done at Kodai, using her rotation star map to locate unfamiliar (to me) constellations. I believe she enjoyed the mind-probing almost as much as I did.

"I think I had always noticed things about me," she wrote long afterward, "but I learned a lot from being with you—to see and hear and feel the little things that add so much to daily living. What a good time that was!"

Since she as head of the radiology department was involved in a grueling schedule at the hospital, however, my guide on many expeditions was often Treva Marshall. Treva had been at Vellore since 1923, functioning as dietician, X-ray technician, hostel matron, as well as a dozen other roles, and the book would become almost as much her baby as Ida B's. Dr. Ida herself often accompanied us on these trips. At the old mission bungalow where she had started her work in 1900 I took her picture standing in the same window through which she had handed out medicines for two years to an ever lengthening line of patients, saw the little room where she had put first one bed, then two, finally six for the treatment of in-patients. Nearby was her first hospital built in 1902 by a Mr. Schell, who had heard young Ida tell of the needs of Indian women and had donated $10,000 in memory of his wife, Mary Taber Schell. Here Dr. Ida had carried on her work until 1923, when the new big hospital had been built down in the center of town and this building had become its eye department.

How to compress those twenty years of struggle, frustration, triumph into a few hundred three-by-five bits of paper? There were many to help, like Mrs. Cornelius, widow of the minister of the little Tamil church, who had helped Dr. Ida in those early years of famine, bubonic plague, swarms of patients.

"When she performed her first major operation there was no one to help her but Salomi, the butler's wife, who had never even given anaesthetic. She was so frightened she almost decided she couldn't do it. But during the first year she performed twenty-one such operations, all successful, and treated over 12,000 patients."

There was Mary Taber Sebastian, namesake of the hospital, the little Muslim baby born on an "unlucky day" who had been given to Dr. Ida at birth and brought up as her own daughter. Now a happy, highly intelligent wife and mother, she told me with many chuckles about her wedding, arranged Indian fashion by Dr. Ida. Like her life, it had been a strange merging of East and West, long skirts and flowered hats side by side with saris and turbans.

We visited the nursing school near the big hospital, lusty child of the little training class which Dr. Ida had boldly started in 1907 at a time when any profession, especially nursing, was considered degrading, tabu, for women in India. It had grown through the years to one of the finest schools in the country, accepting only high school trained candidates and giving college and post-graduate degrees, during its first half century sending over 700 of its graduates to meet the needs of this land where there is still only one nurse for every 11,000 of its population.

But soon she had another dream, for no matter how hard or how long she worked she could barely scratch the surface of

56

India's need. Nor could any or all of the Western woman doctors or the few Indian ones scattered through this land of 150 million women. Moving in and out of little dark rooms behind courtyards, crawling up under the stifling hoods of bullock carts to deliver babies, fighting losing battles over the bodies of young mothers tortured by barber's wife obstetrics, she came to one conclusion: *She must train young Indian women to be doctors.*

I climbed the high rocky mound on the edge of the campus where in 1913 Dr. Ida had taken two prominent Baptist women and tried to sell them the dream of a medical college in the mountain-girt valley below, empty save for rice fields and a few grazing goats. She did. Lucy Peabody, a woman of dynamic leadership, caught the vision.

"You are going to build that college," she vowed, with a flare of enthusiasm kindled from Ida's white-hot purpose, "and you are going to build it here, in this valley."

Fascinated, amazed by her sheer audacity and consummate faith, I followed her struggle through years of diaries, letters, clippings, speech notes: the frustrating war years with money going to liberty bonds instead of missions; the happy choice of Vellore by the South India Medical Association for a women's college; securing consent of the British Medical Department in 1918 to start a small school.

"But you have no buildings, no money, no staff!" protested Colonel Bryson of the Madras Medical Department.

"We'll get them. Meanwhile we will rent houses near the present hospital. And I myself will teach the subjects for first year students."

"Don't be discouraged," she was warned, "if you get no more than three applications."

She got sixty-nine! Rigid in her standards, she accepted only eighteen, and one of these dropped out before the school opened on August 12, 1918.

"Seeing is believing," declared the skeptical Colonel at the formal opening of the Union Missionary Medical School for Women.

I was able to visit one of those first students, Dr. Ebbie Thomas, superintendent of a fine south Indian hospital, and relive with her the struggles and triumphs of those early years when the little class, soon reduced to fourteen, had been the focus of Dr. Ida's vast energy and concern. Rising often at

57

three after studying half the night, she had taught them, trailed them after her through the hospital and into villages, making every patient an object lesson, every surgical triumph an educational adventure. They had been her work, her play, her joy, her despair, her first and last anxiety both sleeping and waking, the very air she breathed. Never could they move quite fast enough to suit her.

"Once," Ebbie remembered with a tender twinkle, "she sent for one of us, a bright pupil named Kamala, and in spite of hurrying it took her a long time to arrive, for she had to come a long way. 'Did you crawl?' asked Dr. Ida tartly. It became a byword with us: *'Did you crawl?'*"

"Don't be discouraged, my dear doctor," the Colonel told Ida kindly when she took her class to Madras for their first year's examinations, "if all of them fail."

"All of them?" she repeated bleakly.

"It wouldn't be surprising. Only a small percentage of men pass it."

Ida was as terrified as her students huddled in a room of a mission bungalow waiting to hear the results. And when they became known she was jubilant. Every one of her girls had passed, four of them in the first class. They had led every medical school in the Madras Presidency!

Standing on the rocky mound I gazed down at the valley with its glorious fulfillment of the dream, a dozen and more stately buildings of native stone, in their midst the beautiful domed chapel with its lily pool and sunken garden, and remembered the long struggle which had brought it to fruition. Surrounded by the mountains of materials I followed her through not only the fulfillment of her dream but also its near annihilation, for in 1938 the new Indian provincial government, worthily intent on raising educational standards, decreed that all medical schools unable to qualify for the Bachelor of Medicine, Bachelor of Surgery degree, must accept no more students. It was a staggering blow. Any less indomitable spirit would have yielded to the inevitable.

Not Dr. Ida. Lose her beloved college? Over seventy, with the world rocked by war on its foundations, she trekked across America in quest of her third million dollars. I pursued her through almost four years of travel, from 1941 to 1945, riding jammed trains and buses, competing doggedly with war charities and glaring battle headlines, speaking often three or four times a day, fighting a life-and-death battle to save her dream.

And it was her inexorable zest for pioneering which made the miracle possible, for she saw that a new day was coming to India. The isolation of women would soon be a thing of the past. By permitting Vellore to become a coeducational institution supported by men and women of all major Protestant denominations, she not only saved it but equipped it with new potentials to meet the demands of a young free nation emerging into the modern world.

Dr. Ida was as concerned with the welfare of the new men students as she had ever been with the women. She noticed that they were still living in makeshift quarters, eating in a mud and thatch building.

"This is no way to treat your students," she accused the men's dean. "Why don't you build them a decent hostel?"

"I want to, Aunt Ida," he explained ruefully. "We're just waiting for the money to come."

Her blue eyes scored him. "Huh! If I'd waited for money to come, we wouldn't have anything. Let's get going."

A *lakh* of rupees (about $20,000) had been sent her by women all over the world for her jubilee and there was another half lakh she had intended to leave to Vellore in her will. True, a lakh and a half would not go far toward an eight-lakh building but she had never been one to sit at the foot of a mountain because she couldn't see the top. She made the decision in the morning and broke sod for the new building in the afternoon.

The college Council, though grateful, was still cautious. "After the one and a half lakhs are gone," it warned, "you must stop." Dr. Ida only smiled.

Now, in 1957, I was able to visit the beautiful new hostel, fully completed and landscaped with everblooming gardens.

Yes, the tiny seed planted more than a half century before had grown into a huge tree like the banyan constantly putting down fresh tendrils which taking root had become themselves sturdy trunks. If Dr. Ida had not herself created all of them, they were as much a part of her achievement as the offshoots of the banyan are native to the original stalk. I must study every one of them.

With Pauline King, an American public health nurse, I traveled into villages, watched her and her student assistants treat leprosy, dysentery, malaria, anemia, hookworm, roundworm, scabies. Pauline was a worthy successor of Aunt Ida. For three months of her previous year's vacation she had lived in the untouchables' section of a village in order to really know the people. "If you just treat them," she believed, "you are continents apart." I saw her and one of her students show a mother how to bathe a tiny baby and treat him for scabies, while the village midwife, probably not a trained woman, looked over her shoulder. Vellore had four active village centers with vans of workers going frequently to each one.

I spent a weekend in one of the eye camps started by a famous specialist, Dr. Victor Rambo. A place was appointed to which people in surrounding villages could come with eye ailments. Sometimes it was a church, sometimes a school or just an open veranda. Here it was an old mill warehouse. I saw sixty people operated on for cataract, one of India's curses, then stretched on mats on the earth floor with skilled attendants left to care for them; I also saw patients previously operated on fitted for glasses and watched them discover the miracle of sight. How Aunt Ida had exulted in this outgrowth of her vast concern. "Whereas I was blind, now I can see!"

I visited Karigiri, site of the Schiefflin Leprosy Research Sanatorium related to the hospital, where Dr. Paul Brand and his wife Margaret were revolutionizing the treatment of leprosy, restoring crippled hands and feet to usefulness, correcting facial disfigurements through plastic surgery and teaching doctors from all over India and other countries. But it was in retracing Dr. Ida's trail on "Roadside" that I had some of my most exciting adventures.

It had begun with a trip each week to Gudiyattam, a city twenty-three miles from Vellore, where starting in 1909 she went every Wednesday to hold a dispensary in the churchyard. Rising at five she would drive her pony cart four miles to Katpadi station, stow herself in a railroad compartment with all her equipment, ride to the Gudiyattam station, also miles from town, hire a *jutka* to take her to the churchyard where she would treat between fifty and a hundred patients. Then later that same year she wrote in her diary in capitals: "SEPTEMBER 23, 1909. THE NEW MOTOR CAME TODAY."

It was a little French Peugeot, high and open, with a folding top, wire-spoked wheels and two seats. Now, swathed in duster, *topee* secured with a long veil, a mechanic to drive them, she and Salomi could ride straight to Gudiyattam, such a confusion of dust and noise that people rushed off shrieking, "The devil is coming!" But soon those along the way were running toward them instead, as villagers discovered that
60

instead of a devil the strange apparition bore an angel of healing. Dr. Ida could not stop to treat them all so she appointed certain stations where she would meet and treat patients each week and "Roadside" was born.

I went with Dr. Ida to Gudiyattam and visited the little mud and thatch hut in the churchyard where for long years she had come each Wednesday to hold her dispensary. As she sat in front of it behind a low table surrounded by some of her early helpers and the nurses in the new Gudiyattam hospital, women came and knelt beside her, as once patients had come to be treated. The picture I took is a graphic memento of those early days, but only a picture. The trip I took on a Friday Roadside nearly fifty years after its beginning was reality.

We left the hospital early one morning in a big ambulance, burly descendant of the little Peugeot—two Indian doctors, a medical student, several nurses, two seniors in the School of Nursing wearing the deep blue sari of the public health nurse, two compounders, an evangelist, a clerk, a peon or general handyman, Dr. Ida B., Mary Taber Sebastian, myself and the driver. Leaving the Vellore streets we turned off on the road to Odugathur. It was a narrow bumpy road but all along its sides were gems of beauty—brimming rice fields reflecting the blue sky, fields of waving sugar cane just springing into silvery tufts, little green plots of land—and it wound through long tunnels of arching banyans and tamarinds. Suddenly a huge crowd appeared ahead, a garden of bright red and green and yellow saris. The ambulance pulled up under a tree at the roadside and we poured out. My head whirled. Hundreds of them there must be. Surely we would be here all day—a week—before all were treated.

But order emerged from chaos and the roadside turned as if by magic into an efficient, departmentalized dispensary. The crowd tightened into a circle. Prayers were said in Tamil. Then Dr. Ida B. followed in English with a plea that the staff might be guided in Christian love and sympathy and skill in their day of service. I could hear Dr. Ida praying just so on forty years of other Roadsides and as I stood with eyes closed I was no longer on a roadside in India but on a dusty lane in Palestine, hearing a strong, assuring voice say, "Come unto Me."

The weekly routine proceeded—long queues of patients coming to the doctors' tables to be diagnosed; the nurses at the surgical shelf dressing abscesses, giving injections, cutting hair and applying ointments to horribly inflamed scalps, putting drops in sore eyes and infected ears, treating worms, malaria, scabies and a hundred other things; the two compounders exchanging chits for packets of pills and powders, pouring medicine into the makeshift bottles which each patient must provide for himself; Mary Taber Sebastian doling out precious stores of dried milk and wheat and ragi, measured into battered and often rusted tins; the religious worker surrounded by a group of children using a flannelgraph to tell the story of the Good Samaritan; the lines of leprosy patients with their special doctor.

"No real need of *telling* it," I thought. "They can see it being *lived*, right here and now."

Sitting beside Ida B. on a folding stool, I was no longer a foreigner, aloof. With the crowd pressing around me, dark faces bent close to mine, ragged saris brushing my shoulders, I was submerged in all the poverty and sickness and suffering which still enslaves so much of India. And in the concern and skill of this woman who shared both her name and her dedication I saw Aunt Ida's forty years on Roadside reenacted.

A dignified Muslim in beard and turban called Ida B. to look at his wife, hidden inside a bullock cart behind the *gosha* curtain protecting her from male eyes. Dr. Ida, I knew, had delivered babies in just such carts, the thermometer soaring to 110, in a day when missionary ladies were expected to wear high necks, tight waists and billowing skirts. I watched Ida B. examine three pregnant patients on the ground within protective curtains formed by the floating ends of their saris held by obliging females. "The gynecology department," she told me with her dry humor.

We made three more stops before the day was over and at the last one, Odugathur, Dr. Ida herself joined us in her car. She could not sit quietly watching. One of my most treasured pictures shows her squatted beside Ida B. as the latter probed by lantern light into an abscess beneath the hard horny flesh of a young woman's foot. The surgery must have been agonizing but I was sure the pain was made easier because Dr. Ida's hands and voice were there to comfort.

"Patients say," one of the doctors told me, "that they don't care who operates on them if only Dr. Ida is there to hold their hand.'" Yes, even Dr. Paul Brand's leprosy patients whose hands possessed no feeling sensed somehow the healing magnetism of her touch on their clawed fingers.

The day's reckoning showed over a thousand patients treated. As we rode back through the dark the team started singing "We Are Climbing Jacob's Ladder." "Every round," I repeated silently and humbly. Forty years, perhaps forty weeks out of each year Dr. Ida had made just such a trip. Sixteen hundred times. A long way from the chugging little Peugeot to this versatile ambulance with its skilled team and efficient, sterile equipment. Thousands of miles . . . hundreds of thousands of patients. Back in the bungalow I clacked out the story of the day on my little typewriter and called it "Christ Rides the Indian Road."

The finer lines of Dr. Ida's portrait were beginning to emerge—patience softening the indomitable purpose, skywide vision coupled with intense love of the smallest manifestation of beauty, ambition and self-assurance tempered by devout humility, boundless energy spiced with adventurous zest and gaiety. Fresh insights came through conversation, observation, reading, actual experience.

"She was such a careful surgeon, so meticulous, not brilliant but so patient and painstaking. There was one operation on women for which she became famous. A nun once came from Europe to have her perform it. She seemed to have a way with human tissues. It was almost as if she could—could recreate them, she cared so much."

"On the day of my impending operation," Dr. Hilda Lazarus told me, "I found her sitting on the steps weeping. When I asked her why, she confessed half ashamedly, 'I'm just so sorry to have to hurt you.'"

Almost every interview yielded one pungent anecdote, like the gem from a friend of Dr. Ida in Madras. One blisteringly hot day Colonel Paton, resident surgeon of the Vellore Government Hospital, asked Dr. Ida to help him with a difficult case. She came promptly, as always, looking as fresh and vigorous as if she enjoyed having the thermometer register 107 in the shade.

"Sorry to bother you," he apologized. "Shorthanded. Such a beastly day."

"I know." She smiled sympathetically. "I'm having one too."

Feeling guilty for calling her from her own work on such a busy morning, he was glad when, later in the day, she was obliged to call him to Schell to assist with another emergency case. It was ten that night when he finally finished his rounds. "Poor Dr. Scudder!" he thought ruefully. "She must be half dead with exhaustion. I wonder how her patient is." He called a conveyance and rode to her compound to commiserate with her. Arriving at the bungalow entrance he saw a pinprick of lantern light in the nearby garden and thought, "Poor woman, she's probably out there on her knees praying."

Quietly he crossed the grass. It was Dr. Ida but she was not praying. He stared. She was *digging*. Heavens, had her day been that bad? Had it driven her a little—

She greeted him merrily. "How nice of you to come! When I found out both of our patients were all right, I was so happy that I invited some friends in to celebrate. Then I remembered this basket of nasturtium plants that had been neglected all day. I just had to get out and get them in the ground. Everybody else had been working hard and was too tired," She sprang up, looking as unwearied as if it were early morning. "Come into the house," she invited gaily. "We'll have some more coffee and music. You've had an exhausting day."

I went with Dr. Ida while she climbed slowly and painfully to the top floor of a hospital ward to give a flower to each patient. I watched her in the out-patient dispensary giving advice and comfort to mothers with mites of sickly, undernourished children. In the sunken garden by the lily pool I saw her sit surrounded by students, laughing with her, sharing jokes, ideas, problems, in their eyes a respect approaching adoration. *Darshan*, they call it in India, the blessing accorded one by the sheer presence of a Great Soul, a Mahatma.

One day I traveled with her through the hospital and marveled that this smiling white-haired woman could have created this vast medical center, one of the largest in all Asia, supported by over forty church groups in more than ten different countries.

"Don't you feel a great satisfaction," I asked her, "seeing all this and remembering that you started it all?"

"Oh, yes, yes," she replied fervently. "God has been very good to me."

I gazed at her in wonder. No pride, only gratitude. *God has been very good to me.*

She reached for my arm with one hand, for her cane with the other. "What are we doing standing here? We still have places to go, things to do. *Juldi, juldi!*"

Juldi, hurry. Only one other Indian expression did I hear more frequently on her lips. *San thosham*, happiness.

The three months were nearly gone. Did I have enough

material for a book? It looked so. Packing most of my clothes and acquired souvenirs in a little Indian tin trunk to follow me I filled suitcase and brief bag with letters, pamphlets, pictures, clippings, diaries, a dozen and a half exposed films and the hundreds of little three-by-five papers, all typewritten on both sides, single spaced. It seemed almost like leaving home, so much had I become a part of the staff, the campus, the medical center, the colorful, teeming, sprawling city of Vellore, the beautiful, tragic land which had long since become my second country. Especially was it difficult to leave Dr. Ida. Already the process had begun which for the next year would link her life inextricably with my own.

"Don't worry. It will write itself," a noted editor who knew Dr. Ida had reassured me. He was nearly right. My subject grew almost without my volition—the child in India, doling bread to starving children crying *"Pasi, pasi,"* never enough in her basket to fill them . . . the teenager at Northfield poignantly revealed in scraps of diary ("Got to laughing in chapel, and oh how I was squelched by Miss Hall! She very kindly told me I had been a stumbling block to some . . .") . . . the carefree young woman changed by those "three knocks in the night" . . . the medical student, radiant, beautiful, besieged by admiring suitors, especially one whose letters were to follow her to India ("So my Bonny dreamed of me! Was it a pleasant dream? In my mind I have had Bonny in my arms many times, but never once in reality . . . Take time from your little detail work to contemplate the vast, worldwide things. . . . Now good-bye, little girl.") . . . the doctor pioneering, dreaming, agonizing, praying, building, achieving, never resting.

The manuscript went to Dr. Ida B. in India piecemeal, on onionskin paper, and she corrected, suggested and, to my joy, approved. In early 1959 she came home on furlough and we consulted, read proof, pleaded with my editor to retain certain incidents which he feared would add too much to the price of the book. They did! When my first copy arrived in October and I saw the price, low by today's standards, I was appalled. Surely it would not sell! In New York on my way to teach a course on religious drama writing in Mexico City I called the publishers to see if it could not be reduced. Useless, of course. As well try to persuade Uncle Sam to reduce one's income tax!

But we need not have worried. Not in vain had Dr. Ida trekked the country on numerous furloughs, delivered hundreds of lectures, roused the women of many denominations to pray mightily and contribute millions to make her dream come true. She was beloved by thousands. Though never attaining best-seller status the book sold well, went through eleven large printings, was the selection of a religious book club, was published in England and translated into German, French, Hindi and Danish. Recently it appeared in a paperback edition. Of the more than one hundred letters from all over the world in my files the one I prize most was written by Dr. Gwenda Lewis, a British member of the Vellore staff, on May 15, 1960.

"During the holidays," she wrote, "I have had the very real pleasure of reading your book aloud to Dr. Ida herself. She has enjoyed it much, making frequent remarks such as, 'Isn't it interesting?' or, 'I had forgotten that.' Several times she said, 'Who wrote this book? It is very well written.' Just now I mentioned that I had thought of writing to tell you how much she has enjoyed it, and she said, 'Please do that, and I will sign it.'"

And did she sign it? Yes. On the back of that letter, written by Dr. Ida's nurse, Helen Preston, is a postscript:

"Dr. Gwenda Lewis has asked me to finish this. Well, I can only say that Aunt Ida enjoys every chapter. She lives in the past now, poor old dear, so it comes back to her afresh. I have only read as far as Chapter 12 to her but the various visiting members of the household pick up and read a chapter here and there. The Gudiyattam incidents ring out more clearly than anything. She is awake now and I shall ask her in her own words to finish this up.

"'Please give her my very dear love and blessings and say how much I enjoy having "Dr. Ida" read to me. So glad some-one was able to make a book of all the wonderful experiences God has brought along my way. With much much love.'

This letter was written at Hill Top on May 15. Just nine days later on May 24 she was gone. Like Dr. Ida B. who was on her way back to India from furlough and whom I met in Oberammergau a few days later I would have liked to be in India to witness her triumphant homecoming. But through the accounts of many friends I was able to relive these last hours of the woman whose life I was privileged to chronicle.

Yes, it was May, hottest of all months in south India. Vellore broiled in the suffocating heat yet crowds by the hundreds moved en masse into the center of town; others poured in unending streams from the surrounding countryside. Stores were closed, shops shuttered, bazaars deserted as for a holiday. But it was no holiday. An awed hush accompanied the crowds. Hindus, Muslims, Christians—all were fused into one by a heat of emotion stronger even than India's blazing sun.

"Aunt Ida has gone!"

The news had sped to Vellore from Hill Top. The great hospital became hushed and stricken. The most skilled surgeon was one in emotion with the humblest probationer. Though the huge medical center continued to function mechanically it was a body from which the spirit had fled.

The town was scarcely less stricken, for Dr. Ida was as much a part of its life and tradition as its founder, Bommai Reddy, builder of the great 700-year-old stone fort in the center of town. More, for Bommai Reddy's monument was dead but Dr. Ida's gave new life daily to a thousand people. Men she had brought into the world stopped work and became silent. Women whose lives she had saved lifted corners of their saris to wipe their eyes. Even the large percentage of the town's population who had never known her personally felt bereavement. A group of boys playing an exciting football game on the town playing field heard the news and with sober faces quietly disappeared.

Now to do her honor they came in such crowds as only India can muster. For the public service they poured into the courtyard of the hospital because there was no church or hall that could begin to hold them. They followed in dense masses after the flower-decked open carriage, lined the streets as the beloved figure, face visible to all after the Indian custom, made its last slow journey along the familiar road where so often it had rushed in pony cart, *jutka*, ancient Peugeot, modern ambulance or on its own tireless, swift feet.

They crowded through the gate and over the wall of the little foreign cemetery, filling every inch of ground space, climbing trees and almost causing a crisis until a persuasive voice over the broadcasting system helped clear a space for those who were to conduct the burial service. Then finally they filled her resting place to the brim with the flowers she had loved, that glorious abundance of beauty which is India's compensation for this season of drought and dearth and dust. It was fitting that they should leave her here to be mingled in body as well as spirit with the earth of her adopted country.

She lived her ninety years to the tune of trumpet calls and they always sounded reveille, never taps. This last and clearest for which she had waited long with faith and expectancy was no exception. For never has she been more alive. Her skilled hands and brisk feet are multiplied by thousands, all dedicated to her sublime task of healing. Her energy flows through the pulsing arteries of a great subcontinent, creating the new life, both physical and spiritual, which she did so much to bring into being.

I was blessed indeed to have relived this life with her.

3

DR. CLARA SWAIN: 'PALACE OF HEALING'

It was some years later that I began reliving the life of a predecessor of Dr. Ida, Clara Swain, the world's first woman missionary doctor. In 1970 the hospital she had founded in Bareilly, North India, was having its hundredth birthday.

When its superintendent, Dr. Ernest Sundaram, wrote asking if I would prepare a history of the hospital for the occasion he doubtless envisioned a little pamphlet, certainly not a book. But research for the pageant celebrating one hundred years of Methodist work in India had impressed me with the dramatic story of Clara Swain. Moreover the worldwide Methodist women's society would be celebrating the hundredth anniversary of the founding of its parent organization in 1969. A book about these beginnings and the hospital which grew out of them would be my contribution to the two events.

Another journey to India! Though I had visited Clara Swain Hospital briefly in 1949 and had accumulated many historical records more first-hand experience was necessary. I planned the trip for November, 1966, when I could combine my research with a visit to Vellore coinciding with the dedication of a Memorial Auditorium to Dr. Ida on her birthday, December 9.

I flew into Delhi at four in the morning of November 12. Being, I hoped, a seasoned traveler, I had written Ella Perry, principal of the Butler Girls' School and a friend of previous visits, that there was no need of meeting me. But remembering a *tonga wala* of 1950 vintage who had once taken me on a hopeless and somewhat frightening detour through the dark outskirts of old Delhi, finally inquiring at a remote gas station the whereabouts of "Boulevard Road," I was glad I could give this taxi driver the more specific direction of "Tis Hazari." This time we went straight and arrival at the big stone bungalow close by my first headquarters at Bishop Pickett's was like coming home.

Some of my most memorable experiences in India have been on trains and the overnight trip to Bareilly was no exception. My compartment was one of those closed-in affairs common to European travel, with doors at both ends and a long leather seat on either side on which to spread one's bed roll. Imagine my surprise when my roommate appeared, a sedate, bearded Indian gentleman in white flowing garments and impressive turban! He was a professor of Delhi University traveling to Bareilly for a veterinary convention. Having known occasions when for reasons of safety I had welcomed a male presence in a compartment (usually with other women, however, and never before *en deux*) I adjusted to the situation with aplomb and we had a pleasant conversation before retiring to our respective bed rolls.

My hostess in Bareilly was Frances Allen, a missionary nurse from Virginia, who proved a competent guide to both city and hospital and an excellent source of information as well as a congenial companion. One of the bonuses of such research is the lifelong friends one makes in the process of delving. On one of our trips to a village clinic conducted by the hospital's excellent department of public health I took the picture of Frances and her student helpers which appears on the jacket of *Palace of Healing*.

It seemed good to be back in a mission bungalow where poinsettias grew lavishly on bushes instead of in pots, where even though there were screens in the windows I tucked myself into a cocoon of mosquito netting at night. I was glad of this for I was a bit leery of mosquitoes in Bareilly which is in an area where encephalitis is endemic. In fact there had been an epidemic of this viral disease the preceding summer when 300 persons had died.

Bareilly is the birthplace of Indian Methodism. Here came William Butler and his wife Clementina in 1856 and from here they fled for their lives in the Mutiny of the next year, being
70

among the few foreigners who survived. Here I found the results of their labors—a church, a theological seminary, a school, the first Methodist printing house and the hospital. For it was Mrs. Butler who was responsible for Clara Swain's coming to India. On the long journey from Calcutta to Bareilly by bullock cart, stopping by the Ganges, she saw human figures lying on the sand with their feet toward the water.

"Who are they?" she inquired.

Oh, those were only women, she was told, so sick they were sure to die soon. As an act of mercy they had been brought there close to the sacred river so their misery might end as soon as possible. A male relative waited on the bank to push the body into the water when death came, thus assuring salvation. No food, no medicine, no tender care for the sick, only sips of water. A doctor? No, impossible. No male was permitted to look on the face of a caste woman. She was shocked and distressed. Forty years before Dr. Ida received her call Mrs. Butler knew she would not be happy until she saw a doctor in India who could treat women.

Nine years later, back in Massachusetts, she aroused the Methodist women of the Boston area to a concern for India's needs. On a rainy March day eight women met in a little room in Tremont Street Church and organized the Woman's Foreign Missionary Society. "Good," approved the all-male Board of Missions. "You raise the money, we will of course administer it." But to their dismay the women had other ideas. They would administer their own funds . . . and did. A little later they voted to send Isabella Thoburn, a young teacher, to India.

But Mrs. Butler was not satisfied. She wanted a doctor. Finding a young woman, Clara Swain, who was graduating that year from the Women's Medical College in Philadelphia, she proposed with fear and trembling that they send two missionaries instead of one. Pandemonium! It was hard enough to get money for one . . . but two! Why, it would take another thousand dollars! Then came a historic speech which was to ring in Methodist ears for the next hundred years. "Shall we lose Dr. Swain just because we have not the means in sight to send her? No! Rather let the Methodist women of Boston walk the streets in calico gowns and save the expense of more costly apparel. But let us send these two women to our sisters across the seas!"

The two young missionaries met for the first time when they

set sail from New York for Liverpool on November 3, 1869. Each recognized in the other her own intensity of purpose and deep spiritual commitment, yet both were too seasick to establish intimacy on the voyage to England. The letter announcing their arrival was delayed so there was no one to meet them in Liverpool. They had to go through customs and to Clara the thought of opening her two trunks and six boxes was not pleasant.

"What's in this one?" demanded the brusque inspector.

"Only my personal belongings," she replied politely.

He lifted the lid, pawed roughly through the contents. An expression of horror crossed his face. "Blimey, what's this!"

"What—Oh, you mean my skeleton," explained Clara. "You see, I'm a doctor."

Hastily the inspector jammed the articles into the trunk, his face as pale as if he had seen a ghost. "All right, lady. You can go through."

The trip which took me less than two days took Clara Swain more than two months. Ship to Bombay, bullock train to Nagpur, horse-drawn *dak gari* to Jubbulpore, train to Cawnpore, *dak gari* and *dholi* to Bareilly. When she came out of her room the first morning, she found a large company of Indian women and girls eagerly waiting to meet the Doctor Missahiba and ask her help. She had fourteen patients that first day. Isabella Thoburn was appointed to Lucknow where she started a little school in the bazaar with six students. Little did either of the two young women realize that one of them would found the first college for women, the other the first women's hospital in all of Asia!

My principal source for details in the life of Clara Swain was a book titled *"A Glimpse of India,"* a collection of extracts from Dr. Swain's letters published some years after her death in 1910. Long before this trip to Bareilly I had steeped myself in its contents. Out of its early pages emerged the irresistible title for the book, *"Palace of Healing."*

By the end of her first year Clara Swain had treated 70 families, visited in 250 homes of the city, prescribed for over 1,000 patients at the mission house. But frustrations far exceeded satisfactions. Long ago her morning clinics had outgrown the size of her living quarters. What she needed, what she *must* have, was a hospital. Her eyes turned yearningly toward a fine open tract of land adjoining the compound.

72

"The Nawab's," she was told. "All that land, forty acres, with its mansion."

"Would—would he sell a little of it, do you think?" She voiced the hope timidly.

"The Nawab? Sell his land to Christians? Not a chance."

Months passed and Clara grew more and more determined. "We *must* have a hospital and I want it on the Nawab's estate." Through the Commissioner of Bareilly she asked for an interview with the Muslim ruler and it was granted. With the Thomases and the Parkers, two missionary couples, and an Indian who understood court manners she traveled the forty miles to the Nawab's palace. After being received with royal painted elephants, feted for several days and given tours of many palaces and gardens, they were conducted to the throne room. At last they were in the august presence of the Nawab of Rampur.

As the time came for Mr. Thomas to present their request Clara held her breath. Only an acre! she prayed. Surely he could spare that. Perhaps, said Mr. Thomas, His Highness had heard of the work being done by the lady doctor for the women of Bareilly. If they could only buy a small portion of land for a hospital—

"No, no!" The Nawab gestured him peremptorily to silence. "The land is not for sale." Clara's heart sank. She was almost too numb with disappointment to absorb what followed. "But I *give* it to you. Take the whole estate. I give it with pleasure for such a noble purpose."

So they had not only an acre but forty acres and on them a mansion almost like a palace. In fact, Dr. Butler immediately dubbed it "The King's Palace." It became the first hospital. Here Clara moved and carried on her work until more adequate buildings could be built. Here she started a small class of medical students, conducted her dispensary, from here made visits into the town and superintended the building of her first dispensary, dedicated in May, 1874, with the thermometer soaring to 120.

"It's strong enough and fine enough to last a hundred years!" she exulted, little realizing that she was speaking prophecy, for it was still there, the office building of the big hospital complex, when I arrived nearly a hundred years later.

The "palace" was a boon, but it was not a building adapted to oriental woman patients. Her new hospital, begun that same

73

year of 1874, was built Indian style around a courtyard with a well. Here high caste Hindu and Muslim women could come, bringing members of their family, supplying their own food which was cooked on the verandahs outside their rooms, and they could be quite protected from the view of strange men. Clara Swain worked here for two long terms. Then in 1885 she left Bareilly to become the doctor in the palace of the Rajah of Khetri and other women doctors took her place in the hospital. Most of them served alone under trying conditions, operating in leaking rooms with poor lighting, only a primus stove to boil water which had to be carried by a coolie in goatskin sacks, long hours of work, never enough beds and always a dearth of money.

When I arrived in 1966 all that remained of the "palace" was an old print, though a visit to the palace of the old Nawab forty miles away yielded a view of the throne where that dignitary had sat and his portrait in all his panoply of elegance. There was little to remind one of Clara Swain—the first dispensary, dazzling in a fresh color wash, the tiled roofs of its projecting front and side porches supported by sturdy square posts interspersed with graceful columns, just as when it was built; one long wing of the old hospital; a bed and chair and Victorian sofa which she used; and, in the old dispensary, her picture. Out of it she looked down at me serenely, hair drawn back neatly atop patrician features, eyes soberly intent behind gleaming glasses.

"If only you could come alive," I thought, "and see how this dream of yours has grown to such rich fulfillment!"

In imagination I walked with her through the compound, saw her eyes sparkle behind the clear glasses as they noted the changes nearly a hundred years had made—the new dispensary, the dental and chest clinics, the maternity wing, the physical medicine unit, the nursing school buildings, the wonders being performed in the shining operating theaters. I pictured her staring incredulously at the dental and X-ray vans starting out on tours of ministry to school children and at a public health bus leaving on its mission of outreach in a distant village. Surely she would be awed and radiant at the sight of sixty-six nursing students, lovely in their blue and white uniforms, sitting with heads devoutly bowed in chapel, performing dedicated and efficient service in the wards, learning new skills in classroom, laboratory, dispensary.

74

"Men and women," she would exclaim wonderingly as we looked into the male and female chest wards where one of India's most terrible scourges was being combated, "all here in the hospital together."

"Yes," I would reply, "India has been changing too and growing. It's no longer necessary to treat women in seclusion."

She would be even more surprised to watch skillful fingers, darker than ours, performing delicate surgery, white-uniformed men and women of another race hurrying past us bound on important missions. "It's true." I would answer her amazement. "Most positions of leadership in your hospital are now held by highly trained and qualified nationals of a new free country."

It was all sheer imagination, of course. For days I walked alone through the compound, accumulating facts, taking pictures, interviewing. And since the story was to be of the hospital as well as its founder, it was to have three parts: the first about Clara Swain and the work she started for women and children; the second a period of rapid growth, with men as well as women among the staff and patients; the third, only beginning, a time of even greater fulfillment, with the Christian leadership of an indigenous Indian church assuming more and more responsibility. But the whole, I decided, must be the story not of an institution but of *persons*.

It was Dr. CharlesPerrill and his wife Wilma, also a doctor, who personified the second stage. I well remembered the exuberant zest with which Dr. Charles had exhibited the hospital's improved facilities on my first trip to Bareilly—a chapel in process of erection, a new dispensary, buildings with basement tunnels for equalizing temperature, an X-ray department, Dr. Wilma's maternity department.

A few days in Vrindaban, where Dr. Perrill was superintendent of another hospital and in process of building a third, added to my understanding of the period they represented. Charles, intensely dynamic, versatile, imaginative, found the hospital small, understaffed, poorly equipped. He left it one of the foremost institutions of its kind in North India.

On to Hyderabad, where I spent a week with Dr. Ernest Sundaram, superintendent of Clara Swain, and his lovely wife Sheila, learning about the third phase of the hospital's growth, the period of national leadership coming skillfully into its own. Dr. Ernest was recuperating from a severe illness in the home

75

of his father, Bishop Sundaram. Here, as so many times, I found my lives overlapping, for, in addition to his graduate work at McGill University in Montreal and at Duke University in the States Ernest had pursued his training in chest surgery at Vellore. He had worked with Paul Brand on a rare case which they had written up and published together.

Ernest's superintendency was marked not only by increasing Indianization of staff but by intensified specialization and the introduction of many new departments. Attempts were made to secure specialists in each area, nationals if possible, but missionaries when they were better qualified. And the hospital placed major emphasis on increasing involvement in the life of the community and in the health programs of the Indian government.

The week in Hyderabad was all too short. There were bonuses along with the furious typing of notes—near burial beneath mountains of garlands; a festive dinner at the beautiful Rock Castle Hotel with my friend, Bishop Mondol, as host; tours of one of India's most beautiful cities. Even the acquisition of a severe respiratory infection which kept me bedridden for days under Ida B. Scudder's expert care after I arrived in Vellore was but a minor imperfection of the trip's conclusion. At least I recovered sufficiently to attend the dedication of the new auditorium on Dr. Ida's birthday.

The research was not complete. Much correspondence followed—with Dr. Robert Peterson, who had left his lucrative dental practice in Portland, Oregon, to spend years at Clara Swain where he established one of the most modern dental clinics in all of India. "What shall I bring?" he had wired Dr. Charles. "Everything," was the reply. So he had packed up his entire office and shipped it to Bareilly.

There was much help from the Riels of Dayton, Ohio, who went to Clara Swain in their retirement, Dr. Eugene to provide a mobile dental clinic, his wife Alice to build a department of physical and occupational therapy from rock bottom; then both of them to raise funds for a new physical medicine block with the most modern facilities for rehabilitation.

Palace of Healing was published in time for the hundredth anniversary of the founding of the Women's Missionary Society. At a jurisdictional meeting in Boston I was privileged to autograph many copies, also to meet for the first time Janette

Crawford and Theresa Lorenz, two of the workers for many years at Clara Swain who had provided me with much rich material and who had crossed the country for this celebration. Greeting guests in that little room in Tremont Street Church where the eight women had met on that rainy day in March years earlier, I wore the same black dress with white lace bib and kerchief which Mrs. William Butler had worn on that historic occasion. The little room is gone now, along with the beautiful stone church which has succumbed to the demands of the devouring inner city. It can be seen only in pictures, like Clara Swain, who still looks down from her frame on the wall of the first building she dreamed into being over a century ago.

Gone? No. Dreams fulfilled outlive the dreamers. The little room with its eight women now has the world for its boundaries. And just as the "palace" lives on in the huge complex of buildings which have supplanted it, so Clara Swain is still the vital moving spirit of a continuing healing ministry.

4

DR. MARY VERGHESE: 'TAKE MY HANDS'

You must write the story of Dr. Paul Brand," said my new friend Albert Jefcoate or 'Jef' as he was affectionately known.

It was October, 1960. I had come to England to give lectures, illustrated by the kodachrome slides I had taken, on my book *Dr. Ida*, which was being published that month by Hodder and Stoughton in London. Julie Sharp, the executive secretary of Friends of Vellore, the British organization supporting the work of Dr. Ida's medical center in India, had arranged the tour, which took me to seven different branch meetings in the United Kingdom ranging from Folkestone and St. Leonards in the south of England to Edinburgh and St. Andrews in Scotland.

My first stop was Amersham, the home of Albert Jefcoate and his wife Phyllis, a charming redhead and a delightful hostess. Whoever categorized the English woman as dowdy and a poor cook did not know Phyllis! Jef, as most people called him, was a human dynamo who had made Vellore his avocation, a concern almost exceeding in interest his successful business career. In energy and singleness of purpose he was another Dr. Ida. As impresario of numerous concerts held in the Royal Albert Hall with world renowned artists giving their services, he had helped raise thousands of pounds for Vellore. And his skills in the art of persuasion were equally vigorous.

His eulogies of Paul Brand, his British friend, the Vellore doctor whose pioneer work in surgery and rehabilitation for leprosy had won worldwide attention, were unnecessary. I knew from seeing the surgical miracles at Vellore that he was a subject of Dr. Ida's calibre. But—write his story? It would mean another trip to India, delving into subjects of which I knew almost nothing—British education, customs and idiom, leprosy, reconstructive surgery. It had been difficult enough probing into tropical diseases and remedies for *Dr. Ida.* The life of a specialized surgeon would be even more complex. However, my appetite had been whetted for biography, and I was looking for another subject. Then suddenly a chance remark sparked another possibility.

"Did you see Mary Verghese in India, that wonderful doctor? She was here last December, spoke to our group and flew on to do graduate study in New York."

Dr. Mary Verghese. The name instantly aroused memories. I was back in Vellore hearing and reading about a remarkable young woman and the operations she was performing. So vivid was the description by one observer of this surgery that I felt as if I had witnessed it myself.

"Bundled into white jackets, caps, and masks, we followed the nurse into an operating room. The young surgeon, Mary Verghese, was already at work, seated at a small hand table. There was nothing unusual about that, for the tendon transplant for restoring function to a hand marred with leprosy is always performed with the surgeon seated. We watched fascinated while Dr. Verghese freed a good unparalyzed tendon in the forearm from its insertion, retunneled it through the hand to the fingers, substituting it for the paralyzed intrinsic muscle. Her work finished, she stripped off glove and mask revealing a deeply depressed scar across her right cheek. But her smile was so warm and radiant that one's first shock was immediately dispelled—only to be stirred to new depths when an attendant entered, released the brake from the surgeon's wheelchair, backed it down a short ramp and wheeled her away."

Paralyzed from the waist down Dr. Mary Verghese was probably the only paraplegic surgeon actually performing operations anywhere in the world. Surely a dramatic subject for any biographer!

Back home I submitted the idea to my editors, and they

urged me to approach her at once. I wrote Dr. Mary, who was doing graduate work at Bellevue Hospital and the Institute of Physical Medicine and Rehabilitation of New York University Medical Center on a fellowship granted by the World Rehabilitation Fund. A shy and modest person, unwilling even to have her name used in eulogies of her achievements, she was first horrified, then extremely reluctant, finally, under the added persuasion of the publishers and some of her friends, willing to sacrifice her natural aversion to publicity if by so doing she could encourage other disabled persons and arouse concern for the cause of rehabilitation in India.

It happened that Dr. Paul Brand, who had been closely associated with her, was in this country lecturing in January, and one morning we all met at the McGraw-Hill offices—Ed Kuhn, the editor who had worked with me on *The Gifts* and *Dr. Ida*, Leon Wilson, my new editor, Dr. Mary, Dr. Brand and myself. While arrangements were being discussed I studied my new subject with the awe and anticipation of one about to partially submerge her own life in that of another.

She was not beautiful. Attractive, yes. She sat straight and proud in her wheelchair, as poised and dignified as a queen on her throne. The rugged, slightly angular features, their soberness relieved by the occasional smiling of an overgenerous mouth, witnessed to a strong will, determined purpose (stubbornness?) and a sense of humor. Skilled plastic surgery had made the scarred cheek far less noticeable. And the eyes, dark, shadowed by heavy brows, hid depths of moods and emotions yet to be explored.

This deeper exploration into the inner recesses of personality must be a long slow process. Soon however I was able to fill in the broad strokes of the portrait, thanks partly to the man whose terse and dramatic description of Dr. Mary's work had obviously enthralled my editors. Dr. Brand had been her teacher in orthopedics, had trained her in her work with leprosy patients, had attended her after the accident which caused her disability. Through his and others' writings and through preliminary interviews with Mary herself an outline began to develop.

The accident which shattered her hopes of a normal life occurred just after she had completed two years of residency at Vellore and was fully trained to practice medicine as a gynecologist. A dozen or more residents and nurses were bound for a

80

picnic when the station wagon in which they were riding careened off the road, toppled over a bank, and strewed both itself and its occupants along a hundred yards of roadside.

The victims were taken back to a stunned hospital, rushed through examinations, given major or minor surgery and restored finally to near normalcy. All, that is, except Dr. Mary. Days later she came to consciousness in a hospital bed, but weeks passed before she knew that the most obvious and painful results of the accident were the least of her injuries. When she learned that her limbs were paralyzed and that she probably would never again walk she faced a blank wall of despair.

"Why," she prayed silently, "couldn't God have let me die?"

Reared in South India's Syrian Christian community which traces its history to the alleged visit of St. Thomas to India in the first century Mary had discovered at Vellore a faith more deeply personal and vital than her own church with its ancient rites and liturgies had been able to give. Now that faith was strained almost to breaking. She had wanted so much to serve as a doctor. Must she spend the rest of her life useless, being served?

"Of course not." It was Dr. Brand who first kindled her hopes of continuing a medical career. Her specialty of gynecology was out of the question, to be sure, but there were other areas such as bacteriology and pathology.

But Mary's first flare of hope became tinged with disappointment. Bacteria, dead tissues? She had wanted to work with *people*.

"I suppose," she asked wistfully, "there's no chance of my doing some kind of clinical work?"

"Why not?" Dr. Brand's eyes lighted with understanding. "We'll pray hard, Mary, and perhaps a way will be shown."

From the window of her hospital room she could look across a path and a strip of lawn to the leprosy clinic where Dr. Brand and others worked. A sudden idea occurred to her. Might this be a place where she could serve? Once she was able to sit in a wheelchair, she offered her services and they were gladly accepted.

But as she was wheeled toward the clinic that first day, anticipation became chilled with doubt. Leprosy patients had enough to depress them already. Some had insensitive hands and feet. Many had facial and other bodily deformities. Might

81

not the sight of someone with even worse disabilities arouse their resentment?

She need not have worried! Bitterness and self-pity vanished from patients' faces at her approach. Eyes lighted. Tongues which had been complaining clucked in sympathy. "Look, a new doctor—our doctor?" . . . "What's the matter? Can't she even walk?" . . . "*Ayoh*, her whole body like our hands and feet!" . . . "*Pavum*, a pity!"

"Dr. Mary has done more for the patients in an hour," commented one clinic worker to another, "than we could do in days."

After perhaps a month Dr. Brand suggested that she try her hand at surgery. She was astounded. "But—have you forgotten? I'm a paraplegic!"

"What of it? You don't operate with your feet. In fact, the hand operation I do is one of the few that has to be performed with the surgeon seated."

Her excitement kindled. She loved surgery. "I—I'll try."

At first she merely assisted. Even this was not easy. The problem of maintaining balance while her hands were busy, the heat, the discomfort, were almost unbearable. But as time passed she became more proficient. Could she perform such operations herself? She could and did. When she had finished, her body felt almost as drained and lifeless as her limbs. But her spirit soared.

Then one day: "I'm sorry, Mary," Dr. Brand told her regretfully. "We have to recommend a fusion operation on your spine. It won't be easy, but it will enable you to sit up without support."

"I know," said Mary calmly. "Go ahead."

It took not one operation but three. She used the long weeks of convalescence to strengthen her own spiritual life, to pray for others, to share the problems of students and nurses. In her wheelchair at last after many months she returned to work and was soon carrying a full operating load.

"She is one of the most skillful hand surgeons in the East," Dr. Brand reported in an address at the Mission to Lepers' annual meeting in 1958. "The operations you can do sitting down she has mastered after four years of apprenticeship with such devotion and keenness that she is now an absolute master of her subject."

But most galling to Mary was her lack of independence. When Dr. Gwenda Lewis, a British anesthetist who was a victim of polio, returned from an Australian rehabilitation center with the scope of her activities widened to an astonishing degree, Mary's hopes soared. If only she could go there! Fortunately her family was both sympathetic and financially able to help. She spent nine months in the rehabilitation center of the Royal Perth Hospital, learning skills which made her increasingly independent. Then an idea began to form in her mind. There must be a department of rehabilitation at Vellore! She wrote to Dr. Howard Rusk of the Institute of Physical Medicine and Rehabilitation in New York and was granted the fellowship which had brought her to this country.

These were the bare bones of the story I was privileged to write. Now I must supply flesh, blood, nerves, muscles, and imbue them hopefully with the breath of life.

There was time. Mary would be in New York for at least a year. While rewriting my novel *The Gifts* into a juvenile called *The Journey*, I would spend the rest of 1961 gathering material for the book about Mary which from its very inception I had titled *Take My Hands*. Most of 1962 would be spent in writing it.

How could I collect the mass of details necessary to write the story of a person of another race and culture with all its diversity of language, home life, religious creed and custom and education? Fortunately I had some assets to aid in preparation: a brief visit to Kerala, Mary's home state, on my first trip to India in 1950, first-hand experience in Vellore, the hundreds of little three-by-five papers containing information on South India, the meager knowledge of tropical diseases and medicine acquired in researching *Dr. Ida*. Of course there must be long personal interviews with Mary, but spending weeks in New York, catching her at odd times in her grueling schedule, would have been impractical. In planning a mode of operation my editor, Leon Wilson, was most helpful. It happened that he lived not far from the Institute on First Avenue where Mary was studying, and he and his family became her personal friends, even inviting her into their home. With his help a tape recorder was installed in Mary's room, and I sent her a list of questions to be answered in her spare time.

No wonder poor Mary was appalled when the questionnaire arrived! I have it here before me now, eighteen pages, typed single-spaced. It began with six pages on her early life, starting with the heading "Family."

"My memory is very vague," Mary wrote back, "and I never

kept a diary. Now I have to scratch my brain to find answers for your questions." She gave me names and addresses of family and friends who might give helpful information, adding the warning, "Some of the folks may hesitate to tell you about my weak moments. It will be a mistake if you paint a picture of continuous victory. That will be far from truth. It is the story of God's abundant grace working in a weak ordinary human being in spite of and through her many weaknesses and failures."

Due to her rigorous schedule, examinations and the constantly recurring setbacks in paraplegia—fevers, pressure sores, skin problems—it was late summer before she was able to complete the questionnaire. I waited expectantly, apprehensively. Would she prove the kind of person able to remember and articulate concrete details, incidents, insights into personalities, all those dramatic events and nuances of local color necessary to an interesting life story? When the first tape finally came I set it spinning with both hope and trepidation.

"This is Mary," the voice came clear and confident, "remembering her early life back in Cochin, South India, now a part of the state of Kerala. I was born in 1925 on a small island called Vypeen, just off the coast in the Arabian Sea. It is a thickly populated island, with about four hundred and eighty thousand people. We lived in a little village called Cherai. . . ."

She was not disappointing. Some of the questions were difficult and involved, some embarrassingly personal. Others, I am sure, seemed to her foolish and unimportant. Who in the world, she wondered, would be interested in knowing what sort of house she had lived in as a child, what games she had played, what her brothers had quarreled about, what foods they had eaten! But she tried to answer each question honestly, her scientific mind probing patiently for details. Soon the microphone became a friendly companion during her enforced hours of rest, accompanying her into well-loved and familiar places.

Her family came alive: *Appan*, Father, strong, slightly stern, short but impressive with his curling white hair and .mustache and spotless white garments, manager of prosperous coconut groves and respected leader in church and community; *Amma*, Mother, strict but kindly in discipline, surprisingly well-educated and independent for a woman who had left school to be married at twelve; Mary's three older brothers, John the mischievous, George, hot-tempered and outspoken but very reliable, Joseph (nicknamed Babi) who when Mary
84

was a baby had wanted to give her to a fisherwoman; her three older sisters and a younger one, Kunjamma, more talkative and competitive than Mary but her beloved companion. She described her home and its surroundings in both words and drawings and her Orthodox Syrian church with its white-washed walls and carvings of old gray stone, its two-hour service when the congregation stood because it was the day of resurrection, its exciting holidays at Christmas and Easter. And thanks to my travels in Kerala I could picture the church service (for I had attended one), the giant coconut palms, the Indian Ocean with its sprawling blue lagoons and lazy backwaters, its lavish green foliage, the spotless white saris and *dhotis* worn by the Syrian Christians, the big black umbrellas they carried.

Mary herself came alive—a keen and tireless student, determined to show *Appan* that a daughter could be as capable of scholarly achievement as his sons; fearless in supporting the struggle for Indian freedom; shy but fiercely independent, defying custom and family disapproval in her decision to become a doctor; in her years at Vellore finding a deeper, more personal faith; awakening to human needs in villages and on Roadside; graduating in August, 1952, one in the procession of white-saried girls winding from the women's hostel into the sunken garden, around the lily pool, over their shoulders the long white jasmine chains that for years had been traditional.

"Childish!" some of her classmates protested. "We used to carry garlands in primary school. Let's not do it this year."

"But Dr. Ida likes it!" That settled it. Though seventy-six when Mary entered medical school and ten years past the age of retirement, Dr. Ida had been for a time acting principal, and Mary, as well as her classmates, had fallen captive to this woman with eyes the color of the Arabian Sea in bright sunlight and hair like a mesh of silver silk, whose lined face seemed to glow with youthful vigor and a faith that was ageless and contagious.

After graduation came the two years of residency with Mary specializing in gynecology and obstetrics, performing operations with skill and ease, exulting in the superior strength which made it possible for her to do the work of two or three doctors. Until on January 30, 1954, a day of mourning for India, the anniversary of the assassination of Mahatma Gandhi, came the accident which changed her life.

Letters from her friends were beginning to come in. One

from a fellow student, Chandrahasan Johnson, gave a graphic description of that ill-fated trip. There were twelve in the picnic party plus Dr. Carol Jameson, who had planned the outing for the house surgeons finishing or starting their internship in her maternity department. Johnson remembered all the details: the names of all thirteen people including Thamby, the driver; the type of station wagon, a 1946 Chevrolet; the gay songs once the soberness of the day had given way to natural holiday exuberance, even the songs sung, including "She'll Be Coming round the Mountain"; the request of one of Dr. Jameson's medical students to let him drive the van ("He assured us he could drive well and that he had a license, which I later found had expired and had not been renewed"); Dr. Jameson's refusal, his persistent appeals, finally her reluctant consent; the overtaking of a bus whose driver would not allow them to pass him; the new driver's loss of patience, his attempt finally to pass, just missing a culvert, a swerve to the left, just missing the bus, the driver's apparent loss of wits, careening from right to left and back, screams, the toppling of the station wagon over a steep bank, taking three somersaults before it hit a milestone . . . tragedy.

The bus driver was reluctantly persuaded to take the victims back to the hospital. He wanted to leave Dr. Mary and Dr. Sojibai Samson, who were lying unconcious and apparently dead, but Johnson insisted that they be included. The shocked hospital sprang into action.

"Mary Verghese was so badly injured," Dr. Johnson wrote, "that everyone was just fighting for her life, overlooking an injury to the vertebra and spinal cord which needed immediate surgery. It was only after two days or more, when the friends staying with Mary noticed no movement of lower limbs, that x-rays of vertebrae were taken and the site of the fracture recognized. But the decompression operation was too late to save the injury to her spinal cord."

Others of the dozen or more letters I received in answer to my requests gave further details and insights into Mary's sufferings, her incredible courage and faith.

"A week after the accident," wrote Helen North, an Australian physiotherapist, "most of the victims were on the road to recovery, but there was one lying very still, hardly recognizable as her face and shoulder were heavily bandaged, and she was unable to move her legs. She was not complaining, though in much pain. What words of comfort could one offer to one who knew full well the implications of a fractured spine? Yet Mary knew personally 'that peace that passeth understanding.' She told me years later that she would have taken her own life many times except for that fact.

"The weary weeks and months dragged on. I was asked to give her physiotherapy. It was not easy but we prayed about it, and my memories of her room are always of a deep peace even in her despair. I shall never forget eight solid months of complete immobility following the operations to fuse her spine. She could not even turn her head. The pain was unceasing.... Slowly, with determination and great effort, she practiced sitting up with support, then balancing, lifting herself with overhead bars, moving from bed to a wheelchair. One morning I walked in to find her sitting beautifully dressed in a sari in her chair. How had she put it on? With her usual 'research mind' she had worked out the best way without actually taking it round her body, and it looked perfect."

"When I did the plastic repair of her face," wrote Dr. Hugh Johnson, a plastic surgeon from Rockford, Illinois, who was working for a short time at Vellore, "Paul Brand and I thought we had anticipated every conceivable complication, but Mary's surpassed them all. I have never seen such a monumental hematoma as the one that developed. Through it all I never received anything but a kind word and a smile when I should have been heaped with shame."

Many of the letter writers provided the incidents I was so anxious to use. Ramani Pulimood, for example, wrote, "One day about three years after the accident I saw Mary looking in the mirror that was fixed to her bed. 'You are pretty, Mary, don't worry,' I said teasingly. 'Not quite. Look at the scar on my face,' Mary said. 'A scar—on your face?' I was surprised. Till then I hadn't noticed the big scar. Mary was so full of smiles and radiance all the time that the scar passed unnoticed."

But the most significant tribute came in a statement by Dr. Paul Brand from an address given at the Mission to Lepers' annual meeting in 1958.

"When I sit in my office I can look through my window and see down the path that leads from the main hospital to our leprosy clinic with Mary Verghese coming down the road busily wheeling her wheelchair for her morning's work. But as I see her in the distance I love to look not so much at her but through the other window where I can see deformed, crippled, paralyzed patients waiting. I love to see their faces as Mary comes round the corner. Before her coming I look at these boys—in their dependency, their despair, their apathy—and then I see Mary coming. She still has the scar right across her face. As she comes round the corner I see a light, a new light, come on the faces of these leprosy patients. They see somebody there who has come to life out of death, somebody who even now is only partially alive, but who has dedicated all her life, all her strength, all her skill, all her love, all her compassion to their needs; somebody who is more paralyzed than they will ever be, who has more disability than they will ever have, who has won through to a high degree of skill, and all of that skill she has put at the feet of the Master on behalf of those who are suffering and need her."

Of course neither the questionnaire nor the letters provided the necessary facts and insights. I must spend long hours of interviews in depth with Mary herself. Plans were made for her to come to my home for several weeks, first in the summer of 1961, then as examinations, pressure sores and fever complications made postponement necessary, in the fall, finally in the winter. My husband's six years in the district superintendency had terminated and we had moved to Orono, the university town where he had once been pastor and where he was to spend two years in an interim job for the Maine Methodist Conference, then retire. Fortunately most of the house we had bought was on one floor; otherwise it would have been difficult to entertain a patient in a wheelchair. We prepared for her coming by removing a couple of doors from a bathroom and bedroom, moving some furniture, adjusting the height of a bed so she could swing herself onto it from her wheelchair. My husband moved into an upper guest room, leaving one section of the house for Mary and me.

She came to Bangor by plane, was lifted down the steps to her wheelchair by obliging stewards and brought to our home eight miles away. Already the house was in Christmas array, as pictures of her by the decorated tree and in front of the gaily adorned fireplace reveal. We spent hours of each day in my study with her in her wheelchair and me at the typewriter delving into details on every phase of her life I could think of, probing into her most intimate thoughts, reactions, desires, ambitions, beliefs, physical difficulties, strengths, weakness-
88

es. She was especially anxious that I should understand all of her weaknesses and failures, and that I should write frankly about them.

She had to rest much of each afternoon, lying motionless as she had done for weeks, months on end. What did she think about, I asked her, as she lay there so long, often in positions which made reading impossible? She spent much of the time praying, she told me, for all the people she cared about and were in some special need. Thinking of the responsibility facing me I hoped she included me in that category!

We took her to church meetings and she made many friends. One day we went for a ride on the roads about our small town. What did she find most unusual and interesting, we wondered, about this environment so different from her own? Was it the huge piles of snow, the evergreen trees, the cold that in spite of a warm coat must penetrate the thin folds of a sari? No, she replied, it was none of those things. What impressed her most was the scarcity of *people*. Of course. Vellore, with its crowds swarming every street and outlying road . . . Kerala, most densely populated of any state in India . . . New York City . . .

She stayed with us for two weeks. Then I set to work. As the pages flowed from the typewriter (rather seeped, for I am a slow worker) they went on to Mary for suggestions and corrections. She sent further information—pictures of her home and family, stories from her brother about the Apostle Thomas and St. George and the Dragon. (The name Verghese means "George.") Letters kept coming. One was from her nurse after the accident, Effie Wallace.

"When I compare the modern special beds and equipment which we use here for similar types of cases I realize how much greater must have been the pain and discomfort she went through. There were times when I walked into her room that I couldn't find words to say. There were other times when I'd see that she had been crying, but I don't remember a time that she didn't smile a greeting through them. . . . I remember when we first started getting her up in a wheelchair. The doctor had a brace made for her from a solid piece of stiff plastic for back support. Imagine wearing this in an area where the temperature ranges from 75 to 110 degrees a good part of the year and where for long periods the humidity is very high. Not only is it irritating to the skin but painful pressure areas would appear. Still she didn't give up."

Meanwhile Mary's dearest dream was being realized. A new Department of Physical Medicine and Rehabilitation was being established at Vellore, first of its kind in all India, and a building was in process of erection. The changes taking place back there seemed far closer to her than the raising of steel girders for a new building two blocks west of the school on 34th Street where she was studying.

This pioneer project could not have been set in motion, at least as soon, without the stimulation of Mary's accident. With all her fierce determination and energy she applied herself to the study which would equip her to become head of the new department. Her task was monumental. Not only must she master all the medical and clinical subjects but learn how to adapt Western rehabilitation techniques to India. Here the greatest problems would be in the area of appliances. In a country whose per capita income was sixty dollars the people she would be treating could not afford braces, artificial limbs, wheelchairs. Dr. Rusk's "Horizon House," a model home designed for the physically disabled with low push-button appliances and sanitary fixtures, would be an absurdity for a nation whose average family had yet to secure a smokeless clay stove and a bore-hole latrine. She spent hours studying self-help devices, preferably handmade, simple, ingenious.

"I want my share of the royalties," she had told me, "to go to a 'Loaves and Fishes Fund' to be used to furnish appliances— braces, artificial limbs, wheelchairs and such things—for those in India who cannot afford them."

That spring of 1962 she was involved in the most strenuous months of her training, preparation for the comprehensive examinations given by the American Board of Physical Medicine and Rehabilitation in Chicago, which if passed would qualify her to head the new department at Vellore. True, she would need to return in two years for her orals, but this would give her temporary qualification. She used every available moment outside her full schedule of hospital duties, spending long hours in the library, and in the evening, obliged to lie down to compensate for the exhausting periods in her wheelchair, taking the heavy volumes, briefs, lecture notes, theses, to bed with her. She must be prepared to answer any question in the areas of neurology, orthopedics, arthritis and physical medicine.

"It is impossible for me to do anything much on the manuscript before the exams," she wrote me in April. "In the meantime I pray to God that he may guide you and that he may use the book as a testimony to his saving grace and power in helping his weak children."

She had been doing other things than study. She had decided to buy a car. Before leaving India Dr. Gwenda Lewis, a paralytic from polio, had given Mary lessons in driving her hand-controlled machine, and now Mary made arrangements with a driving school which specialized in teaching the handicapped.

"Of course you want to go outside the city," said the instructor. "You'll find it easier for your first lessons."

"No," she replied firmly. "It would take too long."

The instructor looked startled, then grinned. "O.K. But I hope you know what New York traffic is like."

The sessions were nerve-wracking. Her arms ached with the tension of synchronizing the multiple demands of eyes, brain and the voice of her instructor. A tendon operation would be child's play beside this. After three months of weekly lessons, followed by two months delay, she took her test. "Stop . . . Park . . . Make U turn." In failing to make the turn she knew she had failed. More lessons, more practice.

The trials of the paraplegic! A week before the examinations she came down again with fever. Serenity? She was expected in Vellore in the fall. The ground floor on the new rehabilitation center was already opened. The physiotherapy school had five pupils. She *had* to go to Chicago. She did. Happily she had distant cousins there. To manage their bathroom door, which was only 22 inches wide, she had borrowed a child's wheelchair. She took the examinations, the only student in a wheelchair. When she left the building at six in the evening she felt drained of energy. Now she must wait. Even praying would not help. The following days spent in touring Canada while visiting friends of Vellore in Montreal, Ewart and Connie Everson, were marred only by the suspense. When word came that she had passed, the relief was overwhelming. She relaxed into complete enjoyment. Visiting Niagara Falls with Kay Smith, once a nurse at Vellore, she could gaze at the thundering flood with all the rapture of a carefree tourist viewing the Taj Mahal.

That summer I went down to New York for days of final conference on the manuscript, finding Mary in a hospital bed battling another bout with fever. We went over every word together, and she made many corrections, suggestions, deletions, additions.

"That isn't exactly the way it happened," she said more than once, then, her eyes twinkling, "but it's all right. It could have been that way."

She flew to England on September 1 and spent time with Julie Sharp visiting rehabilitation centers and studying British techniques . . . then on to home in Kerala and the new work in Vellore. Still suggestions for revisions continued to come on the use of Malayalam words, church customs, name spellings, the objection of one of her doctor friends to having the details of his romance published. Through some oversight this was never corrected, at least in the first American edition. Even the galleys, which came in December, elicited fresh revisions, but at last the book went to press.

I faced publication of the book in the spring of 1963 with misgivings. Would it sell? Could a story about a woman of another country and another culture have appeal for the American public? Results were surprising. Physical disability is no respector of nationalities. A courageous faith which not only endures adversity but *uses* it in a creative way is a goal of universal aspiration. The book sold in its American editions better than any other I have written, except my first novel, *The Brother.* It was the selection of a religious book club. It is still selling. It has gone into many printings both in hard cover and in paperback in England, where it has become almost a textbook in rehabilitation. It has been translated into German, French, Dutch, Danish, Arabic, Indonesian, Chinese, Thai, Hindi, Bengali, Tamil, Malayalam and several other Indian languages. In Germany it has sold more copies than in this country. This has all happened not because it is a remarkable book but because it is the story of a remarkable woman.

Letters still come to me bearing tribute to Mary's story. Now numbering more than 160, they are some of the most rewarding fruits of a writer's labor. They bear the postmarks of many states and many foreign countries. A number are from disabled persons or those connected with them.

"I have just finished reading the wonderful story of Mary Verghese. I am a muscular dystrophy patient and am confined to a wheelchair. I am told by the doctors that I will never walk again."

"I read the story with a heart spilling over with pain for my mother who recently suffered amputation of one of her legs. As Mary said, 'At first the threads seemed to be so tangled and broken.' And I am trying hard to find that the great Designer may be able to use even broken threads. Thank you for this help."

"A friend of mine is reading it now. She has multiple sclerosis and has to use a cane to get around. She is a tremendous person! Her faith! I would like to write Dr. Mary."

Others spoke merely of the inspiration of Mary's life.

"I am deeply touched by this wonderful woman and her strong faith which matched her courage. Having read *Dr. Ida*, I was familiar with the hospital and surroundings at Vellore, and it was like returning to a beloved place."

"I can't tell you how much the book has stirred my heart for the people of India."

"My heart is overflowing with praise and joy and tears, too, as I finish the book. 'Take My Hands' is my favorite hymn. I have had cataracts on both eyes, so I read sparingly. When I do read I choose books similar to this wonderful story."

"I am a Baptist missionary working among students in northeast Brazil. Surely this book serves not only to encourage those who are handicapped but will encourage all those who seek to serve God to the fullest." She would like to translate it into Portuguese.

These are only a few samples from quotations which I sent on to Dr. Mary.

She did return to America in April, 1964, completed her orals satisfactorily, won membership in the American Board of Physical Medicine and Rehabilitation and secured her final accreditation as a department head. In August, after she had traveled in this country and in Canada visiting rehabilitation centers, I met her in New York where we were entertained at a tea in the Interchurch Center. My small part was an illustrated talk on her story, and Mary, the chief speaker, gave a vivid account of her work in Vellore.

I have visited her twice in India since she returned the first time. Earlier in that year of 1964, on a trip for further research at Vellore, I took her picture in front of the new building, saw her at work with the disabled children she so much loves, had dinner in her cosy apartment with many of her friends who had shared with me their impressions and knowledge of events and at last met *Amma*, Mother, a gentle white-haired extremely intelligent woman whose smile was a prototype of Mary's own.

One of the pictures I took which I love best shows a waiting room in the new building with two lines of disabled patients in the foreground looking toward an open door. Outside in the sunlight is a boy standing straight and tall with braces on his legs and a cane in each hand.

"He is learning to walk," I think when I look at it, "because Mary will never walk again."

In the fall of 1964 Mary introduced another innovation at Vellore, a sports meet for the disabled. A busload of crippled children came from Madras, another group from Bangalore, and there were her own present and former patients. Mary welcomed the guests. There were wheelchair races, crutch races and many other events. The participants gained in self-confidence, saw new possibilities for their future. It was an experiment to be repeated.

In 1966, when I traveled to Vellore from northern India where I had been doing research for the book on Clara Swain Hospital, I saw Mary again. Another dream had been realized, a center for in-patients for whom there had been but few facilities for treatment at the hospital. This new Rehabilitation Institute, a beautiful gray and pink building of native stone in a mango grove on the edge of the college campus, had been dedicated on November 26 and officially opened by Sushila Nayyar, Union Minister for Health and Family Planning of the Republic of India. Built partly by the anonymous gift of a generous Canadian donor who had heard Mary speak of India's needs, it would make possible a far wider ministry to the disabled.

Much has happened to Mary in recent years. Her "Loaves and Fishes Fund" has made possible not only appliances for those unable to afford them but also a workshop and a house to accommodate five patients for continuance of vocational training after their medical rehabilitation. A research grant from the Vocational Rehabilitation Administration, U.S.A., has made possible a study of the simple adaptive equipment including wheelchairs which can help severely disabled patients go back to their rural areas and lead independent lives. The final report of this study and others was recently published in a large booklet, "Investigation of Methods Suitable to Village Conditions for the Rehabilitation of Paraplegics and Quadriplegics," illustrated by many fascinating pictures of prosthetic devices applicable to Indian village life.

In 1973, when the Rehabilitation Institute celebrated the World Day for the Disabled on March 17, the Prime Minister of

India and many other distinguished persons recognized the Institute's achievements. During the preceding six years 637 patients had been admitted from nineteen Indian states, one from the United States. They had included 277 paraplegics and quadriplegics, 18 cases of rheumatoid arthritis, 102 sufferers from poliomyelitis. It is a place where miracles are being performed, new life created.

Honors, richly deserved, have come to Mary. On Republic Day in 1972 the Indian Government conferred on her the Padma Shri Award, one of the country's highest possible recognitions of achievement. And more recently the Indian Council of Medical Research honored her with the Dr. P. N. Raju Oration Award for her original research on the rehabilitation of paraplegics and quadriplegics. This was the first time such an award had been given for research in rehabilitation.

But the years of strenuous activity have taken their toll. In 1976 after struggling for more than two years with bouts of fever and asthma and with the heavy duties of the department becoming an increasing physical burden, Mary felt it necessary to leave Vellore for semi-retirement. There was no longer a home to welcome her. In 1974 *Amma* had died so suddenly that Mary could reach the church in her home village only in time for the funeral. But she planned her retirement years at a mission hospital run by her church at Kolenchery, Kerala, where a nephew, a nephew-in-law, and some close friends were on the staff and where she was permitted to build herself a small house in the staff quarters. At last—her own "Horizon House," equipped with all the special aids for living which she had been providing through the years to others. Here, if health and funds permit, she hopes to participate in another pioneer project of rehabilitation.

In my home in addition to the shelf of books in many languages, the letters from readers and the research files, there are two reminders of Mary's presence. On a Governor Winthrop desk there are marks in the wood, made before we discovered that there was too little room in the hall for a wheelchair to pass. I am glad that furniture polish, while dulling, has never been able to eradicate them. They are a reminder of a person who has made scars things of beauty and blessing.

And on a shelf in my living room stands one of the most precious of my India souvenirs, a bird exquisitely carved from buffalo horn with wide outspread wings. It was the gift Mary brought me when she came to visit. Unwittingly she chose a perfect symbol of her own life, aptly illustrating the words with which I closed our book, its final paragraph bearing her upward in the plane on her return to India into sunlight and clouds and infinite skies. The German translation has taken the final words as its title.

Um Füsse bat ich und er gab mir Flügel. "I asked for feet, and I have been given wings!"

5

DR. PAUL BRAND AND HIS MOTHER, EVELYN BRAND: 'TEN FINGERS FOR GOD' AND 'GRANNY BRAND, HER STORY'

Albert Jefcoate was to have his way after all. Dr. Paul Brand had so impressed my editors during the interview with him and Dr. Mary Verghese that after discussion of a few other possibilities it was decided that he must be the subject of my next book—that is, if he was willing.

Again, as with Dr. Mary, it was selfless dedication to his ministry of healing and a compelling desire to extend knowledge and concern in the area of his pioneer activity that conquered his natural aversion to publicity and his fear of possibly violating the British medical code of ethics which frowned on any obvious seeking after personal promotion.

So I was committed to far more complex and specialized research than I had dared to attempt thus far—the history, symptoms and treatment of a strange tropical disease; techniques of surgery and rehabilitation utterly foreign to a layman; a personality to be interpreted within the framework of British culture, idiom, traditions. A man, too, whereas my previous biographical subjects had been women!

Dr. Brand, at that time associated with the British Leprosy Mission, was making a lecture tour of the United States with his wife Margaret in the fall of 1963 and was to be in New York City for three days early in October. I went down to New York and spent as much time with him as he could spare, though his schedule (already I was learning the British pronunciation, *shedule*) left little leeway for interviews with a mere biographer. For two or three hours only, sitting in a hotel lobby, we conducted a preliminary talk. Interview? Not exactly. For an interview implies questions, and I found them almost unnecessary. Dr. Brand was by far the most communicative of the contemporary subjects of my biographies. For the most part he talked while I attempted furiously to keep up with him in my longhand notes. I have them before me now, more than thirty pages in a stenographer's notebook, illegible to anyone but the frantic writer. Intense in speech and manner, with keen eyes and whimsical smile, this youthful-appearing doctor (he was then not quite fifty) was already world famous, the impressive initials after his name including not only a M.B., B.S. (Bachelor of Medicine, Bachelor of Surgery), but an F.R.C.S. (Fellow of the Royal College of Surgeons, which had elected him Hunterian Professor in 1952) and C.B.E. (Commander of the Order of the British Empire, just a step below knighthood). Three years before he had been given the Albert Lasker Award for Outstanding Leadership and Service in the Field of Rehabilitation. Yet he was obviously as humbly objective toward honors as toward his own God-given bounty of skill and energy, prizing both only for their contributions to his chosen medium of service.

He began with a tragi-humorous story of an airplane trip he had taken to the West Coast in 1960. He was one of three doctors invited to address a meeting of the American Society of Plastic and Reconstructive Surgery in Los Angeles. One of the three had died of a coronary before the program was printed. As he was taking the plane from Denver to Los Angeles, Paul received news that the second had also died. As the plane crossed the Rocky Mountains it suddenly hit an air pocket, gave a sickening lurch, and plummeted. "Well," he thought, "this makes it unanimous." He was not particularly frightened or disturbed. He had never considered length of life important, only quality. Once he had been talking with another doctor who was avoiding butter for fear of a coronary.

"As for me," he said, "I wouldn't mind at all dying of a coronary. Quick. Work finished. No hanging around, useless." Jesus, he continued, was not concerned with how long people lived, only that they should live a full life, body, soul, and spirit.

He had lived his creed, I was to discover, for with Paul Brand self-preservation had always been secondary to an adventurous zest for bold living, from the time he had nearly hung himself swinging from banyan tendrils in Southern India, to the time a bit later, when as a youth in England, he climbed up the corner stones of his school to carve his initials on the sandy red brick forty feet from the ground. He had been risking life and limb for far nobler goals ever since.

Paul could paint pictures with words as skillfully as his mother could with brush and palette. I saw him as a child on the mountains, in Southern India, climbing trees with his small sister, Connie; left alone one night when his father was camping and his mother was called out to tend the sick, frightened but assured that God would care for them; sweating with malaria; experiencing his first awesome sight of leprosy when three men bearing the stigmata came up the mountain; watching his father treat people with running sores and worms and rotting teeth and hating it; learning the lore of nature from a father who was a genius, and the three R's from a mother who let him do his sums high in the branches of a jackfruit tree, and a dynamic Christian faith from both of them.

I was glad that Jef (Albert Jefcoate) had insisted on taking me to see Paul's delightfully British maiden aunts, who brought up Paul and Connie from ages nine and seven respectively after their parents' return to India. I could better appreciate their shocked but adoring acceptance into their proper, luxurious home of two little jungle savages who climbed lampposts as substitutes for trees, considered thickly carpeted stairs fascinating media for sliding down on dinner trays, proceeded down the aisle of their grandfather's Baptist church carefully carrying their shoes, the devout procedure in Father's chapel in India.

"They were saints to stand us," Paul commented fervently.

But, remembering the radiant tenderness with which the old aunts had reminisced about their "dear, darling Paul," I knew all sacrifices had long been forgotten.

It is astonishing what vivid impressions of his early years he was able to communicate during those brief hours. I saw him at age fifteen going to the ship to meet his mother after his father's death in India, felt his almost unbearable emotion—remembering her as he had seen her last, tall, stately, lovely; shocked rigid at the sight of what seemed a tiny, shrunken old

99

woman, frail, stumbling, face wet with tears; unable even to kiss her; sitting in the boat train trying to force himself to speak the work "Mother"; lying in bed unable to sleep and thinking, "Their love was so wonderful. If this is what it does when one of them goes, I'm never going to let myself love anybody like that."

The outline of his maturing years is all there in those scribbled pages. At age sixteen he started to learn the building trade because his beloved father had done it before him. But the building training was only preparation for further emulation of his father.

"We must go all over the world," he had told Connie earnestly when they were little more than babies, "in trains and motor cars and jutkas and bullock carts and maybe even airplanes, *all* over the world and tell people about Jesus and God's love."

It had always been assumed by the family, himself included, that he would be a missionary. His mother, back in India, was expecting him to come and join her in the mountain work she and his father Jesse had started. His building training, like his father's, was an almost indispensable asset in an environment of mud and thatch huts where schools, hostels, chapels, infirmaries, orphanages were needed and the poverty-stricken people were desperate for education in new skills. Dutifully, after four years of such training, he applied to the missionary society and to his utter amazement was turned down. He had assumed they would snap him up! All his years of church work, conducting deputations, organizing youth camps, even preaching, and they said he was not ready. It was missionaries they wanted, the committee told him, not technicians.

What should he do? Perhaps, after all, he wasn't "called" to be a missionary. He had never heard a voice, seen a vision. And—what was a call, anyway? Again it was memory of his father that pointed the way. Jesse Brand had prepared for his service by taking a year's course in tropical medicine. Much as he rebelled against memories of his father's loathsome medical duties on the mountains, his son would do the same. To his amazement he found he loved both the work and the study.

"You like medicine, don't you?" asked one of his professors.

"Like isn't the word," he replied. "I love it."

"Then you should take up medicine as a profession, enter medical college."

In the fall of 1937 he entered the University College Medical School in England. I saw him plunging with zest into a new life completely in harmony with his deepest desires; sharing a first year chemistry bench with a sober but attractive blonde named Margaret Berry; to his amazement finishing his first term second in his class, Margaret being first; in a world suddenly gone berserk with war taking a fierce delight in the orderly wonders of human anatomy; starting his clinical work as London went up in flames and the blitz overflowed the hospital with hundreds of mutilated bodies; spending hours picking bits of glass and metal out of chests, intestines, arms, legs, feet, hands; coming to feel a special interest in hands, such things of beauty, such exquisite yet vulnerable tools; marrying Margaret; working toward his F.R.C.S.; firewatching one night on the roof of Great Ormond Street Hospital, while two miles away in the Royal Northern, where the bombs seemed to be blazing worst, his son Christopher was being born; acting as assistant for a year at the hospital under one of London's finest surgeons; and then—his life and that of thousands of others suddenly changed by a simple telegram.

"You must come at once. We need you here desperately. Cochrane."

The writer was one of the world's great leprosy specialists and at that time the temporary Director of the great Vellore Christian Medical College and Hospital, his assignment the upgrading of the institution to meet the new medical standards prescribed by the Indian government. All Paul's objections— he was slated to enter the army, he had had too little experience, his wife was having another baby soon—were brushed aside. Paul was amazed when Dr. Cochrane's powers of persuasion proved as potent with the British government as with himself. His daughter Jean was born as he was in the very act of packing his bags for India. Though he did not realize it at the time, he was forced to conclude later that the telegram was the "call from God" that he had been waiting for for so many years, the opening of a door into a new life.

"All right," he told Dr. Cochrane when he arrived at Vellore in December of 1946. "You have bullied me into coming. I'll stay, but only for a year, to see you through this shortage on your teaching staff."

The thirty pages were a good beginning. Just from that

101

short interview I had a fairly comprehensive outline of Paul Brand's early life, again a collection of bones which might be assembled into a passable skeleton. But to imbue them with flesh and blood and sinews, especially to depict their movements through years which were to bring new life to afflicted thousands, a hundred such interviews would not have sufficed. I must go for a third time to India.

It was arranged that I should be there in February and March, 1964, when Dr. Brand would be spending six weeks at Karigiri, the leprosy research sanatorium connected with the Vellore hospital. I almost failed to make it. In January our house was partially consumed by fire. A change of wind or five minutes' delay by the fire department, and I would have been reconstructing my own life rather than another's. But the damage was remediable. I could leave my husband with even less unease than usual, knowing that loneliness would be somewhat mitigated by two workmen's daily presence and the excitement of rebuilding.

Dr. Ida B. Scudder met me in Madras and took me to her little house on the Vellore College campus. I had seen it being built in 1957, a project of her Presbyterian church women, and shared in her excited plans for its gardens, its comfortable room for Aunt Ida, its sun-yellow drapes and paintings of Indian life, its casement windows opening on the vistas of wide plains with their encircling mountains where Dr. Ida had dreamed her college into being. It was like coming home. For the six weeks I would make this my headquarters, happily sharing its menage with Dr. Ida B., her housemate Dr. Mary Dumm (a Methodist specialist in nutrition from Madison, New Jersey), Ragi, their competent cook, and Nannette, Ida B.'s golden spaniel with her four new puppies.

Six weeks! And three months had seemed far too short for the research on Dr. Ida! Even the six weeks were a misnomer, for Dr. Brand would be spending one of them in Africa. And he had not come to India to feed me material, but to spend long days operating, teaching, organizing, instructing trainees from several Asiatic countries in his techniques of surgery.

But the few hours in New York were a sample of his power to communicate. Conferences with a tape recorder in the evenings were worth days of interviews with an average subject. Stretched comfortably on a couch in Ida B.'s living room after his grueling day's schedule, prompted only by an occasional question, he would record incidents, medical data, personal revelations in such lucid and dramatic language that they could have been used almost verbatim. If, transcribing the next day, I found the tape garbled or, worse, blank (Indian mechanical gadgets, like American, being unpredictable), he would patiently go through the same sequences with the same dramatic zest.

Thanks to interviews with him and others, literature on leprosy, visits to the hospital, numerous articles and letters, I was accumulating more bones to be assembled and breathed into life. The story was taking shape.

One day not long after his arrival in India while visiting with Dr. Cochrane at a hospital devoted to treating leprosy, Paul stopped to examine a patient whose hands showed the paralyzed, claw-like deformities typical of the disease. The hand had lost all sense of feeling and the fingers were curled tightly against the palm.

"What are you doing for claw hands like these?" he asked the specialist.

"Nothing," was the reply. "We know of no real treatment."

Paul was astounded. There were perhaps fifteen million leprosy patients in the world, two out of every hundred persons in that part of India, and many with just such deformities. He himself had done corrective surgery on hundreds of hands injured by other causes. Was it possible that no orthopedic surgeon had ever bothered to study the deformities of leprosy?

"You see," explained Dr. Cochrane wearily, for he had been fighting a long battle against the very ignorance and incredulity Paul was deploring, "people, even doctors, have never really considered leprosy a disease. In their minds it carries an aura of the supernatural, as though its victims were no longer people but somehow accursed, outcasts."

Curiously Paul pried open the stiff fingers of the patient and placed his own hand in the man's right hand. "Squeeze my hand, please," he said. "Press as hard as you can."

To his amazement a sharp pain shot through his palm. The man's grip was like iron. It was not a normal handclasp, of course, because of the curled fingers, whose nails dug so hard into his flesh that he almost cried out. But he felt a thrill even sharper than the pain. The hand was not all paralyzed! It still had some mighty good muscles. Was it possible that surgery might be effective in making a clawed hand usable? He determined to find out.

It was about a year after coming to Vellore that he was ready for his great experiment. "If you will send me a patient whose hands could not possibly be made worse," he told Dr. Cochrane, "I'd like to see what can be done with them."

The patient was Krishnamurthy. Paul regarded him with dismay—huge ulcers on his feet, bones exposed, clawed hands unable to grasp any object, dulled eyes, hopeless. But he started in, first on the feet, then on the hands. The surgery took months, two fingers at a time. He took a good muscle from the forearm, split it into two parts, withdrew it into the palm and retunneled it to the fingers, to substitute for the paralyzed intrinsic muscle, testing its tension, testing, testing again. Then there was nothing to do but wait and pray. More operations, on the other two fingers, on the thumb, then a long period of physiotherapy. Then—much later—a miracle.

"Look!" greeted Krishnamurthy triumphantly. Proudly he arched his fingers, scooped up a big ball of rice and curry and popped it into his mouth. He was a new person, bright, alert, laughing. After being in the hospital about a year, he was discharged, equipped for new life with two useful hands and two healed feet, a good brain and an abundance of hope and energy. A new name also, for in the process he had become a Christian and wanted to be called John.

Then about two months later he returned, sad, hungry, holding out his two hands. "These are not good hands you have given me, Sahib doctor," he said mournfully. "They are bad hands."

"Bad?" Paul stared. "They look good to me. What do you mean?"

"Bad *begging* hands," returned the young man sadly. Because he still bore the telltale marks of leprosy, nobody would employ him and give him a place to live. Before, seeing his useless outstretched hands, people had thrown him coins. Now they had no pity.

Paul was aghast. Was he merely creating beggars with less ability to beg? The answer was obvious. They must be taught means of livelihood. But how? There was no money. Then "Mother Eaton," a patient from Pasadena, California, hopelessly crippled with arthritis, gave him all her money, over one thousand dollars, to use for his work. Up on Dr. Ida's college campus he built a little community of village huts, mud walled with grass thatched roofs, centered around a training shed where his patients could learn to become self-supporting. They called it Nava Jeeva Nilayam, the Place of New Life. It was the first leprosy rehabilitation center in the world.

A week or so after I arrived in Vellore we started on a trip to the south Indian mountains where Paul had spent his childhood.

"What a trip!" I wrote home. "Wonderful but indescribable. The car was a four-wheel-drive Willys, with the truck back lined with two seats along the sides, protected from the elements by a few remnants of curtains. We rode 150 miles the first afternoon to Salem on very good roads. Paul is an excellent driver, competent and *fast*. I never did make out the speed because the speedometer is in kilometers, not miles. But I wasn't at all nervous at that stage. Bicycles, pigs, cows, dogs, pedestrians, lorries, buses and donkeys, usually get out of the way if you know how to handle them. A donkey stands still, a goat keeps going, a pig also, a cow—well, you know what cows do. Bicycles never look, just charge out where they please."

Granny Brand, Paul's mother, met us in Salem. Dr. Howard Lewis, of the International Gospel League, which was supporting her work on the mountains, had come to India to accompany us on this mountain trip. He had arranged with me to write her story also, so it was with both anticipation and trepidation that I approached this meeting.

Never shall I forget my first sight of Granny. Small of stature, stooped, gaunt, she looked as fragile as a dry reed. A fringe of short straight white hair, untidily confined by a ribbon, gave her face a witchlike quality. Her feet and limbs were encased in heavy leather sandals and stout braces, and she walked with a slow shuffling gait, clutching two unmated bamboo sticks. She was then eighty-six.

"Poor creature," I thought, "queer and completely senile." Within minutes I changed my mind. Queer, yes, if you could call a St. Francis or a Schweitzer queer. And her mind was as vigorous as her tongue and as keen-edged.

"A hotel!" she spluttered, as we entered the modern building where we were to spend the night. "Utter unnecessary luxury!" And, as we sat eating a modest meal in the dining room, "Oh, my dears, think of all the poor people on my hills who can't eat like this!"

It was hard connecting this image with the knowledge I acquired later of Granny's early life. Evelyn Constance Harris was born into the luxury and protection of a well-to-do family

105

in suburban London that included nine daughters. She was an acknowledged belle, lovely in her furbelows and flowered hats, which she wore even into the slums where she went to play Lady Bountiful and dispense charity. It would have been patronage, she felt, not to look her best.

Evie, as she was usually called, was well educated, first by older sisters, then at a school in France. She showed marked talent in art and joined an art colony in St. John's Wood, her classical patrician beauty so appealing to both students and teachers that she became a model as well as an artist, even sitting for one young sculptor whose admiration was not entirely professional. But as the years passed she became more and more restless, dissatisfied with the unchanging deadness of colors on canvas. She longed to work with people.

Central to the family life was the strict Baptist church they attended, and here Evie became imbued with the longing to carry the Gospel to far places. One day a young missionary named Jesse Brand came to the church to speak. Evie listened spellbound to his account of the thousands of people on the mountains of south India who had never heard the Gospel, of a trip he and another missionary had taken up these "mountains of death," so cursed with malaria that few white men had ever dared to go there. The people had begged them to come back, but there was no one to go.

Evie felt faint with excitement. "Here I am," she responded silently. "Send me."

Later the young missionary came to the house for tea. She longed to talk with him, but something in his abounding vitality, the black vigor of his thick wiry hair and big mustache, the dark intensity of his eyes, like glowing coals, repelled her. He seemed to be staring at her. She shrank back into the shadows, leaving her sisters to pass the cake and sandwiches.

But she had heard the call and knew she must go. Her father was grievously shocked. Already he had lost three of his daughters by marriage, one by death. "But—you're over thirty years old!"

"I know, Father. It has taken me a long time to decide. Now I know. It's what I was meant to do."

"But—my darling, why?"

"Because it's God's leading, Father. I want to serve where I'm needed most."

And, since it was his own stern creed of obedience to God

that she insisted on following, he had to consent. At a farewell party for her in the church, she wore her usual silks and frills, including a large lacy hat.

"She looks more like an actress than a missionary," someone remarked.

This was the woman whose hair was now a witchlike fringe, her dress a shapeless bag of cotton, and who, they told me, had for many years not owned a mirror.

I never did visit the mission station in Madras to which Evie was assigned, but, having stayed in many mission bungalows of that era, I could easily picture it—high ceilings, broad verandas lavish with bougainvilleas and poinsettias in season, in the living and dining rooms in those days before electric fans a huge *punkah* pulled by a rope to agitate the sluggish air in the months of extreme heat. Evie loved everything about India—its cacophony of sounds from wails of hawkers, pounding of drums, to the raucous cawing of crows; its smells both pungent and sweet, of jasmine, sweat, sandalwood, spices; its colors so sharp and clear they made her eyes smart and her artist's fingers itch; but especially the *people*. Everything, in fact, except the language study which every missionary had to endure (Tamil was her Nemesis) and the heat. By noon in the hot season the temperature soared high into the hundreds. During siesta even breathing made one sweat, and the mosquito-net cages into which one crawled at night were smothering cocoons.

But even more unsettling than the heat was the presence in the big bungalow of young Jesse Brand. Repelling? Frightening in his dark intensity? How could she have thought him so? The dark eyes twinkled. Beneath the vigorous mustache the lips could flash the most appealing smile. "I thought you'd be coming," he told her one day. "I could see it in your face when I talked about the hill people. I knew you were hearing the call." "Yes, oh yes," she replied. And she soon discovered that it was not only the call of the hill people which she had heard. She was falling deeply in love with Jesse Brand. And he was practically engaged to a young woman in England.

As the heat mounted, became almost unbearable, she was sent to the hills to continue her language study. "This is where I belong," she avowed with thanksgiving and hope, "not down there on the plains, but up here where there is room to stretch and breathe." Yet even more stimulating than the mountain air were Jesse's letters which followed her. It was soon evident that he returned her love. "My darling . . ." "Precious One . . ." She would read the words with flaming cheeks, then rush off to her secret place of communion to give thanks. Though she almost died of typhoid in the weeks that followed, the hope of becoming his wife and going with him to the hills made her fight for life and win. She even managed to pass her examinations in Tamil, not with honor, like Jesse, but at least with passing rank. The mission board would never have consented to her marriage and hill assignment if she had proved too stupid to talk to a villager in his own language!

The Kollimalais, Mountains of Death. I saw them for the first time the morning after our night in Salem. Just so Evie must have seen them, rugged, mysterious, dark purple in the morning sunlight, when she went to Sendamangalam, the plains town where Jesse had worked, for her wedding. That same day she and Jesse set off for their new home in the mountains—not by the road we were traveling now. In those days there had been no road. Up we traveled with a mountain-trained driver around seventy-two hairpin turns. Once we had to back up to the edge of a precipice in order to get around a sharp bend. Only later did I find out that the car had no emergency brakes!

This was Granny's world. The higher we climbed the more vibrantly she same alive. When we stopped to enjoy the view she was out of the car, hobbling about with her bamboo sticks. *"Stotherum, stotherum!"* she would acclaim over and over, Tamil for "Praise the Lord!" "Isn't it wonderful, Paul, to be up here again where you can breathe!"

Was she remembering the first time she had climbed these mountains on her wedding day in 1913, no car to ride in then but a *dholi*, that hammock-like affair carried by four coolies? Monsoon clouds were gathering, thunder rumbling. It was August and stiflingly hot. Tensed by the rolling motion, hands clutching the bamboo sides for security, Evie felt her white dress wilting, her neatly parted hair becoming stringy and sodden. It was almost a relief to feel the first gentle drops of rain. Soon came the deluge, the *dholi* became a bathtub. "Are you all right?" asked Jesse anxiously. "Fine," she replied gamely. "I was needing a bath." Finally she got out and walked with Jesse along the narrow path. It was pitch dark, for night had long since come. After much traveling up and down hill she felt

108

her foot sinking deep into mud and water. "Almost there," assured Jesse. "Here we are at the rice fields." He shouted, and after a time a little light came flickering down the hillside. With Jesse guiding her they moved up a hill, and, shivering, wet to the skin, she walked through the dark rectangle of a doorway. "Life is not going to be easy." she thought. "It's good that all this happened. I may as well know it now." But she had not come for an easy time. She had come for love of God and of these hill people and of the man whose strong arms were lifting and carrying her over the threshold.

We also came to the rice fields, stretching golden-green across a broad valley. Beyond was a little settlement on a high hill. A great crowd came out to meet us. As Granny and Paul emerged from the car they burst into shouts of welcome. Granny tottered toward them, the bamboo poles, seeming extensions of her eager arms, reached out to enfold them. She had come home.

That day in the little Christian community she and Jesse had founded I saw their years together come to life. There was the little house he had built before her coming. I could imagine it the way it looked first, as she had loved to paint it, with a thatch roof, beautiful and thick, but a dangerous fire hazard when the hill people came for medical help at night with their flaming torches. Jesse had replaced it with corrugated iron, safer but noisy as a kettle drum in the monsoons. The plain board shutters letting in drenching clouds of mist when opened and shutting out light when closed had been changed for plain glass casements.

Later I was to read the diary telling of their first year together, full of thanksgiving, prayer, hope for a swift acceptance of the Gospel they had come to bring. Surely, thought Evie, if one loved the people enough and tried to meet their desperate needs, they could be made to understand and accept quickly the message of divine love! I saw them going on long camping trips to the villages, Jesse treating the sick, Evie gathering the women and children about her and trying to teach them; attempting to start schools and after repeated disappointments slowly succeeding; teaching new methods of agriculture, training young men in building skills, digging wells deep and full of clean water; instructing the villagers in ways to improve health and prevent disease. I saw their frustration when, for all their camping, teaching, preaching, laboring, healing, for six years they were unable to make a single convert. "Never," they had been warned, "will a Kolli man break caste and follow your way." For accepting the Yesu way of life meant giving up the old gods and leaving home and family. One of the strongest opponents was the *poosari*, the Hindu priest who lived just over the hill.

"Yes," he told the tribesmen who wanted to worship the Christian God," worship this Yesu-swami if you choose, but you must worship the other swamis also."

Then in 1919 came the first breakthrough. "See that gap in the hills?" Paul pointed across the fields toward a break in the mountain range. "It was through there that we saw the boy coming."

Already I knew the story. It was the time of the terrible influenza epidemic which was sweeping the world. The Brands went all over the hills treating the sick, taking them gruel. The *poosari* and his wife became victims of the scourge. Since Jesse was in bed with malaria, Evie went alone to the priest's house. She found him and his wife dying. "You must—take our—children," he gasped. "Please—" Evie came running home, so excited she could hardly speak. "We're—going to have—another baby!" she blurted. Sick though he was, Jesse rose immediately and went to the *poosari*. "You must send the baby to me," he told him, "and your son must come willingly. Otherwise I cannot take them." He wanted to risk no chance of being accused later of taking the children home against their father's wishes.

Would the priest send them? They waited anxiously. Finally they saw the boy coming through the gap in the hills, a forlorn little figure with a small bundle in his arms. "Don't be afraid," Evie comforted him, knowing what frightening tales he had been told about the foreigners. "We'll take good care of her."

They named the baby Ruth. This was the opening of the door. For the *poosari* had died with the name Yesu on his lips. In the camps the hill people flocked to watch little Ruth being bathed, fed, clothed, and tenderly nursed. A different sort of *swami* it must be, they told each other, who bade his *poosari* care for a helpless little orphan instead of leaving it to die!

That was the beginning of the little Christian community that I saw all around me. The schools grew in number. New stations were opened on the range. Not far from the house stood the chapel which Jesse, with the help of his pupils, built
110

with his own hands. We were served dinner in this chapel, sitting barefooted on strips of straw matting, our backs against the whitewashed walls. The hot rice and curry were served to us on big plantain leaves by smiling women in bright clean saris, smooth hair drawn back into neat braids and decorated with flowers. After the meal hill men came to greet Granny, sitting crosslegged before her on the floor and telling her their problems. She advised, encouraged, berated them for their backsliding. "Oh, he's naughty, naughty," she observed more than once in English. "Granny has a nose for sin," Paul told me in a smiling aside. But she was always ready to forgive, and her scolding was prompted solely by love.

Presently four long strips of matting were laid on the floor, and the Christians began to assemble, seated on the strips, men and boys on one side, women and girls on the other. I was amazed at the neat clean appearance of the worshipers in contrast with the villagers we had seen coming up the mountain. It was a worshipful service, followed by a discussion of the problem of finding a new leader for the work the Brands had started here long ago.

Unable to follow the service in Tamil, I sat on the platform with Evie and Paul and tried to reconstruct some of their memories. Was Paul thinking of the times he had laid the strips of matting here each Sunday as a boy, and of the day when at age nine he had been leaving with his parents, worrying about who would lay the mats when he was gone? And Evie—was she too remembering that furlough for which they had waited ten years? Home to England, a year of blessing—and of torture. For it meant leaving the two children with the aunts, Eunice and Hope, those two quaintly delightful sisters whom I had met. They must remain in England to be educated. The day of departure for India came, when Evie and Jesse must leave. The family knelt and prayed together. Then Paul and Connie hugged their parents. "As I said goodbye," she confessed later, "something just died in me."

Five years more they worked on the Kollis, and the community grew. They built a Girls' Home, started an orphanage, taught more practical skills—weaving, gardening, a silk worm industry. Where before there were only rough mountain paths, dirt roads were built, Jesse himself laying them out and doing much of the work. Besides being doctor, builder, agriculturist, teacher, preacher, he was lawyer as well, more than once

111

acting as mediator when the hill people were treated unjustly by men on the plains.

Already their dreams were reaching far beyond the Kollis. One day Jesse and Evie stood on a high crest where they could see four more mountain ranges. "We must go to them," he told her eagerly. "You hear, Evie? Before we die we must go to all those four ranges and take the saving message of the Christ."

"Yes, oh yes!" she agreed, and the word held all the solemnity of a vow.

I stood on the hill at the edge of the compound looking down at the symbol of what seemed the end of this dream, the rough stone marking the grave of Jesse Brand. When he died of blackwater fever in 1929, from all over the hills his people came, those he had healed and taught, whose lands he had restored, whose minds and souls and bodies he had struggled to save. Evie thought life was ended. She could not go on without him. But, being Evie, of course she did.

This was Paul's world, too, and here his first nine years came alive. There was the little house his father had built, set on stone posts with inverted frying pans at the top, to keep out the white ants. I walked through the three rooms, built tandem "like a train of cars," empty now, imagined the two small beds in the bedroom corners where the two children had been tucked at dusk under mosquito nettings to avoid the deadly malarial mosquitoes, entered the little bathing cubicle where snakes had once lived in a crack between the earthen stove and the wall. There on the hillside were the tall trees where he had climbed to do his sums.

Even his eloquent descriptions of his childhood could not have supplied the vividness of this on-the-spot experience. For a few hours I *was* the wide-eyed, lithe, adventurous boy running wild over the hills, shinnying up the lofty jackfruits and spindly bamboos, exploring the wonders of nature with a father whose knowledge and love of God's world was equaled only by his concern for human beings.

Down we came from the Kollis, around the seventy-two hairpin turns, and after a night on the plains we started once more to retrace Granny's steps by climbing her second mountain range, the Kalryans.

For even after Jesse's death she did not give up their dream. During enforced years as a missionary on the plains she marked time, waiting. For about five rupees she hired a little

screened hut to be built, in sections so it could be easily transported, and on holidays she would take this with her up the
mountains. Then she would roam over the hills, camping near
villages, treating gummed eyes and dysentery, doling out qui-
nine for malaria and medicine for big and little worms, wind
guinea worms off a bit at a time so they would not break and
cause dire infection. She would instruct in cleanliness and
hygiene, show pictures, play hymns on her gramophone, and of
course repeat endlessly the story of Guru Yesu. All over the
mountain range she would carry her little portable shelter,
enclosed in mosquito netting, sleeping contentedly inside,
seeking its meager protection from monsoon rains, often gathering children about her within it and teaching them to read by
the light of a hurricane lantern, then of course to pray. Still she
was only marking time.

Ten years passed before her next furlough, for war had
disrupted the world. It was a year of momentous events for the
family. She saw Paul, already a skilled surgeon, off for India to
fill an emergency at Vellore. She rejoiced with her daughter
Connie, home on furlough with her missionary husband from
Africa, on the birth of their little Jessica. But for herself . . .
When the mission board told her she was to retire, she was at
first dismayed. Retire! Why, she hadn't even begun to fulfill
the vow she and Jesse had made! True, she was sixty-eight
years old, and, the committee told her firmly, it was the "rule."
Through her storm of tears Evie glimpsed a sliver of rainbow
hope. She was not above using a bit of guile.

"Please," she begged," send me back for a year. I promise
that at the end of just one year I will retire."

The board was in a quandary. Rules? Precedent? Evelyn
Brand *was* precedent. She had been breaking rules all her life.
They remembered that for some years she had been returning
her pittance of salary, using her small inheritance to finance
her work, buying property in the name of the mission. Reluctantly they yielded.

"Only a year this time, Evie, dear." Her sisters sent her off
with tearful yet hopeful farewells. She gave them reassuring
murmurs. A year, yes, and then . . . She and Jesse had set out
to take the Gospel to five mountain ranges. There were still
four to go. If God gave her time, she would go to all of them.
And let nobody try to stop her!

She fulfilled her promise to the board and was formally

113

retired, with a beautiful lamp as a farewell present, not so useful as a hurricane lantern in the places where she was going. Then at age sixty-nine she started to really live. Of course her friends were shocked. "But—you're nearly seventy!" . . . "To go up into those jungles, among those primitive people, a woman almost alone!" . . . "Well, if you must go, God go with you!"

"He will," returned Evie confidently. And as she climbed the Kalryans in a dholi, she felt like that young eager bride of long ago riding up, up, with new life beginning and Jesse traveling just ahead. "I'm coming, Jess," her heart cried silently. "At last I'm coming!"

And now it was our privilege to follow her. What a road! They assured us it was "jeepable." The word was mildly descriptive. Pebbles, stones, boulders, sheer ledges, ruts as deep as small gullies, forty-five degree ascents, center ridges which would have scraped the belly of an army truck, hairpin turns . . . everything but mud, for this was the dry season. The reddish soil was like powder, the grass rank and brown, the jungle scrub coated with dust. But thanks to Dr. Paul's skillful driving, the road was "jeepable." To Granny, remembering the time when there were no roads, it must have seemed like a king's highway.

After leaving the road and driving for two miles across dry fields and rice field bunds, we left the jeep and took other means of conveyance. First—horses. For Granny it was a familiar means of travel, for she had ridden hundreds of miles over similar rough terrain on her little mount. But for me it was not at all familiar. Only once, going in to Petra in 1950, had I ever ridden a horse, and then my guide had indulged in obvious amusement at my expense.

At Munglepetti, an outstation where we were greeted by a big crowd, another mode of transportation was waiting. Having sampled almost every other kind of conveyance in India, I looked forward to the *dholi* with relish. Like Granny on her wedding day, I arranged myself on the strips of canvas, set my feet against the front crosspiece, and the four bearers hoisted me to their shoulders. The initial impact was like mounting a camel, but the jogging pace was not unpleasant—as long as we remained on the level. But mountain trails are not level. As the bearers started up a rocky slope I clutched the poles harder, relaxed with relief at the top, stared aghast at an even steeper

114

path leading down. I recalled that Granny had once been dropped when riding in a *dholi*. When we came to a ribbon of path with a sheer drop on one side, I turned coward. Deficient though my Tamil was, I made the bearers understand that I wanted *down*. For the last six miles I walked.

"It was a place like this," Granny, still on her horse, told me cheerfully as the path plunged down a stony stream bed, "where I was once thrown right over the horse's head."

For miles and miles, up and down hillsides, through dry river beds, along the edges of deep ravines we trekked, finally climbing the last steep slope to the hilltop which Granny had chosen for her headquarters on the Kalryans. Here also we were given a rousing welcome by some of those who had worked with her during her fifteen years on this second mountain range. We were ushered into the small house which was her home through many of those years, two small rooms and a porch, with a tiny cooking space and bathing cubicle. In a corner of the latter, proudly exhibited as a surprise for Granny and her Western guests, was a flush unit! There it stood in all its porcelain glory. I could see it trekking up those sixteen miles on some coolie's head!

But of even more interest to me was the little hut across the path which had been her first home here. Like the native huts it was made of woven bamboo strips overlaid with clay and whitewashed, surmounted by a high peaked thatched roof.

That evening she gathered the Christians of the little settlement on the veranda for *jebbum*, prayer, a word as omnipresent in her vocabulary as the fervent *stotherum*. Unable to understand Tamil I sat on a striped mat with my head against the wall, watching the play of lamplight on the clean, radiant faces, listening to the haunting melodies, the rhythmic clapping of hands, the firm confident voice of Granny talking intimately about these people and their problems with One who for over eighty-five years had been her constant companion.

The same motley crowd assembled the next morning to see us off. It was a farewell to Granny, too, for she was now working on her third mountain range, the Pachais, starting the process all over again, the slow making of friends and converts, the hundreds of miles of riding over stony mountain trails, camping out in all kinds of weather, the long slow process of bringing new life to people.

Back in Vellore, with Paul off to clinical work in Africa, I plunged into my double research. A tin trunk of family archives in the Big Bungalow yielded priceless treasures—letters from Jesse Brand to his children, copies of a newspaper called "The Superior" edited by Paul and Connie, pictures, diaries, reports. With Granny's consent I shipped a great boxful of such materials back to America. Interviews with helpful persons provided a wealth of impressions, medical information, case histories, anecdotes.

The anecdotes about Paul whether related by him or others, were full of pith and humor. Many of them revealed his complete lack of vanity or affectation, like the time he had been combining recreation with education for his children by teaching them bricklaying. One afternoon the principal of the Teachers' Training College came to ask him to give a Republic Day lecture at his college. It was an official but unannounced visit. Arriving at the house, he saw a coolie tramping about in ragged shorts up to his knees in mud, surrounded by a horde of noisy, happy children.

"Hello," Paul greeted him. "Anything I can do for you?"

"I—I was just wondering if Dr. Brand lives here."

"Yes. This is the Brand place."

"Would he be in this afternoon?"

"He's here," replied Paul genially. "I'm Dr. Brand. May I help you?"

After a speechless moment the man managed to smile and explain his errand.

Then there was the time when Margaret, preparing a pair of Paul's trousers for washing by the *dhobi*, noticed an official-looking letter in one of the pockets. To her amazement she found it was an announcement of the Queen's conferring on him the order of C.B.E.! And Paul had not even mentioned it.

"Oh, yes—that," he replied when she questioned him. It might have been an invitation to a dinner party. "I saw it."

"Did you answer it?" Yes, he had. "What did you say?"

He grinned. "Well, it's not my business to interfere with the Queen's good pleasure, is it?"

Unless he went to England, the honor had to be conferred by the high commissioner within a year of its pronouncement. The time was almost up when Paul, hearing that the dignitary was to be in Madras, asked if it would be convenient for him to call at the government office and pick up the documents and the insignia. A happy arrangement, he thought. No formality. No fanfare.

116

Arriving in Madras on the specified day from a trip north, having spent the night in a second-rate hotel in Delhi, Paul noticed that his traveling suit was rumpled. But, then, he was lucky to be wearing a pukka suit! He often traveled without one. The plane was late, and he was driven directly to Government House. Somewhat to his dismay he found all the elite of Madras there, the mayor and his wife, guests of the Embassy, many doctor friends, the whole throng lined up for his investiture. All were dressed "up to the nines." To his intense embarrassment a wide red carpet was rolled out, and he was told just where to stand. Surreptitiously trying to straighten his suit and tie, he thought cheerfully, "Oh, well, they'll just have to take me as I am!" There was a burst of martial music, and the High Commissioner came down the stairs wearing all his regalia, plus formal morning suit and tails. Paul was just about to start forward to the spot marked for him on the carpet when a doctor friend appeared at his side.

"Pardon me, Paul," he murmured in his ear, then quietly (shades of the Delhi hotel!) removed a bedbug from his lapel.

Unpretentiousness, simplicity—they were as indigenous to his working techniques as to his personal way of life. His colleagues were shocked when, anxious to experiment with simple techniques which could be used under crude village conditions, he proposed performing hand operations in his New Life Center. What! Exchange the white-tiled operating room with it gleaming instruments for the bare interior of a whitewashed hut of mud-brick and tile? "*How?*" "You'll see," said Paul. He made a shadowless lamp by beating a big sheet of aluminum into a concave shape, polishing it, installing a 220-watt bulb, and suspending it from the ceiling with pulleys. A one-bin sterilizer was provided, a wooden operating table fitted with an adjustable headpiece and a hand table support. The only alteration made in the eight-foot-square room was a mosquito netting on the windows to keep out the flies. The first operation proceeded without a hitch, and many more followed. I myself saw Paul at work on the mountains making a rocker shoe for a leprosy patient, using only a few pieces of wood and a sickle.

Visiting the New Life Center, the cluster of whitewashed mud and thatch huts on the edge of the campus, I saw the results of Paul's continued research into the causes of disabilities from Hansen's disease and his techniques of rehabilitation.

One day here in the Center a leprosy patient saw Paul trying unsuccessfully to turn a key in a rusty lock and offered to help. He took the key, turned it hard, and the lock opened. As he handed the key back, smiling proudly, Paul noticed that the flesh of his fingers was torn to the bone. But, the nerves being dead, he had felt no pain. It was his first inkling of a revolutionary discovery. It was not leprosy which caused the mutilation of fingers and toes, as every student of the disease had assumed. It was the use of strength, with no feeling of pain, that did most of the damage. Torn flesh from walking on sharp objects, cuts to limbs, burns on unfeeling hands all resulted in infections which because they could not be felt became serious, often resulting in permanent damage.

The blessing of pain! It became one of the profound tenets of his creed. "It is clear," he said once in a lecture in England, "how important pain must be in the whole pattern of the survival of living organisms composed of many cells. As soon as pain is lost there seems to be a loss also of that body consciousness which makes every part share the success or failure of the whole. . . . In human society we are suffering because we do not suffer enough. . . . With the acceptance of the discipline of pain, suffering for one another, will come also the ecstasy of shared happiness and of new understanding as we glimpse the vision of God for his world."

So here at the New Life Center Paul began a program of rehabilitation. But his second major purpose was research, and, as his startling theory of the origin of shortened fingers and toes became more and more substantiated, the protection of those insensitive members and the education of the patients in insuring their safety became of prime importance. He fitted their tools to long smooth handles, set files in blocks to protect hands from pressure, devised attachments to keep them from dangerous moving parts of metal, like the cutting edge of a plane. He designed wicker frames for the metal plates in which their hot food was served, wooden holders with handles for their coffee cups, so their fingers would not be burned. And unceasingly he dinned into their ears the necessity for constant vigilance to avoid burns, cuts, rough ground, stones or too strong pressures.

Once his theory seemed in actual danger of disproof. One morning a boy came to him with nearly a third of his index finger missing. Paul looked from the raw stump to the young patient's tearful eyes. "What happened, son?"

118

"Doctor Sahib, I don't know. It was there yesterday. You know it was."

"Where is the piece that's missing?" persisted Paul.

"I don't know," mourned the boy.

They went into the room where he had slept and searched the floor around his mat. There were a few tiny spots of blood, but not even a scrap of flesh! Paul felt failure closing around him. It would need only the apparent disappearance of a few fingers without cause to reawaken the old superstitions. They searched more carefully, and not far from the mat they noticed in the dust of the earth floor a few little footmarks. Rats! How horribly simple! Not feeling any pain, the boy had slept on unaware that a rodent was enjoying a meal on his finger. And how often this must happen in village homes where rats could gain easy access! Thereafter he introduced cats into the compound, and every patient who left the colony took a kitten as part of his necessary equipment.

Granny took full advantage of Paul's skills with leprosy. At least two or three times a year she would turn up at the Vellore hospital with leprosy victims she had found at her little dispensary or on her horseback rounds. Often there was no room for them in the hospital, but that did not matter. She had people who needed help, and she meant to get it. If Paul was away, she might employ a highhanded method. "No room? I guess you don't know who I am. Dr. Paul Brand is my son, and these are his very special patients." Or, if he was there, she might become sweetly wheedling. "Look, dear boy, I have quite a lot of patients with me this time." "But, Mother, there are no beds!" "Oh, you'll find beds. Just say it's for your old mother."

I met one of these patients, Karuninasan, whom she found in a wreck of a shed, turned out of his village. She took him to Vellore many times, and Paul operated on his hands, made shoes for his insensitive feet. On our trip to the Kalryans Karuninasan appeared, his shoes worn through, his badly deformed feet showing the ravages of stones and rough ground. Fascinated, I saw Paul make new shoes for him out of the crude materials he had available.

"They're a pair, mother and son," I thought, watching the eminent surgeon spend his mountain holiday examining twisted hands and feet, bandaging sores, inspecting reddened eyes, making shoes out of bits of wood with a sickle. Pioneers of courage, both of them.

But of her own harshly disciplined, austere, and often lonely

119

life Granny would tolerate no eulogies of heroic self-denial. "Hardships! Living here on these glorious hills? It would be horrible to live in those awful cities. I couldn't breathe. Why, just being on the plains gives me claustrophobia!" Of the loneliness she did comment sometimes in grudging admission, "It does have its bad points. The worst is you have no one to laugh with."

Perhaps her physical stamina was less of body than of spirit. Certainly some of her experiences would have taxed the strength of a giant, to say nothing of a reedy wisp of woman between and seventy and ninety-five. One night, alone in her hut, she was crossing the floor, a lamp in one hand, a jug of milk in the other. She went, as she called it, "smash down." Before she was found she lay for some time with a broken hip. Coolies took her down the mountain in a *dholi*, where she was met by a car and taken to Vellore. During the several weeks that she was in the hospital she was the despair of her doctors. She refused to stay put. There was far too much to do to spend valuable time in bed. Maneuvering herself to a mat on the floor, she would inch her way along corridors into wards and private rooms, prescribing large and powerful doses of the Christian gospel to any who would listen. To her harassed doctors' surprise her hip healed with greater despatch than the bones of other patients. She was tough and stringy as a green withe and seemingly indestructible.

But time brought other complications. For some reason she developed a creeping paralysis so that in time her limbs became almost disabled. Hence the two bamboo sticks. But that did not keep her from traveling. Far from it. On the back of her little pony, an Indian boy leading, she journeyed constantly, covering hundreds of miles, up and down rocky paths, falling off but learning to fall easily with a sort of rolling motion, picking herself up and going on, continuing to camp out, sleeping on wood, on stones, on bare ground, living the simple life of her simple hill people, loving and beloved by them.

After Paul's return from Africa I moved to Karigiri, site of the Schieffelin Leprosy Research Sanatorium where much of his work was done, about ten miles from Vellore. Time was getting short, and here I could catch him for interviews at odd times, between operations, at meals, as well as in the evenings. I lived in a very comfortable guest house, occupied also by Dr. Brand and several trainees from other Asiatic coun-
120

tries. Fortunately it was in the room next to mine, not in mine, that a large snake was discovered one day in the bathing cubicle—not poisonous, Paul decided after killing it. It was my closest encounter with such creatures (except for the protegés of snake charmers) in my four trips to India, though I dutifully examined bath cubicles for cobras in wait and shook out my shoes for latent scorpions.

Here I saw Paul perform operations, attended his clinics. In one I saw him examine a man with a foot and ankle so swollen that it was almost unrecognizable. He had broken a bone and, not knowing it, had walked on it. "Isn't it *awful!*" murmured Paul, his face contorted with concern. His work with patients' feet was as noteworthy as with hands. For years he experimented to find the material and style of shoe that would best protect insensitive feet from injuries and ulcers. His search ranged through leather, wood, plastics, sponge rubber; took him to Britain, Nigeria, other parts of India. With the help of John Girling, an enthusiastic helper, he finally found it, a combination of wood and leather called the "rocker shoe." With this, plus painstaking education about the care of feet, Paul's team had reduced the incidence of ulcers in village areas around Vellore by fifty percent. In a workshop here at Karigiri I saw patients making shoes, a double benefit, since it not only created the footware but gave useful employment.

One of the "guinea pigs" in this long process of experimentation was Sadogopan. In talking with him I decided that here was the dramatic story with which I must start the book.

Sadogopan, born of a respectable, educated, artistic family, was about to enter secondary school when his leprosy was discovered. For years he lived as an outcast, shunned, unable to find employment. Someone told him of Dr. Brand. Arriving in Vellore, he was directed to the college four miles away. He tried to take a bus, but the driver noticed his hands and feet and ordered him off. Arriving tired, rumpled, feet bleeding, he met a sweet-faced woman, Mrs. Brand. Learning that the doctor was away, he tried not to show his overwhelming disappointment. As he turned away hopelessly, she called him back, took him home with her, made him feel wanted, respected, even *loved* as a human being.

Here, a dozen years later, I saw a tall, attractive, healthy looking man. Except for the shortening of a few fingers, his hands were capable of normal motion. His feet, though encased

121

in unusual shoes, were free from ulcers and deformity. With him was his lovely wife, also an ex-patient. Their healthy son was being reared like any normal child. Sadan, an efficient typist in spite of his fingers, was well employed and independent. New life, indeed! And he might so easily have been one of the hopeless beggars I had often seen thrusting stumps of fingers toward our car windows!

Paul's creed, like Margaret's, was one of action, but he could also put it into vivid language. Somewhere I got the story of an impromptu talk he gave at Christmas time at Number 10, a little house where leprosy patients were permitted to live while waiting for operations. He came after a hard day's work and was very tired. "Won't you please say something?" he was asked. He felt empty of ideas. But as he rose to his feet he became conscious of hands, many clawed, some with no fingers, some half hidden to hide their disfigurement. *Hands.*

"How I would love," he began, "to have had the chance to meet Christ and study his hands! But, knowing what he was like, I can almost picture them, see the changes that took place in them."

He traced them through the years—the boy's hands, clumsy, learning; the carpenter's, rough, tough, gnarled; the healer's, sensitive, compassionate; the crucified hands, marred, yes, even *clawed.*

"And then there were his resurrected hands," Paul concluded, telling of the invitation to Thomas to put his finger into the print of the nails. "Why did he want to keep the wounds of his humanity? He carried the marks of suffering so he could continue to understand the needs of those suffering. He wanted to be forever one with us."

I could almost see the hands lifted to him then, palm to palm, the same stumps, scars, claws, yet not the same. No one tried to hide them. Somehow even the stumps seemed to have acquired a new dignity.

It was April. Did I have enough material? Not yet, for first I must spend time with Margaret and the children in England. I lived with them for a week in a big house in Kew, not far from Kew Gardens, Paul's headquarters when he was not traveling. Margaret, bless her, was as communicating as Paul. I can see her now, sitting on my bed with the tape recorder, telling in precise and dramatic language the story of her own contributions to the work in leprosy. For she had become as innovative and competent a specialist in surgery and treatment of eyes as had Paul with hands and feet.

Most interesting of all was Margaret's story of their presentation to the Queen when she came to Madras. All the British couples but the Brands received a formal invitation to her reception. Few had correct clothes, and there was much borrowing. Paul and Margaret were teasing the others. They had no worries because they were not invited. A week before the event Paul got an urgent telephone call from the High Commissioner's office in Madras. "Are you coming?" "No, we've had no invitation." "But—you're being *presented*!" "Well," replied Paul, "we'll try to make it."

What to do? Margaret had no proper clothes, and all the decent ones had been loaned. Friends gathered, anxious to help. She tried a short frock. Impossible! Someone produced a long dress about ten years old and certainly outdated, but it had to do. Long gloves being unobtainable, she secured a pair of short ones. "Now what about you, Paul?" He borrowed a pair of black trousers from a student and a rather fashionable Palm Beach frock coat. Tucks had to be taken in the latter, but even then it hung on him like an elephant's hide. Margaret was busy turning the trousers up as they rode to Madras. Halfway there the engine died. Pushing the car to the side of the road, they waited hopefully. A bus came along, and the driver helpfully turned it into express service, making record time.

In Madras at the home of an Indian doctor friend who had heard of Paul's plight, Paul found twelve evening suits lined up for his examination. One fitted perfectly, and he might have issued straight from a Bond Street tailor. Lined up with the half dozen couples to be presented, they were briefed on the proper way to address the Queen. "Just gently hold her fingertips as you do a full curtsy. If she speaks to you, answer and conclude each sentence with 'Your Majesty.'" Certain that she would bungle, Margaret envied Paul his inimitable calm. The moment came. They were the second couple to be introduced. Taking the royal hand gently, by the fingertips, Margaret launched into the full bend curtsy, but something went wrong. She wobbled and would have fallen had she not grabbed the Queen's hand. She completely forgot about "Your Majesty." But the royal couple were so delightfully friendly and informal that the ceremonious terms would have sounded stilted. Moreover the Prince, who remembered Paul from a previous meet-

123

ing, was full of questions. "You're the hand man, aren't you? Tell me, are your patients really able to work now?" Amazed at the man's memory, Paul picked up the conversation where it had been left two years before.

Fortified with such anecdotes, films, and my hundreds of little three-by-five papers, I flew home in April, marveling anew at the anomaly of leaving London at twelve noon and arriving in Boston at one-thirty. The research was by no means finished, though I started the writing immediately. Letters kept coming from the Brands, their family friends, the plastic surgeons who had been spending short terms in Vellore since the project was instigated by Dr. William White of Pittsburgh because of his interest in Paul's work. One from Dr. Hugh Johnson of Rockford, Illinois, the same who operated so successfully on Dr. Mary Verghese, was most helpful. He even sent me a possible opening for a chapter.

" 'The Gospel According to Saint Paul'? Oh, that; it's the title I've given my notes of Paul Brand's gospel of hand surgery. Why? Well, it is a gospel and he's a saint—simple enough. A saint? The chief obstacle in the achievement of sainthood for most is the performance of a miracle. Paul performs miracles in plastic surgery of the hand almost daily."

Remembering that by 1960, about the time Dr. Johnson was in India, Paul had already personally performed more than 3,000 reconstructions of hands, I found his estimate of Paul's achievements not too extravagant.

As I wrote Margaret in one of my numerous letters containing questions, the likely gestation period for my literary brain child was a conventional nine months. By late fall, however, the pages of onion skin were coursing back and forth between America and England, accompanied on their return by many pages of clarifications, fixing of dates, suggestions, corrections. The Brands' Christmas letter in December brought news of the family.

"Christmas 1964 will be an unusual one for the Brands, because we hope to be all together in England for the occasion, the first time since 1945. Then the family consisted of one tiny son. Now, nineteen years and five children later, we have moved into our first home in England and are buying the first furniture we ever owned and we feel like a honeymoon couple except for the towering, husky children who are helping us."

In April when Paul was in the States for a meeting in New

Orleans we met in New York for a final conference on the manuscript, had a profitable visit with Norman Thomas, whose feature article in *Saturday Review* entitled "Paul Brand and His Mission" had appeared the previous year, and of course had sessions with the publishers. True to the usual pattern, I had a new editor, Barbara Collins, my fifth since working with McGraw-Hill, but I found her just as efficient, friendly and easy to work with as her predecessors. As often with my books at this late stage, we were still lacking a satisfactory title. "Brand New Hands," as one patient had delightfully called his miracle of surgery? No, it did not quite suit. Finally one of the girls in the office suggested *Ten Fingers for God.*

By July we were reading proofs, and in October I was in New York again attending a luncheon at the Interchurch Center under the auspices of the Vellore Board on the occasion of the book's publication.

Paul Brand's story had wide appeal. The book remained in print in hard cover in this country for more than ten years. A condensation appeared in the book section of *Reader's Digest* in June, 1966, under the title, "Sahib Doctor: The Healing Surgeon of Vellore." It was a selection of a religious book club. Like *Dr. Ida* and *Take My Hands*, its sales in Germany have been exceptional, and new editions in both hard cover and paperback have appeared there recently. The book has been popular in Paul's own England where it has recently been printed in a new paperback edition. It has been translated into Swedish, Dutch, French, Finnish.

The Brands did not have long to enjoy their new English home. In 1966 Paul and Margaret moved to the United States Public Health Service Hospital in Carville, Louisiana, the only institution for the treatment of leprosy in North America, Paul to become chief of the hospital's rehabilitation branch, Margaret to act as chief of the eye service.

But no one institution could contain Paul Brand and his ebullient, dedicated energy. Carville is only a headquarters, a jumping-off place for the rest of the world. He has three clinical centers which he visits periodically—in Vellore, in Addis Ababa, Ethiopia and in Caracas, Venezuela—where he performs reconstructive surgery and instructs trainees from all three continents in his techniques. He is a consultant on leprosy for the World Health Organization.

The children also are more citizens of the world than of any one country, and all are imbued with the same compulsion to service as their parents. As of last report Christopher, with a master's degree in food science, was doing agricultural work in the deserts of Mexico; Jean, having driven to India in a Land Rover ambulance to be delivered in Nepal, was a teacher-evangelist in Bombay; Mary, a trained nurse, was married to a doctor and living in Minneapolis; Estelle was teaching; Tricia was studying medicine at Paul's University College Hospital in London; and Pauline was still in school in England.

The title *Ten Fingers For God* has for me a double significance. It represents those thousands of hands which have been reactivated to usefulness, transformed from claws to creative tools, every finger made as perfect as humanly possible. But it is also symbolic of the skillful surgeon's hands which perform these miracles of healing. We tried to express this in the last paragraphs of the book, and, as I recall, its closing words are more Paul's than mine. He had been performing a successful operation on claw hands and was now relaxing. Yet he still had a deep sense of frustration, thinking of his team, all of whom contributed so much yet got so little praise, and of all the leprosy patients in the world still needing help. How few he and his team were able to reach.

"In a gesture expressive of his frustration he lifted his hand, its creases lined with little flecks of talcum powder, and impatiently flexed its fingers. Then he looked at them intently. Which one of them had performed that operation? The index finger, perhaps, or the thumb? He laughed aloud. Of course not. They were just instruments, tools of his mind. He could ask only one thing of them, that they be responsive, sensitive, obedient to his will. Just as God asked of him . . .

" 'That's what I am,' he thought with sudden clarity, 'just a finger. Or perhaps a thumb.'

"Frustration? Hardly! What more could any man ask of life than the knowledge that he was a finger or thumb among many other fingers, and that the hand was the hand of God?"

But what about the book about Granny? It was more than ten years in the writing. For Granny had been persuaded against her will, and that will was iron-strong. She soon wrote me a letter. No, she would not let me write her story. No one but herself could tell it as it should be told. She was going to do it herself. Very well. I fulfilled my obligation to the League by writing the story of my trip up the mountains, which was published independently under the title, "Life for the Mountains of Death." She did write her story, which was also published in a little book called "Trust and Triumph."

"Now," I thought, "she has got her version out of her system, and she surely won't mind if I write mine." Taking her permission for granted, I wrote two or three chapters before her letter arrived. *No!* So I consigned the written pages to the big box of materials. Time passed. Surprisingly she kept sending me little bits of information and descriptions. When I was in England at the time *Hilary* was published, my British publishers professed a keen interest in a book about Granny, so I made another attempt. *No* again. "Sister," she wrote, "I hope you understand."

I did. Granny was an individualist. She could not trust another person to thrust probing fingers into her thoughts, her emotions, her precious personal relationship with her Lord. Moreover, she feared that too much credit would be given to herself, when all the credit belonged to God—and her beloved Jesse. But this time the refusal was not quite so final. "Do wait a few months and let me die," she wrote in one letter. "You can write what you like then." So after she died, in December, 1974, at age ninety-five, with the permission of her son Paul and her daughter Connie, I once more started writing.

One bonus accruing from the long delay was the additional material available. Especially helpful was the nurse she worked with for many years on all the five mountain ranges, six finally, for the dream has been more than fulfilled. It was Dr. Paul who first met Carolyn Weeber, a young American missionary in south India, a trained teacher and registered nurse with long experience, and told her about Granny's work. Three years later she climbed the Kalryans and stayed with Granny for several days. Three more years later Dr. Paul met Carol in America.

"And how is your mother?" she asked.

"I wish," murmured Paul as if talking to himself, "that I could find someone to go and stay with her."

"I'll go," said Carolyn Weeber promptly. An appointment was made for her with Dr. Lewis of the International Gospel League, which assumed her support, and she was soon on her way back to India.

Granny could scarcely believe the good news. It was an answer to more than thirty-five years of hoping and praying. Carol was of inestimable help to me also in supplying much information through letters and diaries. She read and criticized the manuscript and drew the beautiful map which lends clarity to Granny's locale and travels. And, best of all, she happened to be in America on furlough when the book was in progress and came up to my home in Maine for consultation.

Another one of Granny's prayers was answered when Dr. David Lister, grandnephew of the famous Dr. Joseph Lister, attended one of the work camps which the students of the Vellore Medical College organized for many years on the mountains, and he felt a call to dedicate his skills to mountain service. In 1969 he returned to become the only resident physician and surgeon among the thousands of people on the six ranges, many of whom had never seen a doctor. Though Dr. Ruth Harris, Granny's niece, whom I had visited on the plains, had at one time lived on the Kollis and had frequently visited the other ranges, the services of this resident doctor filled a vast need. He was appalled as well as challenged by the magnitude of the task he faced.

"These mountain people," a visitor said to him, "must be a hundred years behind the general condition of the people of India."

"More than a hundred years," he replied. "You have to see them to believe that such need actually exists in this world."

Dr. Ruth Harris was also of great help to me in writing the book. On a tour of England in 1975 I was able to confer not only with her but with Connie Wilmshurst, Granny's daughter, who supplied me with many intimate letters from Granny through the years. Paul and his wife Margaret, always so communicative, wrote me numerous incidents, humorous, pathetic, dramatic, which lent color and depth of understanding to Granny's complex and vigorous personality.

Of course her grandchildren, especially Paul's six children whom she knew so intimately in India, were very dear to her, and they loved her in spite of her ways which they thought a bit queer—her long, long prayers over tea when they were nearly starved; her insisting on tending a woman sick with typhoid while the Christmas turkey they had so looked forward to cooked to a crisp; her getting them up in the middle of the night to go walking in the beautiful rain; her living without

128

need of clock or mirror; her habit of putting one dress over another if she was pressed for time and it happened to be more convenient.

There had been a time when her son Paul had worried about her, tried to persuade her to live nearer to medical help, but that time passed. He knew that she would far rather keep on with her work until the last moment than to be under the best medical care in the world. Now located in Carville, Louisiana, Paul spends time in India each year doing surgery and training Asiatic doctors. Granny looked forward to those times and always went to meet him at Karigiri. He was so busy when there that she saw him but seldom, but one time in the day he was hers alone. She would get up before dawn as usual and go to the top of the steps where she could look out over the plains. Paul would come and join her. They would read from the Bible, talk about the family, pray. It was almost as if her beloved Jesse had come back to her.

"The thing so good about these times," Paul wrote me, "was the way she was able to be completely at peace." It had not always been so. There had been anxieties about her work, frustration, even resentment at the mission board for what she considered their indifference to the mountains, their turning over to the government of property she and Jessē had purchased. But not any longer. The near-at-hand had already receded. Her eyes were focused on far horizons.

"In a letter to me this week," Paul wrote not long before her death, "Mother expressed a fear and wish that I feel I must pass on to you. She says her ninety-fifth birthday will soon be here and she feels sure that a lot of kindly people will write and praise her and say how wonderful she is to be still working at ninety-five years of age. I can see the tears in her eyes when she insists, 'I am not wonderful. I am just a poor old frail and weak woman. God has taken hold of me and he gives me the strength I need each day. He uses me just because I KNOW that I have no strength of my own. Please tell the people to praise God—not me.'"

I hope I have done this in her story. Granny represents an older era of missions, a concept which is not wholly in agreement with my own. I could not accept all the tenets of her strict creed. But in love of people and dedicated service she was the embodiment of the Christian gospel, and I feel both proud and humble to have had the privilege of reliving her life. *Climb*

129

Every Mountain—that is the title of the book in its original British edition. Almost to the end she kept riding, fulfilling the dream, visiting the stations on her six mountain ranges. It's so that I like to remember her, always climbing, never satisfied. For one cannot imagine Granny without her beloved mountains. Lines from a poem by Amy Carmichael, who wrote so many beautiful expressions about India, seem to express Granny's life creed as she prepared to climb her last and highest mountain:

"Make us Thy mountaineers;
    We would not linger on the lower slope.
    Fill us afresh with hope, O God of hope,
    That undefeated we may climb the hill
    As seeing Him who is invisible.
    Let us die climbing. . . ."

JOURNEYS INTO HISTORY

INTRODUCTION

What small seemingly inconsequential happenings can change the direction of a person's life! The doctor on whom I am presently doing research would call them "wonder-haps." A chance conversation in the back of a church at a young people's convention, and you become involved in more than fifty years of happy marriage. The greeting of a missions secretary at a church conference, and the result is four trips to India, fifteen years of intensive study of that fascinating country with its diverse cultures, a switch from novels to biography. A simple telephone call from a stranger, and you are plunged suddenly into the world of another century, a project which eventually leads to books about three women whose lives closely paralleled one another's but whose concerns and achievements were in totally diverse areas of social action.

The research would demand a completely different technique, much more like that for the biblical novels. There would be few interviews with living persons, for the materials would be found in books, in family papers, in old newspapers, in historical documents. It would involve travel—to England, to many cities in this country, to an Indian reservation in Nebraska. And it would require study in depth of a variety of subjects of which I had only a smattering of knowledge.

Medicine, for instance. While I had dipped into its mysteries through the lives of Dr. Ida, Clara Swain, Paul Brand and others, I must now explore the progress of medical knowledge

133

through the whole of the nineteenth century, the education of doctors, the lives of prominent physicians and leaders in medical research; later, the history of insanity and its treatment through the ages, the development of concepts of mental illness and its cure.

The American Indian. Here was a totally new study but a most welcome one, not merely of one tribe but of the whole sorry tale of the white man's exploitation. It would be a profoundly moving experience, adding a new tenet to my social creed: long-delayed justice for the first Americans.

Women's Rights. Not the mildly militant movement as we know it today, but a far more daring and revolutionary adventure beginning more than a century and a quarter ago. Those who think the present agitation for equal rights is a radical innovation do not know their history. Gloria Steinem and her cohorts look staid and conventional compared with the pioneers I was to encounter in the nineteenth century—Elizabeth Cady Stanton, Susan B. Anthony, Carrie Chapman Catt, Lucy Stone, Florence Nightingale.

True, the three women of my biographies were not actively engaged in the crusade for women's rights. Each of them believed *human* rights were more important, and each was too busy implementing the principles that their more vocal sisters were enunciating. Yet they probably did more for the liberation of women than those who marched in suffragist parades, demanded their rights most vehemently—and wore bloomers.

It was with zest and anticipation that I prepared to thrust new chambers in my shell back into the world of the nineteenth century.

6

DR. ELIZABETH BLACKWELL: 'LONE WOMAN'

About a month before leaving for India to research the book on Clara Swain I received a telephone call from a senior editor of Little, Brown and Company in Boston.

"I understand you have written books about doctors, in fact, woman doctors."

"Yes," I replied.

The unfamiliar voice continued. "The Reader's Digest Condensed Books people are looking for a biography of Dr. Elizabeth Blackwell. Would you be interested in writing it?"

Would I! Elizabeth Blackwell was well known to me as the first woman in the world to become a full-fledged doctor, with an accredited degree. I had encountered her name in my research of Dr. Ida, also in more recent preparation for the book on Clara Swain, and it had aroused my curiosity. I responded to the possibility like a hound at first scent of the chase. There was only one difficulty, I told the editor. I was about to leave for India under contract for another book. That was no problem, he assured me. They were in no hurry for the Blackwell biography. A brief correspondence settled the matter. I met my new editor in a Boston hotel lobby on my way to the plane for London, and arrangements were finalized.

Since much of Dr. Blackwell's life was spent in England it was decided that I should begin research immediately, spending some time in London on my way home from India. It was not the first time I had researched two books at the same time or researched one while writing another. A professional researcher had been secured, and when I arrived back in London in mid-December he presented me with a sixty-page brief on material available in Britain for the biography. It was an ex-

135

haustive report describing trips to all the areas connected with Elizabeth's life there—Bristol, Hastings, London, Scotland—and included snapshots, contents of museums, lists of books by her, about her and in which she was mentioned, biographies of persons she had known, interviews with archivists and librarians, newspaper and magazine sources, and many other references.

"If I were you," he advised. "I wouldn't spend time here visiting all these places. The information about them is all here. Instead you had better visit a library where her writings, long out of print, can still be found. I doubt if they exist anywhere in America."

It was mistaken advice, but I followed it. For a week I buried myself in a musty basement library furiously making notes on ancient volumes, all of which I later found in Boston, New York, Washington. And I might have stood on the terrace of Rock House in Hastings where Elizabeth spent the last years of her life, looking down over the steep cliff—she was never afraid of heights—to the sea far below; explored the small rooms, read the stone plaque on the back wall facing Exmouth Place: "Here lived and worked for thirty years Dr. Elizabeth Blackwell who died here in 1910. The first woman to graduate in medicine in America at Geneva, New York, in 1849. The first woman to be placed on the British Medical Register in 1859."

I might have visited Bristol and its environs where Elizabeth was born and lived for her first eleven years. I did go there on a subsequent trip to England, after the book's publication. This was not my first experience in research *post facto*. I had written *The Brother* and *The Herdsman* before seeing Nazareth and Jerusalem and Bethel, *Prince of Egypt* before visiting Memphis and Goshen and Karnak and the Valley of the Kings. Though the trip to Bristol made no contribution to the book and other sources had provided the necessary background materials it was like a nostalgic journey into my own past.

I saw the big old red brick house at Number One Wilson Street to which Elizabeth had moved in 1824 at age three and which she described so charmingly in the first chapter of her autobiography—its walled-in garden with fruit trees and flowers and shrubs; its flat roof with a parapet along the front where she and her older sisters had begged Papa to let them climb for a better view with a small telescope, their petition refused in a clever little poem; the banister over which she had leaned to watch a dinner party, with ministers from their "Independent" chapel as guests (Miserable over her banishment for some misdemeanor which had put her name in the Black Book, she had listened to the cheerful buzz of voices and peals of laughter, watched the light stream out from the dining room as the servants carried the dishes in and out).

I stood on the bridge looking down at what was once called Countess' Slip, a little street next to the river where in a small red brick house at the end of a narrow garden Elizabeth was born in 1821. Was it about here that the family stood huddled against the railings watching Papa's sugar refinery burn to the ground, feeling the heat on their faces, even coursing through their hands from the hot railings? I rode past the church of St. Mary Redcliffe (much larger and more impressive in its stone majesty than I had imagined) where during the terrible Bristol Riots of 1831 Samuel Blackwell, though himself a Dissenter who believed that the established Church of England smacked of the "rags of popery," stood facing a mob on the steps, holding his arms across the doorway, literally risking his life by defying the looting mob to enter.

The research for this biography was by far the most formidable of any I had yet attempted. Before it was finished I would have amassed a twelve-inch stack of those little three-by-five papers, typed single-space on both sides; a two-foot filing drawer tightly filled with folders containing correspondence, articles, clippings, xeroxed letter and reminiscences, reports, pictures; a shelf of more than twenty books—biographies, medical texts, histories of women's rights, tales of two cities, Bristol and Hastings.

Research kept pace all through 1967 with the writing of *Palace of Healing*. There are over twenty boxes of family papers in the Schlesinger Library on the History of Women in America at Radcliffe College in Cambridge, Massachusetts; more than sixty in the Library of Congress. Week after week I would go to the Boston area, working each day in the Schlesinger Library. That summer I spent three weeks researching in Washington, arriving each day before the Library of Congress opened and working until closing time, with perhaps a half hour out for lunch. The Blackwell children, all nine of them, were inveterate correspondents, and the letters, all of course longhand, many in tiny script and sometimes written both ways of a page, one penscript perpendicular to the other and overlying it, were difficult to decipher without a magnifying glass. I had dozens of them xeroxed, and they are in my file now, separated into folders covering ten years each from 1840 to 1900.

Elizabeth was unbelievably lucky. She was born at a time when the mind of a girl was almost as restricted as her body. In fact she was not supposed to have a mind capable of absorbing any practical knowledge. But Samuel Blackwell believed that his five daughters were as capable of learning as his four sons. Even more remarkable, he believed they should have some choice in determining their own destinies.

"My daughters have as good minds as my sons," he was heard to say, "and I see no reason why they should not be taught to use them in the same way. As to what use they will put them to in later life, that will be for them to decide."

Independence! Freedom! It was his desire for these privileges not only for his children but for all men that caused Samuel to move his family to America in 1832. He had always felt guilt because the raw sugar he imported from Jamaica for his refinery had been raised with slave labor. He hoped that in the new free world he could pursue his trade without such dependence.

After an incredibly difficult voyage of seven weeks and four days, with Samuel's wife Hannah eight months pregnant, cholera rampant onboard ship, their diet consisting of salt beef, pork, crackers, and brackish water, Elizabeth and her family arrived in New York. Most of their fine possessions had to be left behind, but in the Cambridge home of Elizabeth's nephew, Howard Blackwell, son of the baby born soon after their arrival, I saw one of the salvaged treasures, a beautiful set of china. Hannah's uncle was a goldsmith, and for her wedding present he had wanted to give her the finest set in his shop. But, no, she said, that would be far too elaborate for the wife of a sugar merchant. Looking at the ornate gold and flower design on the one she chose, I wondered what the other might have been! Howard Blackwell and his wife, both in their nineties, were helpful in providing other information.

Samuel's hopes were not realized in New York. His sugar refining business did not prosper. (They were living in what is now Newark when the great New York fire of 1835 destroyed one of his sugar houses.) And to his great grief he found slavery more deeply entrenched in America than in England. But for Elizabeth these years of adolescence were a period of swift and intense growth. With her older sisters, Anna and Marian, she became an ardent abolitionist, intimate with such leaders as

138

William Lloyd Garrison, Sarah and Angelina Grimké, Reverend Samuel May. At one time the Blackwells hid another New York minister, Samuel Cox, in their home because he was mistakenly quoted as saying that Christ was a Negro and was in danger of being mobbed. Because of such experiences Elizabeth became imbued with the passionate concern for human rights which was to motivate her throughout life.

At school in New York she was an avid student in all subjects—except physiology. The very thought of dwelling on the physical structure of the body filled her with disgust. One day the professor, attempting to interest his class in the marvels of anatomy, brought the eye of a bullock into the classroom. Elizabeth took one horrified glance and fled precipitately. Yet she despised herself for this weakness. She had always felt a peculiar impatience with any kind of sickness and exulted in her own physical strength. Though small of stature, not much more than five feet, she was remarkably strong both in mind and in body. Romping with her brothers, she could lift them and carry them around the room. She abhorred weakness of any kind, in herself or in others. Once when she fell ill with a fever she refused to yield to it and walked for miles into the country, head swimming, alternately shaking and perspiring.

"I won't, I *won't* give in to it!" she mouthed between clenched teeth. When she found she could go no further she returned home and shut herself in a dark room, refusing to come out or let anybody in until the worst stage of the fever was over.

Samuel was eternally hopeful. He heard tales of the West and its opportunities. Perhaps there he could pursue his cherished dream of extracting sugar from beets and avoid the alliance with slavery. So in 1838 he took his family to Cincinnati. The diaries of the young Blackwells, especially Henry's, were graphic in describing the difficult trip—three days by canal boat huddled in a crowded cabin with scolding women and squalling children, up the Alleghenies by a strange device called the Portage Railroad, cars drawn by a succession of horses, ropes, and steam engines through a blinding snowstorm, canal boat again, Cincinnati at last after a nine days' journey.

On my way home from a trip to the Midwest, I stopped in Cincinnati and delved into records of the Historical Society. Old maps showed the area where they first lived in a big square stone house on Third Street. Newspaper clippings of the 1840s depicted buildings, industries, persons encountered in the many letters I had read, catalogued events which related directly or indirectly to the life of the Blackwells. I came home to fill another folder with Xeroxed articles, biographical sketches, pictures, maps—all of which were invaluable in writing the story of the next ten years.

They were difficult, often tragic years. Soon after their arrival Samuel Blackwell died, leaving his family not only penniless but deeply in debt. The burden of support fell on Elizabeth, for the two older girls had remained in the East to teach. She opened a little school in their home. The older boys, Sam and Henry, got jobs. Soon Anna and Marian came to join her in teaching. And now for the first time Elizabeth and her sisters tasted the economic misfortune of being female. For the boys, though in their early teens and much less educated, were able to earn twice as much as they. And what occupations were open to a woman in those days? She could teach, she could sew, she could keep house for a married relative or live as a dependent on some member of her family. If she belonged to the lower classes, she could work in a mill under incredibly vile conditions.

Her situation, Elizabeth felt, bore the stigma of slavery, which she came to hate more and more. Yet in the area of social reform also there was so little a woman could do! She envied Sam one day in 1841 when he went across the river with other men to witness in a case for establishing the freedom of two kidnapped colored girls. Later, teaching in the slave state of Kentucky, she sat fuming helplessly when a slip of a Negro girl, barefoot and scantily clad, was made to stand between her and the hot fire, her puny unprotected body a defenseless fire screen. Back in Cincinnati where the family moved to a section called Walnut Hills she found some moral and intellectual relief from her growing restlessness in meetings of the Anti-Slavery Society, sewing garments for fugitives escaping by the underground railway, association with stimulating friends such as William Henry Channing, Salmon P. Chase, Dr. Lyman Beecher, and especially his daughter, Harriet Beecher Stowe. But she felt frustrated, imprisoned. If only she had some goal, some all-consuming purpose!

Then one day she went to call on a dear friend, Mary Donaldson, who was dying of cancer, a visit she dreaded, knowing her instinctive revulsion in the presence of sickness. But in spite of her shock at the sight of the wasted limbs, the sunken cheeks, Mary's gaiety made conversation easy. However when she rose to leave a thin hand reached out to restrain her.

"Wait, my dear." The eyes fixed on hers held a fevered intensity. "It's a terrible thing, Elizabeth, to die a slow death like this. But for me there is one thing that would have made the suffering so much easier. If—if only I didn't have to be examined and treated by a man!" Elizabeth felt the clawlike fingers tighten. "You're strong and young my dear. You have a keen mind and like to study. Why don't you try to become a doctor?"

A doctor! The words pursued Elizabeth all the way home. *Doctor . . . DOC-TOR!* She was appalled, repelled. A preposterous idea! Women did not become doctors. And even if they did, it was the last thing *she* would want to do. Why, she hated sickness, despised weakness, even felt contempt for her sister Marian who was sickly, hated to give her medicine. But the idea persisted. After a while she talked about it with some of her friends, with Harriet Stowe. She found her, as usual, in an untidy house writing a story on foolscap, a child balanced on her knee, another pulling at her skirt.

"A doctor? A fine idea, my dear." Harriet spoke absently, pen poised. "But of course entirely impracticable."

Elizabeth asked others, the family doctor among them. Each was shocked or amused or just frankly discouraging. She wrote letters to doctors she had known in the East. All said the same thing. A valuable idea, but impossible of execution. Perhaps it was this very opposition that made Elizabeth determined. She *would* become a doctor.

She was twenty-four years old and had no money. She must teach for a while even to make an attempt. For some years she took teaching positions in North and South Carolina, where she was able to read medical books in a doctor's library. Then she started to apply at medical schools. Always she was refused. Some doctors told her seriously that the only way she could realize her ambition was to go to Paris and don men's clothes. No! That would compromise everything she was trying to do. She had entered a moral crusade, to open the door of a noble occupation not only to herself but to all women. She had finally made applications to twenty-nine medical schools before one finally accepted her—and that was by mistake!

The little college in Geneva, New York, had been founded on democratic principles. Therefore when a letter came to its dean from a Quaker physician in Philadelphia recommending Elizabeth as a student, the faculty were dumbfounded. What to do? They were supposed to be democratic, and Dr. Warrington, the Quaker physician, was a man of high repute. But—

admit a *woman*? An unheard-of thing! Impossible! In a quandary they hit on a happy solution of passing the buck of decision to the class of medical students. If there was one dissenting vote, the application would be refused. Of course there would be many more than one.

Apprised of the situation, the students called a meeting. Being a rambunctious crowd they thought it would be a great lark to have a female in the class. "Yea!" was the resounding vote. Opposed? There was one weak "Nay." The class pounced on the traitor, dragged him to the platform, and held him down until he uttered a plaintive "yea." What a scene! I found a wonderfully graphic account of it written by Dr. Stephen Smith, a member of that class, and I tried to imagine his thoughts as he waited for the new student to arrive. What sort of woman could it be, so bold, so daring? An Amazon, a Lady Godiva—what? And how surprised he must have been when she actually arrived, small, neat, modest, in a plain gray dress and Quaker bonnet!

So in October, 1847, Elizabeth came to Geneva. And there I came also, just 120 years later, trying to find some trace of her. I took pictures of some of the fine old houses, in more than one of which she tried to rent a room and was refused. Finally finding a home that would take her in, she lived in a little attic room, practicing rigid economy. Once she saw a little bottle of perfume in a store window and wanted it terribly, but felt she could not afford it. She ate little for two reasons: she had little money, and she thought that if she was pale she would be less likely to flush when embarrassing subjects were discussed in class.

I walked across the square which she must have crossed many times while people stared at her. Small boys would follow as if she were a curiosity.

"Come on, kids! Here she comes! Let's have a look at the lady doctor!"

The town women fell silent at her approach and drew aside their skirts, looked after her as if she were a strange animal. She was more than a curiosity. It was believed that any female who dared to undertake such an unheard-of career must be, if not a harlot, at least a loose woman. All the time she was there she was shunned, derided, persecuted by the townspeople. The mere words, "Woman" or "Lady doctor," were enough to arouse horror.

Little did they guess that a hundred years later a sign marking the site of the old medical college would bear as its

142

chief claim to fame the statement that "Elizabeth Blackwell received here in 1849 the first degree of M.D. ever conferred upon a woman"; or that even the old medicine cabinet where she compounded remedies would bear on one of its drawers a plaque stating that she had used it, its sole claim to immortality. I saw it in the hall of Blackwell House, on the campus of what is now Hobart and William Smith Colleges, a dormitory for women honoring the colleges' most distinguished graduate. In the college library is a Blackwell room containing her portrait, books about her and other mementos. And in 1974 I received an invitation to "Blackwell Day" on the campus, celebrating the first day of issue of a stamp in her honor.

She won the respect of her classmates and had a calming effect on their exuberance. A droll episode featured one of her professors, who was inclined to be a bit bawdy at certain points in his anatomy lectures and tried to keep her from attending a series which might have embarrassed her—and him. Elizabeth was not only saddened and discouraged, but annoyed. She wrote the doctor a note. She was there as a student, she told him, with an earnest purpose, and should be regarded simply as a student. The study of anatomy was to her a most serious one, exciting profound reverence in all its many aspects. Like herself, these students were being prepared to officiate at childbirth, a holy ministry in which they would be sharing with womanhood the most intimate mysteries of creation. She would absent herself from the lectures if it was the desire of the class, though it was not her wish and seemed to her a grave mistake. The doctor was rebuked and humbled. Elizabeth attended the lecture, which proceeded in an orderly manner, all lewdness and jocularity missing. It set a pattern for the entire series.

Elizabeth's graduation was chronicled in newspapers in both America and England with shock, amusement, horror, incredulity and outrage.

"It is to be regretted," ran one of the milder reactions in the Boston *Medical Journal*, "that Miss Blackwell has been induced to depart from the appropriate sphere of her sex and led to aspire to honors and duties which by the order of nature and the common consent of the world devolve upon men."

Unlike most of her male compeers, Elizabeth was not satisfied with the two terms of medical training, sixteen weeks each, which were the accepted requirement for her famed diploma. Between sessions she spent months in the Philadelphia Alms Hospital at Blockley, resented by many of the horrified doctors and nurses, learning much, helping to treat ship fever (a form of typhus) brought in by Irish immigrants, writing her thesis on the disease and its effective treatment.

After graduation she went to Paris and worked for a year in the incredibly sordid and disease-ridden La Maternité, a veritable prison, learning midwifery. Here she met the one love of her life, a young doctor, M. Claude Blot, but she refused to let their romantic friendship jeopardize her life purpose. Frenchmen did not encourage their wives to become competing surgeons! Here also a tragedy occurred. Bending over a baby with purulent ophthalmia one dark November morning, she felt some of the virulent fluid spurt into her own eye. There followed weeks of excruciating pain, fear, torture and agonizing waiting. Neither the constant ministrations of the skillful M. Blot nor the tender care of her sister Anna, who was pursuing her writing career in Paris, availed to save the infected eye. Eventually it had to be removed, and her fond hopes of becoming a surgeon were gone forever.

But it would have taken more than a glass eye to deflect her from her purpose. No surgery? Very well. At least she could practice medicine. Thankful that the other eye had been saved, she embarked on the next stage of training. To her delight a letter from Sir James Paget had given her permission to attend St. Bartholomew's as a student in wards and other departments of the hospital. She went to London in the fall of 1850.

The months she spent there demanded new lines of research, for she was soon involved in British reform movements. Two young women, Barbara Leigh Smith (later Bodichon) and Bessie Raynor Parkes, with fathers as independent in thought as Elizabeth's had been, sought her out and introduced her to a group of intellectuals which included Lady Noel Byron, Sir John Herschel, Christina Rossetti, Professor Faraday and others. Another who came to her was Florence Nightingale, just beginning her struggle to break the cocoon which enclosed British women and, to the horror of her family, become a nurse.

"I had to come." The words poured from her in a flood. "I hope you won't think me meddlesome, but I have to know. What did your family think of your studying medicine? And suppose they had fought you at every point. What then?"

Elizabeth considered. "It would have made no difference," she said firmly.

"Thank you," said Florence joyously.

Grateful for the biographies which I had brought back from

beth Garrett Anderson—I plunged into them, along with the voluminous correspondence with Lady Byron.

In 1851, back in New York to start a private practice, Elizabeth was ostracized even more violently than in Geneva. She had hard work finding a place to live where she could hang out her shingle, so great was the prejudice against a woman doctor. Doors were slammed in her face. Finally she had to rent a whole floor of a house at 44 University Place, off Washington Square, at an exorbitant rate. But—patients? Even advertisements which the liberal Horace Greeley was willing to run in his *New York Tribune* brought few results. The handful of daring women who came to her were almost all members of the Society of Friends. That fall and winter were a nightmare of loneliness and discouragement and waiting. In the evenings, released from the waiting, she walked the streets. Everywhere she found problems which aroused her concern.

If she walked east toward East River there were the slum sections filled with immigrants from Ireland and Germany, and she longed to alleviate their poverty, their terrible lack of sanitation. For she was generations ahead of her time in believing that cleanliness was a major source of health. Walking north up Broadway she saw young women of the well-to-do classes swathed in high-necked, long-sleeved, wasp-waist dresses with layers of voluminous petticoats. And she did a daring thing. She advertised a series of lectures entitled, "The Laws of Life with Special Reference to the Physical Education of Girls." She went to the first lecture terrified. Would anyone come? Some came, many of them from the highly intelligent women of the Society of Friends.

"The education of children," she emphasized, "should not merely not injure, it should do physical good. If lessons produce headache, lassitude, inactivity of functions, if they make the child pale, quiet, spiritless, then the lessons are bad. If the course of study is not positively beneficial to the bodily organism, it is injurious."

Then—shocking finale!—she launched into instruction in the processes of sex, of birth, of the structure and functions of their bodies. Huge and bitter doses for those Victorian ladies when sex was a synonym for vice, and even the word "body" was taboo! Some choked and did not come back. Yet many returned for more. At the encouragement of friends she wrote the ideas into a book, which was greeted with shocked horror in some quarters, but from many with warm approbation. The eminent Charles Ruskin commended it.

"It has taken fifty years," one of America's first pediatricians was to say a half-century later, "for even the foremost of the medical profession to catch up with her ideas."

For the story of Elizabeth's pioneering activities in New York I spent many hours in the New York Infirmary which she founded, going over the reports of more than a hundred years, interviewing, studying and photographing the long mural on one wall which depicts the successive stages of her achievement. The first view shows her standing, a courageous little figure in billowing black skirt, white jacket and head kerchief, in front of her little dispensary, beside her a woman and baby and a child on crutches.

When she offered her services to the New York Dispensary, she was coldly refused and told to start one of her own. So she did in 1853, hiring a small room in Tompkins Square. She found soon-to-be prominent men willing to support her venture and act as trustees: Horace Greeley, Charles A. Dana, Cyrus W. Field, all of them at that time young. Even here at first the idea of a woman doctor was so strange that, though the service was free, no one dared come—until one woman in desperate need did venture. She told another, and soon the news of the little "doctress," as they called her, began to spread.

But Elizabeth had even more bold ideas. Moving along the mural one can see the next materialization of her dream, a small hospital started in 1857 in the old Roosevelt house on Bleecker Street. It was opened on Florence Nightingale's birthday, a fitting tribute to Elizabeth's encouragement which had inspired Florence to start her notable career in nursing. It was a big house with four floors, with hospital wards on the second floor, even a small operating room where Dr. Emily Blackwell, Elizabeth's sister, who also had the daring to study medicine, graduating from Western Reserve Medical College in Cleveland, performed the operations which were denied to Elizabeth. Emily had also pursued her studies under the famous Dr. James Simpson at Edinburgh University.

Though patients came and the beds were always full, there were crises of opposition. In spite of Elizabeth's insistence on cleanliness and sanitation puerperal fever would develop after childbirth. Once a patient died of it. A crowd assembled in the street brandishing hoes, shovels, raised fists, relatives and friends of the dead patient.

"You killed her, you killed her!" Shouts came. "You in there, female doctors! No doctors, killers!" They threatened to beat down the doors. Then suddenly an Irish laborer appeared, a burly figure holding a crowbar. Looking through the window

146

Elizabeth recognized him as the husband of a woman she had treated at the old Tompkins Square dispensary. Pushing his way through the crowd, he mounted the steps.

"You there! By the saints in heaven, what the divil's goin' on?" It was his booming voice rather than the menacing crowbar which compelled attention. Finally he got the story. "I see. Your woman had a baby, and she died. So what? Lots of women die in childbirth. What's all the hullabaloo?"

The clamor swelled again. "Women doctors... killed her..."

"*Quiet*! Now youse listen to me. My wife had pneumonia, and they made her well again, same as they've made lots of your women well. Ain't it so?" Heads nodded. "I ask youse, too, what other doctors ever done nothin' for youse, care whether youse live or dies? Doctors ain't God...."

When two policemen came running, the trouble was already over. The brandished weapons had become tools again. Once more during the famous Draft Riots of the Civil War the hospital was in grave danger, with houses being burned all around it. They had black patients in the wards, and blacks were being hunted out and killed all through the area. For three days they lived behind locked doors, but this time also the crisis passed.

"Children are born to live, not die," was the text on which Elizabeth constantly preached. One of her dreams was realized when a "sanitary visitor" was added to the infirmary staff, her exclusive object the *prevention*, not the treatment, of disease by the instruction of poor women in practical hygiene through home visitation. It was a startlingly novel program, antedating the network of district nurses, social workers and public health workers by many decades.

Symbolic of Elizabeth's work is the gateway which stands in the center of the mural, because she opened the door not only to new health and life but to new opportunities for the women of her day. Before Florence Nightingale opened her school of nursing in London the Blackwells were operating the first school of nursing training in New York, and during the Civil War Elizabeth and her Infirmary were actively involved with the nursing program of the Union. But, like Dr. Ida, she kept having more daring ideas.

"The practice of medicine by women," she declared in one lecture, "is no longer a doubtful but a settled thing. But there is not in the whole extent of our country a single medical school where a woman can obtain a good education."

It was a long battle, its triumph depicted in the final se-

147

quence of the mural, for in 1868 the Blackwells were able to start their own medical college in a rented building adjoining their infirmary. While doing research I walked down to 126 Second Avenue to find the corner where the hospital and college once stood. I thought it appropriate that the theater now standing near the spot should be advertising as its feature a picture called "Your Own Thing." Certainly that was exactly what Elizabeth was doing a hundred years ago, her "own thing."

Central to my research was a study of the women's rights movement, for all around the periphery of Elizabeth's life its initial action was seething. While she studied medicine in Geneva, only a few miles away in Seneca Falls the first women's rights convention was being held. Her brother Samuel married the Reverend Antoinette Brown, the first woman to be ordained a minister. Her brother Henry courted and married Lucy Stone, one of the foremost leaders in the fight for women's rights, who insisted on keeping her own name when she married. The two of them signed a statement defining their views on a woman's legal rights, a remarkable document in a period when a wife had almost no legal status at all, could not control her own earnings, own personal or real estate, exert guardianship over her children. These two, who edited the *Woman's Journal* in Boston, probably contributed more to the cause than any other two people.

The book grew—to alarming proportions. My editor became apprehensive, until I assured him that I intended to end the major part of it with Elizabeth's departure for England in 1869, to spend the next forty years in traveling, lecturing, crusading for innumerable causes, organizing a National Health Society, aiding Elizabeth Garrett Anderson and Sophia Jex-Blake in founding the London School of Medicine for Women, accepting the chair of gynecology on its staff, serving for many years on its council, seeing its success finally assured by its affiliation for teaching purposes with the Royal Free Hospital, living to see 550 names of women added to her own and Elizabeth Garrett Anderson's on the British Medical Register.

It was a painful decision, necessitating the sacrifice of so much information acquired, hundreds of letters noted or xeroxed, biographies read, reports digested. But after all Elizabeth had achieved her primary purpose—obtained the first doctor's degree ever conferred on a woman, practiced medicine successfully, founded an institution which was to render distinguished service for the next hundred years and more in one of the most needy areas of New York City.

The decision posed two problems. First, how to depict in a few words the developments of those hundred years, which were as much an extension of Elizabeth's life as the next forty? I imagined her being called out on a case, as she so often was, late on the night before she left for England, returning home to stand looking at the infirmary, taking her farewell of this only tangible fruit of her long and difficult travail. She would see the set of high narrow buildings with their four tiers of windows, the wards' faint glimmer, one brighter slit beneath the roof where Emily still worked, another in the adjoining house where a medical intern was burning the midnight oil. Through four decades she was to follow all the details of its remarkable growth, its move to a new site at Livingston Place, far more pleasant, with Stuyvesant Park in front; a fine new building for the college which in 1876 would become second after Harvard in making its three-year course obligatory instead of optional. She would rejoice with Emily when Cornell should open its medical college to women, making their medical school no longer necessary; would exult in all the "firsts," some of which she had started—first to train nurses, to supply a "sanitary visitor," to create a chair of hygiene, to train the first Negro woman doctor—and in the distinguished doctors they had helped to train, like Mary Putnam, Elizabeth Cushier, Martha Wollstein, Josephine Baker.

And with her mind's eye, always so keen, she might even have glimpsed its growth beyond her lifetime as I, her biographer, was able to see it: the ten-story building of shining whiteness filling a whole block, its twelve-story counterpart just across the way on Fifteenth Street; the manifold departments with strange names but with functions not at all strange to her vigorous imagination, pediatrics, physical medicine, psychiatry, neurology; the clinics which would have marched across her vision like the fulfillment of all her dreams: the child guidance clinic, a psychiatric clinic for babies, the Strang Clinic, first in the world devoted to the prevention of cancer.

It was on one late night call such as this that an incident occurred which gave me the title of the book, *Lone Woman*. As she hurried into the orbit of a streetlamp, a group of rowdy boys passed by on the other side of the street. One pointed at her, shouted something, and the others burst into loud guffaws. The words coming to her ears made her chuckle, for she knew they described her so well, summed up the intrepid boldness of her life's adventure:

"See that lone woman walking like mad!"

And the second problem: how to compress into a few pages those last forty years of a superactive life? It was Kitty who helped me do it, the little Irish waif who entered Elizabeth's life back in the mid-1850s.

"Why don't you take one of those little orphan girls," suggested Emily before leaving for study in England, "and train her for house service? A lot of people, you know, are taking them."

Elizabeth did know. The new Children's Aid Society had been placing hundreds of homeless children. Making several visits to the orphanage at Randall's Island, she found her attention attracted again and again to one child, not pretty, thin face sharply aquiline, shoulders a bit stooped, arms and legs like pipestems, hair so jet black and riotous that it gave her a witchlike appearance. Elizabeth interrupted the matron's sales talk.

"Tell me about that child there, please, the one looking out of the window."

"Oh, but you wouldn't want her!" The matron looked shocked. "Now this one—"

"I'd like to know more about her," insisted Elizabeth.

There was little to know, it seemed. She was between seven and eight, of Irish parentage, an orphan, with no living soul to claim her. Even her name, Katharine Barry, was doubtful.

Elizabeth's sister Marian, who had accompanied her, was equally shocked. "Not her, Bessie! I thought you were looking for a nice strong intelligent child, one you could train up to be a valuable little domestic."

"I thought so, too," was Elizabeth's sober reply.

"Then what—why—"

"Because—this child needs me more than any of the others."

Kitty Barry became, not her little domestic, but a beloved adopted daughter, blooming into a young woman of keen intelligence and deep sensitivity. All her life afterward, as long as Elizabeth lived, she served her beloved "Doctor" with loving devotion. As one of the family expressed it, she "fitted Elizabeth's curves like an eiderdown quilt."

At the end of the book I imagined Kitty going back to Rock House, Hastings, where they had spent the last years. It was 1910, and she had laid her Doctor to rest in Kilmun, Scotland. As she went over the things in the house, preparing to leave, she lived over the last forty years, packing the many books Doctor had written, the lectures she had delivered, innumerable letters from family, from friends like Florence Nightingale, Lady Byron, George Eliot, the diaries telling about all the travels they had made in Europe. And when the house was sold and friends wanted to place a plaque on its outside wall commemorating its most famous occupant, it was Kitty who chose lines from Browning, which Doctor had both loved and lived.

> "One who never turned her back but
>   marched straight forward,
> Never doubted clouds would break,
> Never dreamed, though right were worsted,
>   wrong would triumph,
> Held we fall to rise, are baffled to fight better,
> Sleep to wake!"

Perhaps the compression was not altogether successful. One reviewer wrote in an otherwise favorable commentary, "The latter years are somewhat abruptly telescoped." How true! Forty years condensed into ten pages! But even without further detail the book ran to more than four hundred. I called it facetiously the "tome of my life." It had a respectable sale, appeared in the Reader's Digest Condensed Books in October, 1970, later in the British and French editions, and was published also in England and Germany.

I had immersed myself so long and deeply in the 1800s that I occasionally dated a letter 186- instead of 196-. Filing away the innumerable folders and cards I felt a personal nostalgia. It was a century of such gallant and daring women with such brave hopes and bold achievements! I longed to relive the lives of a dozen others. Well—why not? Already I was exploring the possibility of another life or two.

7
SUSETTE
LA FLESCHE:
'BRIGHT EYES'

"**D**o you have suggestions for another character as interesting and challenging as Elizabeth Blackwell?"

I put the question to the book club editor who had worked with me so helpfully on the research for *Lone Woman*. The list she gave me was full of possibilities. I could have tackled any of the subjects with zest. But heading the list was a name I had never encountered. *Bright Eyes*. Intriguing. I went straight to the *Dictionary of American Biography*.

She was all that any author concerned with human rights could desire, an American Indian who in the last century had become involved in an intensely dramatic incident of injustice to her people. In a day when a woman, much less one of a minority race, had no political and almost no legal rights, Bright Eyes challenged a powerful area of government—and won. I had to write her story.

From the East Indian to the American Indian. It was a completely new area of research. This was 1970, and *Lone Woman* had just been published. I was becoming accustomed now to bringing out one book, writing another, and researching a third, all in the same year. I immediately began reading everything on Indian history, life and culture I could find. The university library yielded a treasure-trove in the 27th Annual Report of the Bureau of American Ethnology, titled *The Omaha Tribe*. Compiled by Francis La Flesche, brother of Bright Eyes, and Alice Fletcher, an ethnologist, it was a storehouse of tribal history, legends, rites, songs, customs, artifacts. I was soon in correspondence with Wayne Tyndall, a member of the Omaha Tribal Council.

"You must come out for our annual powwow," he told me.

I agreed, so in August, 1970, I flew to Sioux City, where I was met by Wayne, a vigorous, efficient young Indian, and Winona Porter, a tribal member who was to be my hostess for the two weeks I spent on the reservation. As we left the city limits and took the main road south, my excitement mounted. In Homer we stopped to examine a plaque marking the site of Tonwantonga, Large Village, one of the early Omaha settlements, now long deserted. Once the whole state of Nebraska, *Ni-btha-thka*, Land of the Flat Water, had belonged to the Omaha tribe. In 1854, the year of Bright Eyes' birth, they had been moved from Belleville, near Omaha, to this small reservation to the north. Already I could sense the close relationship of the tribe, like all Indians, to their land, even these few acres which had been left to them. As with the ancient Hebrews, Indians believed that land, like air and water, was free, to be used but not owned, and the white man's idea of the ownership of land they had always found incomprehensible.

"How beautiful," one of the Omaha women has titled a booklet of her memories, "how beautiful the land of my forefathers!"

Here was Bright Eyes' world, these green rolling hills, the high banks edging the Missouri River which they called the Smoky Waters, the valleys where round lodges and tepees had been slowly replaced by square wooden houses, where a rich and ancient culture had been profoundly disrupted and reshaped in its conflict with the white man's world. She herself had been the epitome of that conflict.

Inshtatheamba, Bright Eyes. The name was given her in an age-old ritual called "Turning of the Child," making her a part of the family and tribe. It was one of the few events of her childhood of which I found a graphic description. As she approached the ritual tent alone, suddenly in the tent's entrance loomed a figure, giant-tall, a huge animal skin over one shoulder, a towering object on its head. With a little shriek she turned and fled. It was Grandmother Nicomi—she who in younger days had been called the "beautiful Omaha"—who caught her, took her hand and led her back. "See, little one. There is nothing to fear. He is your friend."

The face between the frightening skin and headdress be-

153

came familiar. She had seen it often in Father's lodge. She went forward willingly. The man smiled down at her. "You shall reach the fourth hill sighing. You shall be bowed over. You shall have wrinkles. Your staff shall bend under your weight. I speak to you that you may be strong."

Though she would remember little of the long ritual, its roots buried deep in the primeval strata of tribal rites, the essence and rhythm of the quest for relationship with the cosmic forces stirred her whole being. As she was turned to the four points of the compass, each turning accompanied by song and the thunder-roll of drums, she felt in the words a strengthening age-old power.

"Turned by the winds goes the one I send yonder;
Yonder goes she who is whirled by the winds;
Goes where the four hills of life and the four winds
are standing;
There in the midst of the winds do I send her,
Into the midst of the winds standing there."

As she went out, wearing new moccasins, she was still shy of the crowd. She always would be. But she was no longer afraid. In her childish way she realized that she had become part of something big, akin to fire and wind and earth and the whole family of living things. And she had a new name, aptly suited to her radiant liveliness. *Inshtatheamba*, Bright Eyes.

But she was also Susette La Flesche, daughter of Joseph, a French-Indian who in those mid-1800s had become the last head chief of the Omahas. Joseph, *Inshtamaza*, Iron Eye, adopted by the old chief Big Elk and designated by him on his death bed as the future head chief, was in all his loyalties far more Indian than white. Yet he saw all too clearly that with the inexorable encroachment of the white man on his land the Indian would have to learn the white man's ways in order to survive.

There was much material about Joseph, all helping to complete the picture of Bright Eyes' early years, but nothing expressed more poignantly his philosophy of life or the relationship between father and daughter than one of the rare recorded incidents of her childhood. One evening she was playing near her father. A small boy, one of her playmates, came and gave her a little bird he had found. Delighted, holding the trembling creature, she showed it to her father, then filled a bowl with water and taking some kernels of corn tried to make it eat and drink. No use. It cowered in her palm, quivering with fright.

"Daughter," called Joseph, "bring your bird to me."

He held it in his hand, smoothing the feathers gently. "Daughter, I will tell you what you might do with it. Take it carefully out yonder where there are no tents, where the high grass is, put it softly down on the ground, and say as you put it down, 'Wakonda, God, I give you back your little bird. Have pity on me, as I have pity on your bird.'"

She looked up at him wonderingly. "Does it belong to Wakonda?"

"Yes, little one. And he will be pleased if you give it back to him to take care of."

Carefully she did as she was told. In the years that followed many memories of her father would become blurred, but not this. Nearly forty years later she would record it, though in the words of another language.

We turned off the main highway into a narrow side road and went down into Macy, the small settlement which is the official center of the Omaha tribe. During the next two weeks I explored the past and present of a people whose claim to American lineage long predated that of the proudest Mayflower descendants. Both past and present were all about me. I lived in a neat modern house identical with others in a new development, sleeping in a comfortable guest room while my host family preferred the age-old custom of spreading their blankets on the living room floor. My hostess was a competent young Indian social worker with two teen-age sons who would have looked at home in any jazz combo and a father who could have posed for a portrait of the noblest and wisest Indian brave. One of my most treasured pictures shows him holding his little sleeping grandchild Lani, apparently impervious to all around him, his deeply lined face expressing all the wisdom and sadness and resignation of the centuries.

I visited the tribal council building, talked with leaders who looked and acted the peers of my own town councilmen, was entertained in homes by couples who resembled members of my local church. I attended a dinner of the senior citizens, served by women who might have been Ladies Aiders, and ate it at a table surrounded by women in Mother Hubbards and pigtails. I was garlanded many times in India, with flowers, Tibetan beads, sandalwood rings, once with a silk scarf, but no garland is prized more than the lovely beaded medallion made by Winona's mother and presented to me that day. I was invited to a birthday feast, to a dedication meal for a child going away to school, to a dinner following an all-night meeting of the Native American Church which combines many of the beliefs of Christianity with the old tribal ways of worship. At all these meals we sat on the ground or on the floor, our plates or bowls filled from a big cooking pot by those who went around the circle serving, reminding me of my many meals in India sitting on a mat, rice and curry heaped in front of me on a plantain leaf. Hospitality is as vital to Indian culture as in the days when Alice Fletcher the ethnologist viewed with dismay the repeated invitations, not to be refused, "Come and eat." Yet no bit of food is wasted. It is the polite custom to take along a container (doggie bag?) to take home what one is unable to eat.

All these were fusions of the past and present, inextricably intermingled. Not so the four days and nights of the ceremonies in the walled circle on the edge of the settlement. The powwow belonged only to the past. True, the colorful trappings, resplendent crowns, huge flamboyant sunbursts of feathers may be designed more for tourism than for authenticity, but the intricate dance movements and the rhythmic beat of the drums, exact in tune and tempo, were as old as the sacred tribal pipes and the Council of Seven.

I watched all the preparations with fascination—the assembling of cars and trucks and wagons and motorcycles, some coming from distant states; the setting up of tepees; the family picnic tables; the booths and tables selling foods, soft drinks, handcrafts. One of the booths bore the intriguing name in large letters of "Custer's Last Stand!" It was all a cross between an old-fashioned Methodist camp meeting and a country fair. Every afternoon and evening for four days I went to the circle and watched the dances, feats in amazing endurance and physical prowess, many of them ancient war dances handed down through long centuries. Every so often the dancing would stop and the crier would announce that a family would bestow gifts, a very old custom. In the early days if a man died or there was some unusual event, often all that he owned was passed out to friends. Hospitality, sharing even one's last cake of maize . . . giving, even if one had nothing left . . . customs which the provident white man has never been quite able to eradicate.

156

The powwow is a sad replica of the old sacred tribal hunt. Its circular setting tries to recapture something of the tribal circle in which the tents of the tribe were always placed at the time of the hunt, the *huthuga*, symbolic of the roundness of all natural things in the universe. Bright Eyes knew this well, for she went on her first hunt at age five, in the "Moon When the Buffalo Bulls Hunt the Cows," called June by the white man. She loved every part of it—almost—crossing the plains in the huge caravan; scampering through the tall grass with the other children; galloping; backtracking; playing *uhebashonshon* (crooked path) in which each one repeated the pranks of the leaders, but always in dread of the terrible tabu, the sacred pole, that dark, long black object carried by one solitary old man.

She loved the pitching of camp when each clan had its own place in the circle; in the evenings, listening to stories of creation and of Wakonda's giving of the buffalo as told by the elders around the campfire; in the nights, watching the shadow pictures cast on the conical tent by the glowing fire; later, wrapped in her blanket, seeing the stars wink through the smoke hole at the top. She loved everything except the confusion of dashing horses, flying arrows, exploding gunpowder, dying animals screaming. Shuddering, she hid her face in her father's robe, but he turned it firmly about.

"No. I want you to see—and remember. Never turn your back, little one. See everything just as it is."

"But—they're killing them," she sobbed, "the poor animals."

"So that you and all the rest of our people can eat and grow strong. They will kill only as many as will be needed to last the winter, and not a scrap will be wasted. Not like the white man who kills for the sport of killing, or for the delicate taste of a heart or tongue, leaving the carcass to rot on the plain."

The last hunt was in 1876, and they found the plains strewn with carcasses. Of the nearly four million buffalo killed in the previous three years, only 150,000 had been killed by red men. To the Indian such waste was incomprehensible. It also disrupted his whole life because legend, religious ceremonies, masculine prowess and major occupations as well as food and other useful items were all dependent on the buffalo. The loss of the hunt was a tragedy which the culture of the Indian could not survive.

So the powwow, though belonging to the present, was an indissoluble link with the past, necessary to an understanding of Bright Eyes' world. Slowly many of its features came to life about me. Some came through people. Wayne's mother, Pauline Tyndall, a public health worker, gave me invaluable material in writings and on tape, a graphic picture of the sensations of a sensitive Indian child in earlier days. Her description of an Indian spring was sheer poetry, and with her permission I used some of it in my first chapter.

"Spring was early that year. The seven geese who returned at the end of the 'Moon of Blinding Snow' to see if the waterways were open did not go back south to wait until after the 'Moon of Little Frogs.' The rest soon followed and after the geese came back things began to happen. Wakonda spoke. With the voice of the First Thunder he wakened Earth from its long winter's sleep.

"Hearing his command the medicine men took out their sacred bundles, opened them, and going to a high hill offered their prayers and songs, blowing smoke from their pipes to the four winds. . . . And, as the sun grew stronger and the 'gonedown' birds returned, the gurgling flute notes of the meadowlark announced loud and clear in the Omaha language, 'It is spring! It is spring!' "

With Wayne and others I climbed to the Council Point high on the bluffs above the river where the seven chiefs used to sit in solemn conclave, then climbed beyond it to the Sacred Fireplace on top of the highest hill where the young men used to go long ago on their Vision Quest, spending four days and nights in fasting and prayer. Standing here looking over the broad expanse of river I could easily imagine Bright Eyes' agony as she must have waited for her beloved brother Louis to return, fearful lest he could not stand the ordeal, praying that his vision might be something beautiful like a lovely bird or a graceful elk, overjoyed when he returned to tell his vision to some old man who had had one like it.

And I walked along the river bank with Winona and her father (a grandson of Wajapa whom the children of Iron Eye had called "Uncle") and climbed the bluffs to the site of the old Presbyterian mission school where Bright Eyes experienced her first, most painful conflict with the white man's culture. For here all things Indian were tabu, "heathen" and "savage." Pupils were not allowed to speak a word of Omaha or even French, one of her father's languages, only English. Here she was not Inshtatheamba, Bright Eyes, but Susette. Here logi-

158

cal names for boys like Flying Eagle and No Knife and White Horse were changed to strange sounds like George Washington, Daniel Webster, Thomas Macaulay. I found life in the school described in graphic detail in a book written by Susette's brother, Francis La Flesche, *The Middle Five*.

The conflict would never be resolved. "I may be a good Presbyterian most of the year," she confessed later, "but when the First Thunder comes, I'll always be an Indian."

Here at the mission school she fell under the spell of books, yearned for more and more knowledge. And she was able to secure it, for through one of her teachers the chance came to attend a fine school for girls in Elizabeth, New Jersey, where she gained high honors and even published some stories about Indian life which appeared in New York papers. She also found that she had real talent in drawing and painting and was able to illustrate her stories with art work.

She returned to the reservation with one purpose, to share her knowledge with her people. At first it seemed impossible. Only white people were supposed to know enough to teach. Though the Indian Bureau professed a policy of giving qualified Indians preference over white employees, it took much red tape to even persuade an officer to deign to make inquiries about her qualifications.

"Deserves highest praise," came the response from the Elizabeth Institute. "She was at my school for over two years. She had pleasant winning ways and exhibited a wonderful courtesy." Her report on scholarship was equally favorable.

Still there was stalling. She must take an examination and send in a certificate from the Nebraska School Committee. The examination was in Takamah, a town outside the reservation, and an Indian had to get permission from the agent to leave. He refused to give it. She went anyway, riding to Takamah on her pony, took the examination and returned with the certificate. But at last she was appointed assistant teacher at the agency day school and plunged into her chosen career with all the vigor of an impassioned crusader. For some years she taught in this government school, in a leaking room with few supplies, her pupils coming barefoot through the snow in winter, her salary half that which less qualified white teachers were receiving. And then all at once she was thrust into intense, history-making drama which made her one of the outstanding women of the century, certainly the most important and well-known Indian

woman up to that time (save perhaps for the legendary Poca-
hontas).

Two weeks in Lincoln in October at the Nebraska Historical
Society, repository of the La Flesche family papers and much
other pertinent material, including valuable pictures, furnished full details of this crisis.

It began in January, 1877, the "Moon When the Snow Drifts
into the Tents." Two men from a tribe related to the Omahas,
the Poncas, brought the news. Joseph's brother White Swan
was a chief of this tribe, whose reservation was northwest on
the Niobrara River. It had been given them by treaty "as long
as the grass shall grow and the waters flow." They had built
homes, planted crops, kept peace according to their treaty. But
the Waxes, white men, it seemed, had made another treaty,
giving their lands to the Sioux, who had not kept the peace.
Now they wanted to move the Poncas to Indian Territory, that
dread land "Toward the Heat."

The Omahas, met in Joseph's house, were appalled. "But
—they cannot take away your land! You have your treaty."

The messenger, Big Snake, shook his head. "So did the
Delawares and the Cherokees have their treaties. And where
are they now? In the land 'Toward the Heat.' So do the Chey-
ennes and the Araphahoes. But they will all be in Indian
Territory soon. And," he added ominously, "*you also have your
treaty.*"

Ten men, including Uncle White Swan and another chief
named Standing Bear, had been taken by the inspector to
Indian Territory to look the land over. Their way had been paid
on the Iron Road. If they did not like it, they were promised,
the tribe need not go. The Omahas burst into swift exclama-
tions of relief. *Ou-daa!* Then the news was not bad. The Poncas
would not like it, of course, and they need not go.

"*Wait and see,*" replied Big Snake.

They waited. One day in March, the "Little Frog Moon,"
eight Ponca chiefs arrived at the Omaha reservation. They
were haggard and emaciated, clothes soiled, moccasins worn
through, feet swollen and caked with blood. One of them was
Uncle White Swan. They had been taken to see the new land
and had not liked it. The water was bad, the ground stony. The
inspector had even refused to give them money to go home.
They had walked in the winter's cold all the way, sleeping in
haystacks, eating dried corn from the fields.

Susette, listening, was suddenly all Bright Eyes. She want-
160

ed no part with the white men, even their God. If there was a God, he must have created Indians for the sole purpose of torturing them. But—no. Remembering the kindness of the Christian women who had taught her, she could not wholly disbelieve. They had talked of America's ideals—justice, law, freedom for all. All, she understood now, bitterly, except for the first Americans.

The chiefs returned home. A telegram was sent to Washington, to the Great White Father, Rutherford B. Hayes. Susette helped to write it. It stated the case and asked for justice. No notice was taken of it. In May 1877 the Poncas were all driven from their homes, their goods were taken away and they were started on their long journey.

From the day-to-day journal of the Ponca agent who accompanied them, I was able to reconstruct that journey of 500 miles—forced marching, sickness, many deaths; then their arrival in Indian Territory in a hot malarial area where no preparations had been made for them and the land was too poor to grow crops. In the ensuing months hundreds of them died, among them the only remaining son of the tall noble brave named Standing Bear.

"Please, *Indadi*," he begged as he was dying, "take my bones back and bury them by the Swift Running Water where I was born. Promise me?" And what could Standing Bear do but promise?

Meanwhile as tribe after tribe was removed forcibly to Indian Territory, the Omahas lived in a limbo of fear and uncertainty. Surely they would be next. When the Commissioner threatened to remove them, Susette was outraged.

"Because I am an Indian," she wrote him, "can you order me any place you wish, and I be powerless to appeal to any law for protection?" Of course, no answer.

Then one day in March, the "Moon When the Geese Return," thirty Poncas headed by Standing Bear, having fled from Indian Territory, arrived in the night after weeks of incredibly hard and dangerous travel. The Omahas welcomed them, gave them land to plant, and tried to hide their presence from the agent. No use. They were apprehended and marched away by soldiers. Helpless, Susette watched them go, Standing Bear straight and tall at the head of his band, behind him the rickety wagon bearing his son's bones in a rough wooden box. She went back into the schoolroom and set about the task of lifting the children from savagery to civilization, using as her tools the

161

white man's language, history and credo of freedom and democracy. If only somebody would do something!

Somebody did. Thomas Henry Tibbles, editor of the Omaha *Herald*, was a crusader with a long record of championing unpopular causes. His colorful career is detailed in a source which I found indispensable, his autobiography *Buckskin and Blanket Days*. One night in March 1879 he was approached by General George Crook, who had been instructed by Washington to return the Poncas to Indian Territory. Crook could not help them. Tibbles could. If he would try to do something for these unfortunate victims of the despicable Indian Ring, Crook would stand by him.

Tibbles would and did. He visited the Indians in the Omaha fort, listened to their pleas for justice, rushed around to churches speaking and getting a signed resolution from four ministers, wrote the story and telegraphed it to papers in Chicago, New York, and other cities, all in the next day, Sunday. At 3 A.M. he stretched wearily on his bed.

"I fought for the liberty of black men with pistol and saber," he told his wife Amelia, "but I swear this fight for the liberty of the Indian with only a pen for a weapon is a blamed sight harder on the body!"

He went to a brilliant young lawyer, John L. Webster, and laid the problem before him. Yes, Webster agreed, they might have a case. With another lawyer, A. J. Poppleton, a petition was drawn up for a habeas corpus. The case came to trial under a very wise and liberal scholar, Judge Dundy. At the request of friends of the Omahas, Susette had written to Tibbles telling all she knew about the situation. Her statement, in the fine slanting script and perfect English taught her in Elizabeth, remained almost a hundred years later firm and black as on the day it was written. She met Thomas Tibbles for the first time on the eve of the trial. At first she was awed and startled by his bigness. The deeply bronzed face framed by the heavy shock of hair reminded her of a lion's. But the steel-gray eyes held soft blue glints, and the stubbornness of the chin was negated by full smiling lips.

"So this is Inshtatheamba," he said. "Bright Eyes."

She flushed. How had he known her Indian name? Surely she had signed her paper Susette La Flesche. At the meeting which followed she was asked not only to interpret for her father, who knew little English, but to speak herself. When she first tried, her voice was little more than a whisper. But soon

162

she was leaning forward, talking eagerly, telling the story as she knew it. She had forgotten herself completely.

At the trial the courtroom was filled. Poppleton made an eloquent plea. But the lawyer representing the Indian Bureau maintained that habeas corpus was a right reserved for *persons*, and an Indian was not a person in the sight of the law. Standing Bear himself was allowed to plead his case, which he did with dignity and eloquence, towering in his impressive, colorful regalia. He held out his hand to the judge.

"That hand," he began quietly, "is not the color of yours, but if I pierce it, I shall feel pain. The blood that will flow from mine will be of the same color as yours. I am a man. The same God made us both."

At the end of his simple but intensely dramatic appeal the courtroom burst into life. There was prolonged applause. People rose to crowd about him and clasp his hand. Among the first to reach him was General Crook.

There followed days of almost unbearable suspense before the Judge rendered his decision. It was a historic one. An Indian was a *person*, declared Judge Dundy, within the meaning of the law of the United States.

I found the whole story of the trial and events leading up to it chronicled in lucid detail in a little book by Thomas Tibbles, *The Ponca Chiefs*, with an introduction by Inshtatheamba. It is told also in shorter form in Dee Brown's *Bury My Heart at Wounded Knee*, in a chapter titled "Standing Bear becomes a Person."

It was victory of a sort, but the Poncas were still exiled from their legal reservation, and the Omahas were threatened with removal. Then something happened which changed Susette's whole life. She was asked to go East with Standing Bear and Thomas Tibbles to plead for the rights of the Poncas. She was panic-stricken. Get up on a platform and speak? No! She was weak with relief when Joseph, *Dadiha*, refused to give his consent. Then tragedy struck the Omahas. It was learned that a bill had been introduced in Congress to remove the tribe to Indian Territory. Tibbles renewed his urging. She *must* go East. Every possible means of pressure must be exerted.

"I have to go, *Dadiha*," she told her father. "I would never forgive myself if I didn't do everything possible."

Joseph finally consented, but only if her brother Francis, Woodworker, went with her.

From Nebraska to Chicago, Boston, New York, Philadelphia, Baltimore, Washington lay the trail of research, into libraries, museums, archives, biographies, newspapers. Especially newspapers. My file on Bright Eyes bulges with more than seventy-five xeroxed press releases, many of them covering long columns and several pages, so sensational was the crusade of this little team and the reception it received.

Ironic! Living among Indians she had been for many years Susette La Flesche. Now, in the white man's world, she was once more Inshtatheamba, Bright Eyes. She had wanted to use her more formal name, but the public would not let her. "Bright Eyes" described her too well.

"As pretty a name as was ever devised," commented the Boston *Lady's Journal*. "Bright Eyes has taken sober Boston captive."

Doubtless the public would have preferred her to conform to the popular conception of Indian apparel—skins, porcupine quills, moccasions, beaded headband and long glossy braids. But fortunately Tibbles wanted all three Indians to dress in "civilized" fashion, and they agreed—all but Standing Bear. Though often wearing white man's dress on the street and looking very much like a New England deacon, he insisted on appearing before an audience in full chief's regalia, blanket heavily adorned with beadwork, necklace of bears' claws, horned headdress, leggings and moccasins. He was a chief, and these were his official accoutrements. But with all his dignity he revealed a marvelous sense of humor.

Bright Eyes interpreted for Standing Bear. And how he could speak!

"You may wonder at my traveling. When a weaker man is oppressed, he goes to a stronger. I am traveling to find someone to help me. I owned a field, and the land was mine. It belonged to me and was dear to me. We had lived on our lands hundreds of years. . . . If you white people had been treated as I have been, you would not like it. If anyone had taken hold of you and forced you into another country that you did not want, you would not like it. I was driven down to the Indian Territory against my will, and I did not like it, so I broke away. You ask why I did so? I wanted my wife and children and all my people to live. That is all."

Bright Eyes herself was amazingly eloquent. Slight, barely five feet tall, painfully shy, almost collapsing after each ordeal of speechmaking and handshaking, she held her vast audiences spellbound as she told of wrongs done to the Indians, her voice low yet rich and vibrant, carrying to the far back of parlors, churches, huge halls. She was probably the first woman ever to speak in Faneuil Hall in Boston.

"When the Indian," she began one speech, "being a man and not a child or a thing or merely an animal, as some of the would-be civilizers would term him, fights for his property, liberty and life, they call him a savage. When the first settlers in this country fought for their property, liberty and life, they were called heroes. When the Indian in fighting this great nation wins a battle it is called a massacre; when this great nation in fighting the Indian wins, it is called a victory."

The party took staid and intellectual Boston by storm. Not for a hundred years had this hub of progressive thought and cradle of independence been so shocked and aroused. Places of meeting were crowded to the doors—Horticultural Hall, churches, the Merchants' Exchange, Faneuil Hall. They made friends for the Poncas' cause among some of the great names of the day: Oliver Wendell Holmes, William Jennings Bryan, John Greenleaf Whittier, Helen Hunt Jackson. In fact, it was because she was so inspired by Bright Eyes that Mrs. Jackson wrote her great novel, *Ramona*. But one tragic event clouded the triumph of Boston. Tibbles received a telegram saying that his beloved wife Amelia had died. It was only Standing Bear's gentle urging that forced him to go on.

"Don't go back home. Don't stop trying to help my poor people. Many husbands have seen their wives die, down in that hot country. You suffer greatly but they suffer more. Promise that you will not forsake them." Tibbles promised.

The crusade continued all over the East, with Bright Eyes and Standing Bear addressing vast audiences in New York, Philadelphia, Baltimore, Washington. Bright Eyes testified before committees in Congress. She was entertained in the White House. And public pressure brought changes in the arbitrary policies of the powerful Indian Ring. The Poncas were permitted to go back to an area near their old reservation on the Niobrara, though many of the tribe chose to remain in Oklahoma. New laws were passed which at the time seemed to make the Indian more secure. At least the Omahas were not removed and were able to keep a small part of their ancestral lands.

It was in the annals of this Eastern crusade that I found the dramatic incident with which to start the story of Bright Eyes. It is described in detail in a biography of Helen Hunt Jackson, who was present on the occasion.

The time was a day in December 1879, the place a luxurious home in Cambridge, Massachusetts, where a party was to be held. Due to a traffic snarl of carriages in the street, the guests of honor were late in arriving. A man kept running to the windows, rather an old man with a long white beard. "Where is she?" he kept demanding impatiently. "Why isn't she here?" At last she came up the walk, a slight figure in black coat and small black hat. The man ran to the door, flung it open, and stood waiting. He was the poet, Henry Wadsworth Longfellow.

He stepped forward to meet her, took both her hands in his and looked long and hard into her face. There were no long braids, no beaded headband, no moccasins, no fringed and gaily embroidered skin tunic. But the light from the open door spread a bronze glow over the softly rounded cheeks, cast a blue sheen on the sable wings of hair framing the broad forehead, kindled unquenchable fires in the great dark eyes. The poet nodded with satisfaction.

"This," he said in a loud clear voice, "is Minnehaha."

In a display case at the Historical Society in Lincoln, carefully preserved, is Bright Eyes' autograph album. Probably it is opened to the page on which that day in Cambridge Longfellow inscribed his name, together with ten lines from "Hiawatha," beginning, "From the wigwam he departed, leading with him Laughing Water," and ending, "'Fare thee well, O Minnehaha.'"

Later Bright Eyes married Tibbles and in the home of the wife of her step-grandson near Providence, Rhode Island, I was able to see the dress she wore and secure a picture of it, worn by her step-great-granddaughter, a girl thirteen years old. It was a beautiful creation, the gift of some of her women friends in the East, a soft fabric of wool challis, with elaborate ruffles, laces, tucks, and furbelows. Secretly Bright Eyes agreed with the Oldest Grandmother's appraisal of its suitability.

"*Na he*! Soft, yes, but not like an *unonzhin* of finest doeskin! And not a proper robe for a bride. How well I remember my own wedding tunic, all embroidered with dyed quill work and fringed, made by my mother, the daughter of the great chief Blackbird!"

Now there was a still further problem of identities. Was she

166

Susette, or Inshtatheamba, or Mrs. Thomas Tibbles, wife of a successful editor in Omaha? It was a problem never to be solved.

There were other trips East, with constant lecturing. Although emotions over the plight of the "poor Indians" had somewhat cooled with the solution of the specific Ponca problem, her appearance in a city invariably fanned the fires of public interest and stimulated further legislative action. She was accepted also as a literary personage since her Indian stories in *St. Nicholas*, *Wide Awake*, and other children's magazines, illustrated by her clever drawings, were gaining favorable attention. Then in 1887, to Bright Eyes' distress, a lecture bureau persuaded Thomas Tibbles to contract for a year of lecturing with his wife in England.

"Bright Eyes in England," Tibbles captioned Chapter Forty of his autobiography twenty years later. The tour started inauspiciously, with the agent leaving them stranded in London. Bright Eyes, much relieved, was all for returning home. Not Tibbles. He approached a Reverend Dr. Fraser with letters of recommendation, including one from James Russell Lowell. The poor cleric explained with acute embarrassment that his denomination believed in the command that women should keep silence in the churches. But a visit to Bright Eyes made him change his mind. He determined that she should speak in his church, whatever happened. After a brief worship service he came down from the pulpit and introduced Thomas Tibbles, then after his address presented the "Princess Bright Eyes from America." There were lords and ladies in the audience, all giving her the acclaim she was used to receiving in America. There was much publicity. An English agent made them a proposition, and they started on a lecture tour which continued for several months. To Bright Eyes' horror the agent printed a supply of folders featuring the "Princess Bright Eyes." She rebelled. They must all be destroyed. Friend of Lowell, Longfellow, Whittier, ardent reader of Emerson and other liberals, champion of freedom for her own people, she found the very idea of royal address repulsive.

"But," argued T. H. (as Thomas Tibbles was usually called), "one must conform to the customs of the country. I had to conform to Indian customs when I lived among your people, even though white men ridiculed them." Reluctantly she agreed, though insisting that the hateful folders be destroyed.

But she could not escape the title with all its implications. Sometimes when she entered a room, all would rise and remain standing until she was seated, since she was considered to be of royal blood. When this happened she could hardly keep from laughing. "Dirty savage! . . . Princess!" What consternation if each group of name-callers could see and hear the other!

Strangely enough, extensive research in England failed to reveal any newspaper publicity of this tour. But Tibbles kept a diary (unfortunately lost), and his account of the trip must be fairly accurate. Certainly the many inscriptions in Bright Eyes' autograph album include well-known names in both England and Scotland, many illustrated with drawings and containing reminders of spirited conversations and visits to various homes. One Edinburgh writer made a poetic acrostic on her name, Inshtatheamba.

It was considered a victory when legislation granted the Omahas the right of allotment. Alice Fletcher, the ethnologist who had studied the tribal history and customs and had accompanied Bright Eyes and T. H. on an extended camping trip, visiting many tribes, was designated by the government as the agent to partition the land into individual allotments. Through the kindness of Mrs. Rosalie Boughn, a niece of Bright Eyes living in Walthill near Macy, I was able to visit the site of Bright Eyes' allotment, just outside of Bancroft, and see the house which she and Thomas Tibbles built and where she spent the last years of her life. It is a small story-and-a-half frame house set in the midst of a generous lot with fine shade trees. A picture furnished by the Historical Society shows Bright Eyes sitting in an upstairs window.

It's fortunate that she did not live to see the results of the allotment which they worked so hard to secure, each man having a title to his own land. For in the long run the white man, always greedy for more land, was able to take advantage of it, as he had done over and over in the past. Though no longer able to take the land, once the twenty-five-year trust period expired in 1910 the white man was often able to buy it. And the Indian, who had been taught the white man's vices, chiefly his thirst for liquor far more than his virtues of thrift and hard work, was in many cases reduced to poverty and unemployment.

Bright Eyes was involved in other historic events crucial to Indian history. It was 1890 when T. H. told her that they were to go to Pine Ridge, where rumors of an Indian messianic era and resultant ritual dances had sparked jittery fears among officials of an uprising. Newspapers were printing avid headlines. Troops were on the way.

"We're to be special war correspondents," he grimaced, "for the *World-Herald* and the Chicago *Express*."

She gasped in dismay. "War correspondents! But—"

"I know. The Sioux have no more intention of starting a war than the Omahas. But tell that to these city editors slavering for bloody headlines. Maybe we can counteract some of their stooges' cockeyed dispatches."

They went to Pine Ridge and lodged in an Indian home instead of the hotel with the other reporters. Conferences with the Indian leaders and attendance at one of the "peace dances" assured them that no hostility was contemplated or desired. No weapons were carried. While T. H. sent dispatches and attempted to nullify the fictitious tales of the war hounds, Bright Eyes spent Christmas with their new Indian friends. Four days later came the massacre at Wounded Knee, when 300 men, women and children camping peacefully in an Indian Village were raked with gunfire and killed. She was in the little church at Pine Ridge when the wounded were brought in, and with other women she did what she could, prying loose caked clothing, bandaging the worst gaping wounds, keeping the half-frozen bodies covered with blankets. She stayed there all night and even the dawn seemed more like an end than a beginning. The Indian was at last conquered, his age-old pride, dignity and ambition ground into the blood-soaked earth at Wounded Knee. Looking up at the Christmas greens still festooning the church rafters, she saw the banner over the pulpit bearing the ironic words, "Peace on Earth, Good Will to Men."

She was not the only member of her remarkable family to achieve success. Her three sisters, Rosalie, Marguerite, and Susan, all children of Joseph's wife Mary, were outstanding in contributing to the welfare of their people, especially Susan, the first Indian woman to obtain a doctor's degree, who spent long years of devoted service to the tribe. And their half-brother Francis made a distinguished record as an author and scientist in Washington. His collaboration with Alice Fletcher the ethnologist preserved the priceless treasure of Omaha lore, songs, customs and artifacts for posterity.

I saw many of these artifacts in the Peabody Museum at

Harvard University with which Alice Fletcher was long associated. There were robes, moccasins, the sacred war pack with all its contents, mystery bags belonging to the secret societies. Most interesting of all was the sacred pole, perhaps the most important and holy of all the relics, its origin hidden deep within the mists of primeval legend. Their presence there signified the passing of an era.

Bright Eyes too preserved many of the tribal memories in words and pictures. Collaborating with Fannie Reed Giffen, a writer long associated with the Omahas, she helped prepare a little book published during the Exposition in Omaha in 1898. It was called *Oo-mah-ha Ta-wa-tha* ("Omaha City") and contained stories told by Joseph and Mary. All her artistic ability and love of Indian life were concentrated in the drawings—a canoe in moonlight, a tepee, a baby on a cradle board, and an arrow with an unstrung bow (a symbol of death).

Her own life was not long, less than fifty years, and her last years were made unhappy by a difference of opinion between some of her family and the strong-minded, often obdurate Thomas Tibbles. They did not agree on the best methods of solving the increasing difficulties of the tribe.

But when her last spring came it brought contentment, as if all the springs wakened out of winter's death by the sound of the First Thunder had been fused into one. Never had the feathery mist of the willows been more golden, the new cottonwood tips aglow with more magic fire. She waited with an almost painful eagerness for the return of the "gone-down" birds, afraid they might come too late, and when she heard the first meadowlark flute loud and clear in Omaha, "It is spring, it is spring!" her sense of fulfillment was complete.

It was May, the "Moon in Which the Tribe Plants," when the end came. Dr. Susan and their mother Mary were with her. When it was over Mary, heretofore calm, yielded to abandoned weeping, in which might be heard an echo of the loud Indian mourning wail, haunting and plaintive. But they did not stay. They went reluctantly, constrained by their men-folk who did not intend to remain in Thomas Tibbles' house longer than necessary nor let their family do so.

"Why?" I was asked by Dr. John Neihardt, the noted poet, when I went to interview him in Lincoln. "I have always wondered why there was none of her family with her that night."

He had been asked by Thomas Tibbles to sit up with his friend during the night before Bright Eyes' funeral. He liked Tibbles. The very qualities which made T. H. unpopular with many—fearless, almost brutal candor, defense of the underdog—were the ones Neihardt most respected and admired. I tried to explain, and perhaps at last he understood. On tape he told me, as only a poet could do, the story of that night.

"Come," said Tibbles soon after his friend had entered the house. He led him into the front bedroom where the still form lay on a bed, white cloths covering the face. He stood looking down at her, shoulders shaking. Dipping the cloths in a basin of cold water fresh from the well he laid them over the face with slow caressing motions. It was an act repeated again and again through the night, and each time Tibbles would say brokenly, "Look at her. My Bright Eyes. Isn't she beautiful?"

Rosalie Boughn took me to see the grave in Bancroft where she lay beside Joseph, Grandmother Nicomi, and the Oldest Grandmother. In the lefthand corner of the stone is engraved Bright Eyes' own symbol of a life fulfilled and ended, an arrow poised for flight within an unstrung bow.

I am glad I could write this story now because it seems so curiously pertinent to today's headlines when Indians are still fighting for their rights after the wrongs of three hundred years, when Women's Lib is exploring the past for just such pioneers as Bright Eyes, when Wounded Knee once more has made the front page, and when the long-exploiting white man is only beginning to respect the red man's philosophy of conservation and unity with all creation.

8

DOROTHEA LYNDE DIX: 'STRANGER AND TRAVELER'

I n the town of Hampden, Maine, about fifteen miles from my home, there is a rest area on the road with a stone gateway bearing the words DOROTHEA DIX PARK. On one of the uprights of the gate is a large metal plaque, its words clearly legible to all who pass:

In Memory of
Dorothea Lynde Dix
who by her devoted care to sick
and wounded soldiers during the
Civil War earned the gratitude of
the nation; and by her labors in the
cause of prison reform and of humane
treatment of the insane won the
admiration and reverence of the
civilized world
HER BIRTHPLACE

Surely here was a life just begging to be relived, and almost on my doorstep. The name had been on my editor's list. How could I have passed over it? Because of the lure of far places which had so often caused me to overlook the here and now? Or had previous research given me a somewhat prejudiced view of Miss Dix? Elizabeth Blackwell, meeting her briefly during the stress of their work during the Civil War, had not been impressed by her personality. Other woman writers of the same period had been lukewarm in their appraisal of her contribution as Superintendent of Nurses. Now some impulse—a happy hunch or the prodding of conscience?—sent me once more to that treasure house, the *Dictionary of American Biography.* I was excited and challenged. Here was a project made to order—a woman whose roots were here in Maine, whose life spanned a period on which I had done intensive research (1802-1887) and, best of all, who had probably done more for the betterment of human society than any other person of her century.

I found it amazing that she was not better known. There had been some juvenile books and many articles written about her in recent years, but the last definitive biography had appeared in the thirties, its subtitle fittingly "The Forgotten Samaritan." When I suggested the subject to my editor at Little, Brown, he regarded me somewhat quizzically, and no wonder. He thought I was talking about Dorothy Dix, the columnist, noted for "advice to the lovelorn." Hardly my area of interest! But he was soon converted to approval of the project, and the contract was signed. Time and again I got the same reaction from persons who heard what I was writing. "Oh? The columnist?"

Stranger and Traveler. The title emerged inevitably during the process of research. The words are from a poem written for Dorothea by her friend, John Greenleaf Whittier. Concerned about the needs of all God's creatures, not just human beings, she wanted to donate a fountain for the horses she had seen dragging heavy loads through the streets of Boston. She remembered a poem which she had heard Whittier read, one that he had found on a fountain in the Middle East, and she wrote asking if he would send it to her. He could not locate it. "But I will write one for you," he said. It began with those words.

> "Stranger and traveler!
> Drink freely and bestow
> A kindly thought on her
> Who bade this fountain flow
> Yet hath for it no claim
> Save as the minister
> Of blessing in God's name."

Stranger and traveler. The two words apply very well to Dorothea herself, for all her life she was lonely and a bit withdrawn from other human beings while being obsessed by the urge to help them, and she probably traveled more thousands of miles than any other person, man or woman, in the nineteenth century.

Of course I went to Hampden first. Though the officers of the Historical Society were most cooperative, we found little information in the town's annals about the Dixes. Dorothea's birth is recorded as occurring on April 4, 1802, and there is a record of the Dix family having purchased a pew in the Hampden meeting house. But the early history of the town is rich in details about the ten years the Dixes lived there—homes in existence, prominent families, schools, the shipbuilding industry, roads, public buildings. I discovered that the impression of the town conveyed in previous biographies—of crude log cabins chinked with plaster, rough floors, small windows covered with oiled paper—was misleading. The houses were sturdy, comfortable, many of them luxurious, homes not only of thrifty farmers but of prosperous shipbuilders and mill owners, merchants whose ships plied the waters all along the Atlantic coast and as far as the Indies and Europe.

True, Dorothea's parents were poor, their house unpretentious. With a Methodist friend who had lived in Hampden all her life I walked down through the park perhaps a mile to the site of the house where Dorothea was born. There is no building there now, only an open field at the end of a long path leading down through the woods, but a drawing of the old house is preserved, apparently authentic—small, square, neatly clapboarded, certainly no chinked log cabin.

Dorothea had an unhappy childhood. In fact, "I never had a childhood," she confessed later. Most of her time was spent in caring for an invalid, rather shiftless mother, doing much of the housework, and in plying a huge needle through endless tracts and sermons for her father. Though Joseph Dix, son of Dr. Elijah Dix of Boston, had been sent to Maine to manage his father's lands and open them to settlers, he felt called to ride over the country as an itinerant preacher, fervent and eloquent in his attempt to save souls who he believed were in imminent danger of the wrath of an angry God and a fate of fire and brimstone.

So torturing was this sewing that it was to color all her

174

memories of childhood. Other activities must be finished with feverish haste, whether housework or sessions during the short terms when she was able to attend the little rural school down the road. Always there was the hurrying to cut and sew and paste those tracts and sermons, work of sheer torture, pushing the big needle through the thicknesses of coarse paper, pulling the threads taut ... pushing ... pulling. Even Mother would leave her sick bed and stagger to the table to help, for their living depended on it. They would bring little cash income at best, many given in exchange for Father's lodging or the horse's fodder, potatoes, maple sugar, yarn, and other commodities, all welcome but useless as tender for rent and flour and calico.

Yet there were compensations even in this drudgery, for the hateful pages held the magic of words, and she hungrily absorbed them as she worked, though finding the idea of an angry, vengeful God repugnant to her sense of reason and justice even at this early stage of her life. Reading, learning, they were her joy and hope.

And even in these barren years of childhood there were brief glimpses of paradise, when she traveled with her beloved grandfather, Dr. Elijah Dix, to his home in Boston. Not that Dix Mansion in Orange Court seemed such an Eden of perfection. Indeed, Grandmother's stern admonitions and derogative references to her clothes, manners and especially her mother kept rearing tiny serpent heads. Madam Dix, as she was usually called, had never forgiven her son Joseph for leaving his studies at Harvard Divinity School and marrying a woman twenty years his senior from a family considered inferior by the aristocratic Lyndes and Dixes of Worcester. It was Grandfather who made these trips adventures into Eden. Some people might call Dr. Elijah stern, stubborn, dictatorial—and did—yet he never frowned at her or chided. He took her walking along the Mall, showed her Old North Church and the place where the despised British tea had been flung into the harbor; took her riding in his carriage when he called on his patients; showed her his drugstore on the south side of Faneuil Hall.

It was another world, beautiful but ephemeral, and always, looking back at the vanishing city from the deck of a schooner, she saw the gates of Eden closing. To start the book with her trip home from what was her last journey with Grandfather I

175

researched ships and seafaring, the history of towns along the Maine coast, corresponded with the curator of a maritime museum and studied a relief map of the tortuous Penobscot River.

Dr. Elijah Dix, this hero of her childhood, had bought over 20,000 acres of Maine wilderness land at about a dollar an acre, founding the two towns of Dixfield and Dixmont. It was on his last trip to the area, in 1809 when Dorothea was seven, that he was taken ill while surveying land near what is now Dixmont Corner and died there. Trips to Dixmont, about nine miles west of Hampden, produced even more materials than Hampden, since two of Dorothea's cousins were among the early settlers there. Of course I visited the cemetery not far from the main road, where an impressive monument was reared in her grandfather's memory.

This time the gates were slammed shut. Nothing left now but the drudgery, the endless sewing and the unsatisfied hunger for knowledge. In 1812 Joseph left the rented farm in Hampden and took his family to what he hoped would be greener pastures. When Dorothea at age ten rode with her family in a rough wagon up through the woods path and left for parts unknown, their going barely noticed, she could not have guessed that nearly ninety years later the whole town of Hampden and many distinguished guests would assemble to dedicate a park, festive with booths, tents, flags, bandstand; roam the graveled path to the site of the old house by the river; listen to speeches and poems and songs honoring the memory of the town's most famous daughter.

They roamed about for two years. At one time they were in a town in Vermont, where Joseph ran a bookstore, importing textbooks from Boston. Here Dorothea was in her element. Books! She could handle them, read them, exult in their treasures. But the interlude soon passed, the unsold books sent back to Boston. Finally they came to Worcester where her father had lived in early years. But if Joseph hoped for a revival of his fortunes in his native city he was disappointed. He refused to seek favors or even casual intercourse from relatives who had disapproved of his marriage. Failing at other pursuits, he turned to his first love, preaching. Again came the cutting and pasting and stitching, the loading of saddlebags, the dirt and clutter, the long days of work never done. Dorothea worried not only about her own lack of education but about the neglect of her young brothers Joseph and Charles who were being reared without proper training.

At age twelve, hungry for learning, frustrated beyond endurance, she ran away. Somehow she made her way to Dix Mansion in Boston. Her grandmother, Madam Dorothy Lynde Dix, was a formidable figure. The picture I found of her shows firm unsmiling features beneath a close-fitting white cap, brilliant dark eyes, aquiline nose, stern lips. Her seven sons and one daughter had often quailed before her and with reason, for her unswerving devotion to family was conditioned by an inflexible will and a puritan perfectionism.

"Why did you come?" she demanded of the dirty little waif in ragged clothes.

The child did not quail. Her eyes, a softer color but equally brilliant, were unwavering. The small chin was just as firm.

"To beg you to take me in, Grandmother. I couldn't stand it any longer, living the way I did. I want to grow up to know things, to be somebody."

Her grandmother took her in and sent her to school, but she had qualities which did not endear her to a young girl of twelve. Austere and intensely righteous, she tried to mold Dorothea into the prevailing idea of the model young woman of the day, sedate, quiet, correct in manners, a perfect seamstress. Dorothea, being an independent soul, very much like her grandmother, naturally rebelled. It was a life without the affection for which her sensitive young spirit was starved. Finally her grandmother sent her to relatives in Worcester who were far more understanding. Then returning to Boston sufficiently trained in manners and skills to suit even her grandmother she was sent to more advanced schools and given every advantage which the burgeoning intellectual life of Boston was able to give.

From the age of fourteen Dorothea taught school, first in Worcester, later in Boston. It was the period of the "Dame School," classes often being held in the teacher's own home. Strangely enough the severity which had aroused rebellion against her grandmother's regime was now accentuated in her own teaching. Whipping, an accepted procedure in education, was not neglected for the boys. With girls her punishments were different but equally severe. One child was made to walk

177

to and from school wearing on her back a placard stating "A Very Bad Girl Indeed." Yet she was an excellent and much beloved teacher. Letters from her pupils in subsequent years attest not only to the quality and thoroughness of her teaching but to an intense and abiding affection between teacher and pupil.

"She fascinated me from the first," recalled one pupil, "as she had done many of my class before me. Next to my mother I thought her the most beautiful woman I had ever seen. She was tall and of dignified carriage, head finely shaped and set, with an abundance of soft, wavy hair."

She wrote books. One of the earliest, published in 1824, was called *Conversations on Common Things* and was a forerunner of the Book of Knowledge. Examining it in the Boston Public Library, I was amazed at the scope of subjects covered, the amount of detail conveyed and the level of interest for young readers.

It was her dedication to teaching as well as her spirit of independence that brought an end to the one serious romance of her life. She was engaged to Edward Dillingham Bangs, a Worcester cousin, twelve years her senior.

"You say—I'm not to teach?" They were walking in Boston and talking of their marriage.

"Of course not." He laughed indulgently. "You'll have other things to do."

"What things?"

"Why, just being my wife. Looking beautiful, as you always do. Entertaining my friends and clients. Presiding over my table. Teaching your own children, not other people's."

Soon after this conversation she wrote him a letter. She would never be content just running his household. She was a *person* with her own abilities and responsibilities. He must not tell her what she could or could not do. And she hoped he would understand because she loved him with all her heart. But he must consider himself free, not bound by any promises. When Edward Bangs announced his engagement to a young Worcester woman, one who would conform to his idea of a proper wife and live to further his career of many years as Secretary of State for Massachusetts, only to one person did Dorothea confess the bleakness of her hurt and desolation. To Anne Heath of Brookline, her dearest friend and confidante, she wrote in the verse which came to her pen so easily:

178

"In the sad hour of anguish and distress
  To thee for sympathy will I repair;
Thy soothings sure will make my sorrow less
  And what thou canst not soothe, thou wilt share."

It is in Dorothea's correspondence with Anne through the years, hundreds of letters which Anne fortunately did not destroy though Dorothea commanded her to, that one finds some of the most intimate glimpses of Dorothea's personality—that is if one can read them! Even Anne complained many times of her friend's terrible penmanship, though resigned to the fact that if Dorothea did not write in such haste during her hectic travels there would have been far fewer letters. When need arose, as I discovered, Dorothea could write with perfect style and legibility. But over this correspondence with Anne I labored many days with a magnifying glass. With others of the Dix papers they are in the Houghton Library at Harvard University where to my satisfaction and that of my husband who had seen me off so many times on extended trips to India and other far places I could work for a few days at a time, always returning home on weekends.

Besides the days spent in the library I immersed myself in the Boston of the 1800s—its changing topography, its history, its art and literature, its buildings familiar to Dorothea. Many of the latter of course were gone. One day I walked along Washington Street (once Orange) and tried to locate the site of Dix Mansion, but it was lost in a complex of modern structures. However, I found part of her locale exactly as she knew it.

Up on Mount Vernon Street on Beacon Hill is the old home of William Ellery Channing. It was here far more than at Dix Mansion that Dorothea found her spiritual home and liberation from the tight walls which had made her childhood so unhappy and stultified. She became an intimate friend of the Channings, teaching their children during two summer holidays at Newport, going with them one winter to St. Croix, an experience which opened new doors of discovery in nature. It was about this time that she wrote her remarkable little volume *A Garland of Flora*, an exhaustive study of flowers and plants from A to Z with much of the literature of the world pertaining to each one.

It was Dr. Channing, the great liberal scholar, who had the most profound influence on her life, freeing her from the two constraining and conflicting creeds of her childhood—the hell-fire angry God of her father's preaching and the cold Calvinist rigidity of Puritan Congregationalism which she found in her grandmother's church. Channing believed in the love of God and the universality of man. He opened her eyes to the needs of the world and awakened the social consciousness which was to become the compulsive passion of her life.

She spent herself on her pupils without stint—rising at dawn; spending an hour on devotional study and prayer; working all day as teacher, student housekeeper, writer and boarding school matron; and retiring long after midnight. With her father's death her two brothers became her pupils, and she lavished on them all the care of a mother. She started a school for poor children in the loft of the Dix carriage house, calling it "The Hope." Her health, always delicate, for she had weak lungs, broke completely. She had to give up her teaching.

There followed a frustrating period: a trip abroad for a year of convalescence with the Rathbones, new Quaker friends near Liverpool; the death of her grandmother, followed by shuttlings between the cold North and warmer climes; futile attempts to satisfy her compulsion by teaching a Sunday school class, writing hymns, sharing vicariously in the achievements of contemporaries—Margaret Fuller, Emerson, Longfellow, Samuel Gridley Howe, Horace Mann. She believed her active life was ended. Ended! It was like saying spring is over when the first crocus dies.

At 85 Mount Vernon Street, next door to the Channing's, is one of the finest old Boston mansions, the Harrison Gray Otis house built by Bulfinch. I studied it with interest, took pictures of it, admired its towering three stories, its cupola, its rose-red brick, its iron gratings, its chimney pots. Like the whole neighborhood it has remained almost unchanged for the last century and a half, to the lamppost in front (once gas) and the driveway between the two houses, cobblestones with two smooth parallel courses for the carriage wheels. It was this house, occupied by Miss Sarah Gibbs, a member of the Channing family, that Dorothea made her Boston headquarters for many years. She was living here when the event occurred which changed her life.

It was one cold windy day in March 1841 when she was nearly forty years old. As an experiment she was spending the cold season in the North against the advice of her doctor. A young man came to her door. He was John Nichols, a young Harvard Divinity student, son of the minister of the First Parish Church in Portland, Maine, in whose home Dorothea had often visited. One of a group of students who had agreed to hold Sunday services in the East Cambridge jail, he had found to his dismay that the twenty persons assigned to him were women. He felt imcompetent to teach them. Did Miss Dix know of anyone who would go?

"I will go myself," she responded instantly.

"Oh, no!" he protested, knowing that she was in poor health. But she insisted. The next Sunday was bitterly cold for spring, an east wind blowing. She had intended taking an omnibus, but Miss Gibbs insisted on sending her in the carriage with the family coachman. "If you *must* risk catching your death—!" Even in the closed vehicle, with a soapstone wrapped in a woolen bag at her feet, she shivered. But she felt imbued with new life. She would take springtime to those poor women icebound in sin. They rattled across the bridge over the Charles, plowed through streets deep with mud. One could smell the prison area before arriving, whether from human odors or the miasma of its swampy environs, it was hard to tell.

She taught the class. Then on impulse she decided to walk through the jail, much to the shock of the jailer. "No place for a woman, ma'am! I can't let you—"

He might have been remonstrating with a cyclone. Had he but known it, he was the first of hundreds of similar protesters who would find themselves equally frustrated. To her horror Dorothea found insane persons lodged with the criminals, enclosed in unheated cells, being treated like animals.

"But—they're freezing!" she exclaimed. "There isn't even a stove!"

The jailer shrugged. "None needed for those uns, ma'am. Mad folk don't known hot from cold."

No use protesting further. The idea of putting insane persons in a jail with criminals was abhorrent, but she knew it was not the jailer's fault. However she made it clear to him some changes could be made. If warmth was not provided before she came again she would go to the proper authorities.

She returned with warm clothes, blankets and food. Nothing had been done. The jailer had regained his confidence, even his arrogance. It was the commissioners who told him what to do and they had prescribed no stoves.

She went to the commissioners. They laughed. She presented the case in writing to the East Cambridge Court then in
session. Her specific request for stoves was finally granted (at
least voted), but the sensational details of her protest reached
the newspapers and aroused a storm of outrage. A woman
meddling in politics? Dorothea cared nothing for the opposition
except that it impeded progress for further reform. A stove
was but a tiny palliative, no remedy for the appalling distress
she had uncovered. Channing advised her to see Samuel Gridley Howe who had once made a survey of prisons, almshouses
and houses of correction in the Commonwealth. She did, finding to her amazement that it was the common practice for local
authorities responsible for the mentally ill who could not be
accommodated in the new asylum at Worcester to lodge them
in jails and almshouses. In spite of all that had been done by
Howe, Horace Mann and others, there was still little provision
for the insane poor.

"What is needed," Howe told her, "is a thorough survey of
the state, not by letter but by person. But—who could be
found to do it?"

Who ... Dorothea was aghast at the possible answer. Objections seemed insuperable. A woman, a *gentle* woman, challenging jailers, accosting strangers, prying into local politics,
prowling about noisome haunts of crime and disease and mad-
ness? An invalid with weak lungs, presumably not long for life,
buffeting the exigencies of travel in railroads and stages, the
colds and snows of this northern climate from which for years
she had been fleeing? Impossible! Yet at her prayers Bible
verses leaped at her from the page. "I was in prison, and ye
came unto me." "Whosoever will save his life shall lose it." ". . .
and who knoweth whether thou art come to the kingdom for
such a time as this?"

She began with an exhaustive study of insanity and its
causes, history and treatment, and of course I had to do the
same. Though a new understanding of mental health was beginning to emerge in those mid-1800s and there were a few
enlightened doctors trained in the new field of psychiatric
medicine who practiced techniques of non-restraint and healing in some institutions, popular concepts of insanity remained
in the Dark Ages. If the mentally ill person was no longer
believed to be demon-possessed (not such a foreign concept
even today!), he was at least consigned to the category of an
182

animal, insensitive to cold and heat, having no need of clothes or decent food, incapable of any form of healing.

There was no money for such a survey. Fortunately Grandmother had left her an adequate income. She would use it all in this crusade. For that was what it was, inspired by as self-renouncing a zeal as the ancient struggle to redeem the Holy Land. To cover the Commonwealth of Massachusetts, to visit every city, town, village and hamlet to discover the existence and condition of the mentally ill in every almshouse, jail, house of correction—a herculean task! She started in the summer of 1841, expecting to be finished before winter and spend the coldest weather in her comfortable rooms in Boston assembling her findings. Time passed ... autumn ... winter ... spring ... another autumn ... another winter ....

Travel was incredibly difficult. There were only three railroads in Massachusetts and those connected only the largest towns. The railway cars were uncomfortable, hard seats without springs, soot and cinders seeping dust through the cracks, reddening the eyes, grinding into the pores. Sometimes she had to sit up all night on a hard bench in a cold bare station. But the railroads touched only half the towns she had to visit. She had to take a stagecoach, carriage or often farm wagon to reach the rest, riding over roads which if not deep in mud or ice or water were often rough with stones and thick with dust.

Yet she persevered. In a day when no respectable female was supposed to travel alone, certainly not to interfere in men's affairs or politics, this tall woman in the plain dark dress and snowy kerchief with her quiet but aloof dignity invariably commanded respect. Barred doors were opened. Jailers, at first hostile, found themselves yielding to the rich low voice which spoke with a quiet but powerful authority. She took copious notes. Sometimes she recorded whole conversations verbatim, as when she asked the way to the almshouse in the town of Berkeley:

"Are there insane persons there?"

"Oh, yes, plenty of insane and idiots."

"Are they well taken care of?"

"Oh, well enough for such sort of creatures."

"Are there any violently insane?"

"Oh, yes, my nephew is there, a real tiger."

"Is he comfortably provided for?"

"Well enough."

"Has he decent clothes?"

"Wouldn't wear 'em if he had 'em."

"Food?"

"Good enough for him."

"One more question. Has he the comfort of a fire?"

"Fire? Fire indeed! What does a crazy man need of fire? Red-hot iron wants a fire as much as he."

Back she came to Mount Vernon Street, to find to her sorrow that the beloved Dr. Channing had died in her absence. But in his house, at his desk, she laid out her meticulous notes and wrote her Memorial to the Legislature of Massachusetts, a deadly indictment of the conditions in the forty towns she had visited, many more than once.

"I proceed, gentlemen," it began, "to call your attention to the present state of insane persons confined within this Commonwealth, in cages, closets, cellars, stalls, pens, chained, naked, beaten with rods, and lashed into obedience."

The memorial was presented to the Massachusetts legislature by Samuel Howe, arousing almost the traumatic shock of that "shot heard round the world." Years later a commentator would refer to it as "the greatest sensation produced in the legislature since 1775." Another would call her investigation the "first piece of social research ever conducted in America." Town selectmen, almshouse masters were outraged. "Lies!" they protested. "Meddlesome tomfoolery!" But the facts were verified by such eminent persons as Charles Sumner, Horace Mann and Samuel Howe. Dorothea protested that it was not persons or localities she was denouncing, but a *system* cruel and outdated. People did not mean to be cruel. They acted through ignorance. And the memorial brought results. A bill was introduced to enlarge the asylum in Worcester, where Dr. Samuel Woodward was the enlightened superintendent. It was strongly opposed.

Once more Dorothea sat in Dr. Channing's study, at his desk, her heart in her throat, waiting to hear the result of the vote. After what seemed an eternity she heard the rattling of wheels on the smooth tracks of the driveway, the pounding of hooves on the cobblestones. Dr. Howe appeared in the doorway. She dared not look up for fear of the disappointment his face might betray.

"Miss Dix," he announced joyfully, "your bill has passed."

So began the long crusade which was to take Dorothea Dix from the house on Mount Vernon Street into all parts of the world, from California to Constantinople. In state after state starting with Rhode Island, then to New York, Pennsylvania, New Jersey, Kentucky, Maryland, Tennessee, many states west of the Mississippi and even into Canada she made the same meticulous surveys, presented the same kind of memorial to each legislature, labored quietly but with uncanny skill with the members, helped choose the sites for new institutions, helped to staff them with competent persons trained in the enlightened new techniques of mental health.

Everywhere she found the same conditions as in Massachusetts, the same cages and cells, chains, treatment which would have been considered cruel if applied to animals. One case, that of Abram Simmons in Rhode Island, was memorable.

"Is this all?" she inquired of the kindly almshouse mistress after visiting two or three insane persons in their cells. No, there was one other, but she must not go near him. He would surely kill her. Dorothea insisted. Very well, she would get a lantern. In the almshouse courthouse was a queer stone structure resembling a tomb. Dorothea heard smothered groans and moans issuing from the place, as from something buried alive. "He's here," said the woman, returning with the lantern and unlocking the strong iron door. At the end of a passage there was a second door, equally solid. Immediately such a stench filled the passage that Dorothea choked and was forced to retreat. Out in the air she drew long breaths before returning.

"He'll kill you!" In spite of the woman's warnings she groped her way into a cave-like room, perhaps seven by seven, all of stone. The inmate stood near the door, motionless and silent, tangled hair about his shoulders, bare feet pressing the wet stone floor. She went toward him, took his cold hands, tried to warm them. He might not have been conscious of her presence except that a tear stole over his hollow cheek. Her foot struck something—a length of ox chain connected to an iron ring encircling the man's leg. At one end it was joined to a solid chain, bars of iron perhaps two feet long, linked together.

"Why, he didn't even try to hurt you!" the woman exclaimed as they left the cell. Her husband, she continued sociably, sometimes raked out of a winter morning half a bushel of frost,

185

yet the creature never froze. Sometimes he screamed, and that was why they had the double wall and two doors. His cries disturbed them in the house.

Dorothea wrote scathing articles, approached legislators, stressed the urgency of this case. Eight months passed and still nothing had been done. When action was finally taken on his removal it was announced that it had come too late. Abram Simmons was dead. But sentiment was aroused, resulting in an excellent new institution in Providence known as Butler Hospital.

Eleven of her memorials have recently been republished in the series POVERTY, U.S.A. under the title, *On Behalf of the Insane Poor.* The details they reveal, such as the above incident, are almost unbelievable. Surely, one thinks, such things could not have happened in my town! I thought so, too, until I visited the old City Farm in Bangor, Maine, and climbing up a steep flight of stairs into the attic found under the roof a long line of cages, far removed from heat, where mentally ill persons used to be confined; then down in the cellar I saw even more solid cages where a person inclined to be violent could be guaranteed not to escape or cause disturbance. It was evidently the common thing to house the mentally ill with the poor in jails and almshouses. Moreover, cages such as these were some of the milder methods of restraint. In the book is included a picture of a "Utica crib" in which a woman was confined in an Illinois institution for fourteen years.

The debt society owes to the work of Dorothea Dix is incalculable. In 1843 when she presented her first memorial there were only thirteen institutions for the mentally ill in the United States. In 1880 when she ended her active career there were 123, 75 of them state owned. She herself had helped to found over twenty of them.

The first one was at Trenton. Her memorial soliciting a hospital for the insane in the state of New Jersey was presented to the legislature in 1845. But then came the most dangerous days of all. She never entered the halls of legislation nor approached the legislators in their homes or lobbies. A small room was usually set aside for her. She worked indefatigably, writing articles, holding interviews, urging, challenging. Sometimes she would entertain up to twenty legislators in the living room of her boarding house. At last the bill passed

186

unanimously. Then she was asked to give advice on the site and plans. Oh, she had wonderful ideas! A high hill, a long stone building with white columns, bright airy rooms. She returned often to Trenton, and when it was finally built so much was it a part of her flesh and blood that she would always think of it as her "firstborn child."

Almost as a twin came the hospital at Harrisburg. When she started her travels in Pennsylvania there was no state hospital, yet she found more than a thousand mentally ill patients in county prisons and poorhouses. Not only did she condemn the same shocking treatment she had found in other states, but she began her long effort to reform the prison system which herded together every type of lawbreaker without distinction of age, color or degree of misconduct. Many of her observations on prison life are as pertinent today as when they were written.

The only hospital which she allowed to bear the name of Dix was one near Pittsburgh. Its name of Dixmont, however, she insisted, did not honor herself but her grandfather, Dr. Elijah. She herself chose its site, on a high hill outside the city with trees, broad fields, a wide view. It is still called Dixmont.

Many of the hospitals were dear to her, like these three and the Army and Navy Hospital in Washington, later known as St. Elizabeth's. But always the one she loved best was her "firstborn" at Trenton. Here through the years rooms were kept for her disposal, and they were as near to home as any place except Boston.

Not that she used them often, for she was constantly traveling. 10,000 miles ... 20,000 ... 60,000 ... Her letters reveal distances which sound almost incomprehensible. For a strong man the tale of her travels would sound like an Odyssey. For a frail woman starting such a career at age forty, constantly battling a chronic lung disease and enduring a body riddled with malaria, it is a tale defying belief. Railroad, stagecoach, river boat, horseback, carriage, farm wagon, ox cart—she rode them all, from the Atlantic coast to the Mississippi and beyond. One account of her travels which I found, covering twenty months from 1845 to 1847, fills three closely written pages and includes the names of 411 cities and towns she visited, some of them many times. Letters to friends reveal untold distance and hardships.

"Jail to jail," she wrote George Barrel Emerson of Boston, her former associate in teaching, "prison to poorhouse, through almost trackless forests, through swamps. Often the way lies through a wilderness, traced by slight cuts on trees, houses fourteen or twenty miles apart, if they can be called houses, single rooms of logs and a stone chimney. Four nights out of nine able to find such rest as I could in two chairs, wide chinks between logs. Cold. Far from well. Finally I discharged a horse, driver, and took the stage for eighty miles. . . ."

It was buried in such accounts that I found the dramatic incident with which I like to start a biography. It happened in Michigan. A young farmer boy was driving her in a rickety carriage through the wilderness to a distant town. Discovering that he was carrying pistols because of the prevalance of bandits, she made him give them reluctantly into her keeping. Sure enough, in a lonely spot a man rushed into the road, seized the horse by the bridle, and brandished a pistol.

"Stop! Don't reach for your gun, or I'll shoot!"

"I—I ain't got no gun!" quavered the boy. "She took 'em."

"Who?"

"The woman in there. My passenger."

"Woman!" The man burst into raucous laughter. "You're lying." Warily he approached the window, peered inside. "By God, it *is* a woman—and alone! Hand over your purse."

Dorothea addressed him quietly. "Are you not ashamed, my good man, to rob a woman? I have but little money, and I need it to defray my expenses in visiting prisons and poorhouses and giving to charity. But if you have been unfortunate, I will gladly give you some."

"My God!" exclaimed the man, staring at her. "That voice!"

In the Philadelphia penitentiary he had heard the woman talking to some of the prisoners in an adjoining cell. He would have known her voice anywhere. They could go on, he told them. No, said Dorothea, not yet. She wanted to give him money, to support him until he could get honest employment.

"Oh, no—no, I couldn't—"

But she insisted, "You might be tempted to rob someone else." The boy heard the clink of coins. "Goodbye, my good man, and God bless you."

Knowing Dorothea, I found the reported incident completely credible.

Her reform work was by no means confined to the United States. All over England, Scotland, Europe, she traveled, probing into asylums and jails, making her keen analyses and recommendations. The story of her manipulation of the higher echelons of British government reads like a stage drama. Through its action she revolutionized the treatment of the insane poor in Scotland. She dared to seek an audience with the Pope and shocked him with details of the appalling treatment of the mentally ill in the shadow of the Vatican.

"And did thee really kneel and kiss his hand?" a Quaker friend inquired later.

"I most certainly did. I revered him for his saintliness." In ensuing months she made sure that he had fulfilled his promises of corrections.

She visited hospitals in Venice, Trieste, Corfu, Smyrna, Constantinople. Here Dr. Hamlin, President of Robert College, wrote of her visit, "Miss Dix made the impression at Constantinople of a person of culture, judgment, self-possession, absolute fearlessness in the path of duty, and yet a woman of refinement and true Christian philanthropy."

She went to Scutari looking for Florence Nightingale and was bitterly disappointed to find her away. Throughout her journey along the Black Sea she had hoped to meet her, and only gave up hope when she started up the Danube for Pesth. They were never to meet, these two women who did more to alleviate the miseries of sick human beings than any others in their century.

Almost no human need was outside the scope of Dorothea's concern. She worked to establish orphanages, schools for the deaf and blind. She provided life boats for sailors at Sable Island, shipwrecked by the terrible storms of the north Atlantic.

I followed her to Washington to retrace some of the most intensely grueling periods of her life.

At St. Elizabeth's Hospital overlooking the city is the small desk she used when writing the bill establishing this institution, first known as the Army and Navy Hospital, which has become one of the foremost institutions for the mentally ill and the training of psychiatric workers in the world. She literally badgered the government into making an appropriation for this hospital. One room, known as Miss Dix's room, contained the immense bed she used when staying there. The Director's room, which was once part of her apartment, now contains this desk on which she penned the basic law adopted by Congress for the organization of the institution.

She was not so fortunate with some other crusades in the city. During the early 1850s, seated at just such a modest desk in the Congressional Library, she labored to secure the passing of a bill allotting twelve million acres of Western land as a permanent fund for work with the mentally ill. Year after year she worked, from one session to another, struggling to gain supporters, frustrated again and again. President Fillmore was her firm friend and backer in the enterprise, and the correspondence between them was indicative of a warm understanding. A hundred years later the belated discovery of such missives was extravagantly headlined as "love letters found," but, though expressive of mutual affection and admiration, they were never that. Unfortunately when the bill was finally passed by a large margin in 1854, Fillmore was no longer president. It was vetoed by President Pierce, the greatest disappointment of her life.

Washington was also the scene of what she considered another bleak adventure, her years as Superintendent of Nurses during the Civil War, serving from 1861 to 1865, in all that time never taking a single day of rest.

This is not the work I would have my life judged by, she was to confess.

If she was unpopular during those years, it was because she was too much the perfectionist, too strict in her regulations, so accustomed to authority that she sometimes failed to delegate responsibility. It was these qualities that Dr. Elizabeth Blackwell criticized. Perhaps her rules for her nurses were a bit overdrawn. She insisted that the applicant must be at least thirty, a plain looking woman, with no bows, no curls, no jewelry, and, what hurt most, no hoopskirts! Yet many of her nurses, like Mary Holland and Louisa May Alcott, were bold in her defense. In fact, Louisa became one of Dorothea's most ardent admirers. In her book *Hospital Sketches* she recorded the time when she was sick in the building to which she had been assigned and Dorothea had taken time to visit her every day.

It was usually the lax and incompetent doctors and other officers who objected to what they considered her meddlesome insistence on cleanliness and healthy care for sick soldiers. And as the war progressed she let her keen judgment of character and innate sense of humor triumph over the puritanical rigidity of her rules for nurses. Secretary of War Stanton was always her keen supporter, and the historian Lossing said of her, "Like an angel of mercy she labored day and night for the relief of suffering soldiers. . . . The amount of happiness that resulted from the service of this woman can never be estimated."

She was eighty when she was finally forced to retire to her rooms in Trenton Hospital; she continued her work of travel and visitation to the end. Her concern for the prisoner and the mentally ill was to her death her passionate goal of involvement. As she had once expressed it in the midst of her grueling travels:

"If I am cold, they also are cold;
  If I am weary, they are distressed.
  If I am alone, they are abandoned."

It was after the book was written that I went to Trenton Psychiatric Hospital to lecture to the staff, and the rooms she had occupied were no longer there. When the new building was planned, they tried to keep intact her apartment over the front portico, but the price proved prohibitive. However, there are many reminders of her which they hope one day to incorporate in a Dix museum—the desk she used, her writing case, the sampler she was working on at the time of her death. The writing desk contains two quill pens, an ink bottle, a seal and a napkin ring. One interesting object is a crude wooden stool, bearing this inscription: "This stool was made and used by Robert Burns in his school days and was given by his brother to Miss D. L. Dix at the time of her visit to Ayr, Scotland, and was presented by her to John W. Ward, Supt. of Trenton Hospital from 1876 to 1907." Another interesting reminder is a great yew tree which, legend has it, grew from a sprig brought by Dorothea from the churchyard in England where Gray's *Elegy* was written.

And of course there is her portrait. Though she was strangely averse to all kinds of publicity and repeatedly refused to have people write her story, such portraits hang in some of the great hospitals of the nation and in many public places. The likeness on the jacket of the book is copied from a portrait in the Boston Athenum. Others, especially the one at Harrisburg, reveal something of the strength and determination which characterized her later days.

The secret of this strength and of her vast accomplishments? She was a soul obsessed by a magnificent dream. She saw vast human need and wherever she saw it she had to try to meet it. She was indeed one of those rare souls who "have miles to go before they sleep."

She did sleep finally, at age 85, after some years in that apartment in Trenton Hospital which she always called her "firstborn child." She was laid to rest in Mount Auburn Cemetery in Cambridge, Massachusetts. I was able to go there and see the place where she lies. It is very beautiful, very simple. A small stone marks the place, as modest and unpretentious as she herself was all her life. She had asked that there be only two words on the stone, Dorothea L. Dix. No date, no tribute. Nothing to show that in the years she lived she changed the whole philosophy of mental illness and its treatment, erected life-giving monuments of healing in half the states of the nation, freed thousands of human beings from cells and cages and dungeons, pioneered in prison reform, served her country with tireless zeal in a time of crisis.

The funeral service too was very simple. A clergyman spoke briefly on the text, "I was an hungered, and you gave me meat. . . . I was in prison, and you visited me." A poem she loved, "At Last," which her friend John Greenleaf Whittier had sent her in manuscript and which had been found under her pillow, was read, a testimony to the religious faith which had guided her all through life. It was just as she would have wanted it, as simple as the bonnet and shawl, the unadorned dark dress with its fluff of white at the throat which she had worn entering cells and dungeons, palaces and halls of state, and which had absorbed the dusts and muds and cinders of the length and breadth of two continents.

I was glad that close by were beautiful gardens that she would have loved, for she was all her life a keen lover of beauty and a naturalist of no mean talent. It was almost as if the *Garland of Flora* which she had created in her book long ago had come to life here, close to her resting place.

There were innumerable tributes, resolutions of distinguished bodies and heads of state, glowing newspaper eulogies. But none could equal the simple words of her old friend Dr. Charles Nichols, long the superintendent of St. Elizabeth's:

"Thus has died and been laid to rest in the most quiet unostentatious way the most useful and distinguished woman America has yet produced."

ADVENTURES IN PRESENT DAY COURAGE

INTRODUCTION

"**C**hoose the close at hand, the here and now for your subjects," English teachers used to warn us would-be writers. "Write about things and places and people you know from actual experience."

I have consistently disregarded this advice. There were the plays, almost all seventy of them about biblical subjects. There were the novels, all concerned with persons and events far removed in time and place and demanding meticulous research to even approximate the accuracy of first-hand experience. There were most of the biographies. India, Palestine, Egypt, England, a gamut of time and space stretching back through three thousand years and halfway around the world! Forty years of writing, for instance, and still I had produced no book, hardly a word, about my own state of Maine, which has proved such a rich and profitable source of material for many writers. Why did I so consistently shy away from the close at hand, the here and now? Possibly because I followed the path of least resistance in which one project led naturally into another—a request for another play or biblical novel, that first trip to India which resulted in three more and as many books, a telephone call from a new editor.

But at least three of my biographies feature persons within my own time range and cultural environment, though I traveled across the ocean to write about one of them. Even they demanded intensive research in areas of which I had little knowledge. One, my only book about a Maine subject, except for Dorothea Dix, involved a study of the state's history, wilderness areas I had never before visited, the processes and lore and language of lumbering. The other two explored concerns in which I was already profoundly interested.

Disability. Rehabilitation. The problems and defeats and triumphs of the heroic handicapped. I had walked humbly in the wheel tracks of Dr. Mary, marveling at her faith and courage. Now I was privileged to follow two others along the same rough, uncharted trail. It was a humbling, chastening, exalting experience. It demanded much more medical and technical knowledge than I had acquired through Mary, much more empathy and vicarious struggle after faith and spiritual fulfillment. I invite you to relive these lives with me.

9

DR. FRED J. PRITHAM: 'THE BIG-LITTLE WORLD OF DOC PRITHAM'

There was an old doctor up in Greenville, Maine, which we had visited often during my husband's superintendency and where we had once spent a summer vacation. There had been articles about him in major magazines. Minister friends who had preached in the church there had regaled us with tales of his exploits, and for years I had felt that he would be a good subject for a book.

"No," my husband had discouraged me, "that's not your line. For one thing you wouldn't be able to handle the language of that rough lumbering country."

But there came a time when such warnings left me undeterred. Certainly the backwoods idioms of my native Maine would be no harder to research than the vagaries of Hindi and Tamil and Malayalam! I wrote to Doc. "I'm not interested," was the substance of his brief reply. But his letter, terse though it was, did not sound absolutely final. I wrote again. Surely, I suggested, his experience might inspire some adventurous young doctors to fill the dire need for medical service in our neglected rural communities. Did he not think that personal reluctance for publicity might be worth sacrificing in such a cause? This time his reply was even more brief and terse. It contained one sentence.

"I will cooperate."

My husband Elwin and I made an introductory trip to Greenville in the spring of 1969, marveling anew at the beauty of this north Maine country, stopping some seven miles out of town to feast our eyes on twenty-two mountains marching along the horizon, again at Indian Hill Farm for our first view of Moosehead Lake, which Thoreau described a century and more ago as "a suitably wild-looking sheet of water, sprinkled with small low islands, covered with shaggy spruce and other wild wood." Turning left at the Indian Store in Greenville we traveled about a mile, and there on the right next to the Methodist Church was a square, rather austere house with pyramidal roof, double bay windows at either side, its outer walls covered by gray asphalt shingles. Beside the front door, small but visible from our car, was a weather-beaten sign depicting an ancient horse and buggy, under it the words, "F. J. Pritham, M.D." It was spring, yes, April, but the snow was still so high around the house you could hardly see the windows. Just so it had stood almost without change, save for the shifting of the seasons, since Doc and his wife Sadie had moved into it after their wedding in June, 1906.

Later I got a priceless glimpse of this event in their wedding pictures. It showed a slender graceful figure with slightly angular but attractive features, long white gown gathered into a high ruching at the neck, full in waist and sleeves but tapering to tight narrow lines at the sixteen-inch waist and in the long cuffs, skirt wide and full and sweeping the floor; beside her, seated stiffly in an ornately carved chair, a small grimly sober male, hair meticulously and sleekly parted, mustached lips unsmiling, glistening boots firmly planted on the floor, neat white bow tie and well-pressed best suit, models of the 1906 proper bridegroom's attire. Since he would seldom be seen in such conventional garb during the next six decades, it was well that he was thus preserved for posterity.

When Doc came to the door that April day, a stooped, gnomelike little figure, aged nearly ninety, my heart sank. True, ruddy cheeks and keen eyes belied his years, but a certain gruffness of manner and that terseness of expression which had characterized his letters gave scant promise of easy communication. Could I possibly extract from this shriveled, close-mouthed little has-been all the information I would need?

We went into his offices on the left of the hall, two rooms

200

whose contents, I was to discover, were as revealing of Doc's personality as his open-necked plaid shirt, work pants, high thong-laced boots. They contained the low folding cot bought in 1906 from the Methodist minister for seventy-five cents ("A sensible gadget, down close to the floor, worlds ahead of those miserable high iron contraptions! Children would gladly jump up on it when you wanted to feel their tummies or look at a sore toe!"); the table made out of a medical supply box, Lilla Clark's oilcloth contributed sixty-five years before still covering it; the medicine cabinet made by Wendell Hubbard; the two worn Windsor chairs bought second-hand ("cussed uncomfortable!"); the battered black bag and back-pack which had facilitated the jumping of trains and treks through mud and slush, over snow and ice—all remaining almost unchanged for those sixty-five years.

Close-mouthed? A has-been? He was as keen as one of his scalpels, as contemporary as salt and pungent spices—though both of the latter had for years been taboo in his diet! As he rambled on coherently and in pithy detail about his early life I tried to scribble notes. Then, wonder of wonders, he produced a loose-leaf notebook of about 175 pages containing a most wonderful array of incidents covering perhaps the first half of his life. It was a hodgepodge, incomplete, disconnected, as rough as uncut diamonds, but the jewels were there, waiting to be shaped and polished. I could hardly believe my good fortune. If only all my biographees had been so considerate! It is now carefully treasured along with other resource materials in the special collections department of the University of Maine Library.

While lecturing on *Palace of Healing* and revising *Lone Woman* for publication, I found time for researching the new project. The book must be the story not only of an unusual man's life, but of one of the world's most beautiful and fascinating regions, of human adventure and history involving Indians, explorers, lumbermen, sportsmen, of a fast vanishing era. For Doc's ninety years had spanned the transition from horse and buggy to airplane, axe and hand saw and peavey to huge impersonal mechanization, operations in remote cabins and lumber camps to sterile surgery in fine hospitals, a little wilderness town "two hundred miles from nowhere" into one of the lush pleasure resorts of the country.

201

A visit to Bowdoin College in Brunswick, where Doc graduated from medical school in 1905, yielded valuable material: the roster of his seventeen classmates, the subjects he studied during the four years, his senior thesis based on his experience at a school in clinical obstetrics in Boston and entitled "Labor Abnormalus, Fredericus Johannine Pritham." The choice of an "abnormal" case was typical of his approach to life, for even in these days he bore the marks of a maverick.

"If I were you, Pritham," advised one of his professors when he was looking for a place to practice, "I would get away from the city and go just as far into the wilderness as possible."

Fred did not resent the inference that he looked and acted like the farm boy he was. In fact, he would have been gratified that the advice bore another implication: that already he bore the marks of a nonconformist.

I never did visit that salt water farm near Freeport, Maine, on the shores of Casco Bay, where Fred spent his boyhood, but his descriptions in the notebook were graphic. Those early years were a dress rehearsal for the three-generation heroic drama in the vast north country. Spreading hay, milking cows and driving oxen before he was seven; learning to swim, skate, scull and hunt ducks in homemade "floats," develop self-reliance in lonely sorties on the bay which except for its bitter taste, its salt-laden marshes and clam flats and seaweed might have been a big inland lake; yes, even probing the mysteries of surgery when at the age of four after amputating the end of his brother Harry's finger when they were chopping pumpkins he had watched curiously as Dr. Twitchell had shortened the bone a bit to obtain flap to cover the end of the finger; when later, after splitting his leg open on a rusty scythe, he had lain on the kitchen table and stared with fascination as his mother sewed the flesh together with stitches as neat and even as in the hem of her pink calico dress. A hundred times in the next three-quarters of a century he would recall the incident when he took needle and thread in hand to perform a suture, and every nurse who worked with him would marvel at his neat fine stitches.

In June and July of 1969 my husband and I spent a month in the Greenville area, living in a cottage on Wilson Pond, while I explored Doc's big and little worlds firsthand. It was the first time Elwin had been able to accompany me on a research expedition, and we both welcomed the opportunity. While he his days fishing for salmon, lake trout and togue, I drove into town and fished for information. I was glad I had better luck than he did!

Doc's little world was not hard to conquer. The square house with its furnishings almost unchanged, the town with its long main street and few offshoots, the Crafts Building on the corner where he had had his first office and watched his first river drive, the old Y.M.C.A. building down by the lake where on the top floor he had had his first operating room, the old and new hospital buildings on the main street, the railroad which had long been the connecting artery with the outside world and, dominating all the town's life, the lakeshore—all could be compressed into a half hour's circuit. But his big world—that was another matter.

I tried to envision it. Taking the ski lift as far as it went, I climbed to the top of Squaw Mountain, looked over the dozens of lakes and miles of unbroken forest. We took many trips by car up the shores of fifty-mile-long Moosehead, to Grant Farm near which Sadie had once gotten lost; to Rockwood and Kineo, the stark headland which had furnished the ancient Indian tribes with its treasures of flint; to the roaring sluices of Ripogenus; to Brassua Lake where Doc had performed his first operation in a lumber camp.

I assembled an album of thirteen geological maps which were to prove invaluable in tracing Doc's incredible travels by horse, boat, train, skates, car, lumber wagon, snowmobile and hundreds of miles by foot. Even hiring one of Greenville's small planes and flying over the wilderness of lakes and mountains, circling his big world of more than 5,000 square miles, is like trying to sense the wonder of the Taj Mahal through the monocle of an airplane window. For it was not just an expanse of little towns, blue lakes and green forests. It was depth as well as length and breadth, time as well as space, the terror of changing seasons, the passing of eras. In fact it was almost a century of a man's life. The only way I could see it was in trying to live that life with him.

Working together for hours at the tape recorder, we reenacted the drama of those sixty-five years. I went with him painstakingly through the precious notebook, and he embellished each incident with further details—names of persons, descriptions of places, of horses, boats, cars, snowmobiles, lumber wagons, weather conditions, numbers of miles traveled, cases treated, operations—his nonogenarian mind as keen as when he had picked out the words with two fingers on his old typewriter. It was a saga of incredible courage, ingenuity, devotion to duty, enthralling adventure. Doc's Hippocratic creed was simple. It had been impressed on him in his youth when he had acted as assistant to Dr. Gray in Freeport.

"It's a doctor's business," he had been told sternly, "to go where he's called, come hell or high water." After coming to Greenville he had been forced to revise his evaluation of a doctor's duty by only a few pertinent phrases. *It's a doctor's business to go where he's called, come hell—yes, or fire, rain, snow, mud, fog, wind, ice—as well as high water.*

My lumbering research proved invaluable. I could follow Doc into his first camp on Brassua Lake where he had found a man lying in a bunk groaning, on his hand a sore fast developing into a carbuncle, picture the scene as Fred cut into the flesh and removed the ugly mass of inflamed tissue, the lumberman sitting on the "deacon seat" as stoically motionless as the split half of log under his solid buttocks, lips not motionless but summoning the aid of the loggers' entire roster of saints. I could tuck Fred into his bunk between the thick spread as neatly fitting into the woodsman's life as the moss chinked into the cracks at the bunk's head. I could color the narrative with some of the popular woodsmen's ballads immortalized by such writers as Holman Day.

Doc always felt far more at home in red flannel shirt and mackinaw, wool socks and moccasins or high boots than in the conventional suit his colleague Dr. Hunt considered appropriate for his professional status, and he wore them almost constantly. This informality of dress was also unpopular with some of his more affluent patients, like the wealthy woman he visited during the grueling influenza epidemic of 1918. She expressed her disapproval of his unprofessional appearance in no uncertain terms.

"Good," snapped Doc, his patience stretched taut by two months when he had barely slept or eaten, his only rest in naps, on a boat, on his horse's back, in a lumber camp bunk or on a floor in a blanket. "If that's the way you feel, then you're not in very serious condition. I'll go and attend some of my patients who are." And he walked out.

Doc cared little about such criticism, even occasional ridicule. Once he attended a big Masonic affair dressed in conventional evening attire. "Oh, look!" someone whispered. "There's Doc Pritham, and he's still wearing his moccasins—*with a tuxedo*!" But before the evening was over, sure enough, he was called out to go dashing off somewhere into the woods, tuxedo and all, where patent leathers would have been far more *de trop* than moccasins in a ballroom.

He was as immune to the crudities of the lumber camps and other wilderness habitats as to criticism—yes, and to their bedbugs. It was during another epidemic, smallpox this time, that he accompanied a physician from the health bureau in Augusta into some camps to assist in vaccinations.

"Hope you're in good form and fit to travel?" inquired Doc. Of course, was the blithe, slightly contemptuous reply. It was a normal trip for Doc, boat to Lily Bay, mail truck to Kokadjo, hired car to Chesuncook Dam and Ripogenus, a hike some fifteen miles to a camp beyond Sowbunge Mountain. Not for the visitor. During the last of the trek he was making little more than a mile an hour.

But he encountered worse discomfiture than sore muscles. At one camp he was enjoying the fine dinner of delicious baked beans which the skilled cook set before them—until said cook started to replenish the dish. As he tipped the big iron kettle, out with the beans plopped a big fat lizard. Even some of the lusty drivers, contemptuous of the foaming furies of Ripogenus Gorge, looked a bit sick and, with the visitor, headed for the door. Not so Doc. The beans had tasted good and, as he expressed it, no darn lizard would make him waste them. He helped himself to more.

Through the years he performed many operations in such lumber camps and other wilderness shelters. Henrietta Bigney, a nurse who had worked with him, told me of one such incident when, on a bitter cold night they had trekked for miles along railroad ties, then traveled by truck for six or eight miles, as far as the tote road was passable, then ridden in a pung for ten miles to a lumber camp, arriving at six in the morning.

"Can't be moved," Doc told Henrietta tersely after examining the patient. "Appendix might rupture. Can't be prepped, either. You get the ether ready while I get the stuff boiled up."

He returned from the cook's camp carrying two pie plates, one over the other, in which he had boiled his instruments. She had heard of other such emergency procedures. One of the plates would hold his instruments, the other his sterile goods. Both were at a minimum. The little leather kit which he used for wilderness cases was not much bigger than a manicure case. It contained pinch forceps, needle holder, catheter, scissors, artery clamp and six knives. There was a flap for needles and suture materials. Sterile pads were individually wrapped.

Henrietta was appalled. How on earth could he operate under such conditions! No table! The narrow space between a bottom and top bunk! Almost no light! But obediently she administered anesthetic, watched while Doc hung a lantern at the head of the bunk, scrubbed with steaming water and strong soap in a tin washbasin, and using his head mirror as a reflector performed the operation. She remained with the patient, and he made a quick and complete recovery. Doc left for Greenville immediately to attend some other urgent cases. How did he get there, she wondered. Walk?

I climbed up to the top floor of the old Y.M.C.A. building where from 1912 until the new hospital was built in 1918 Doc had performed most of his operations. Before coming to Greenville he had had neither training nor experience in surgery. For his first appendicitis case, about 1913, a doctor was summoned from Bangor. Doc assisted. A short time later a man came in at night in desperate condition. No sending to Bangor for a surgeon this time! The job had to be done at once. So of course he had to do it. It was a pus case, and drainage was necessary. The patient made a good recovery.

"Weren't you scared?" someone queried later. "Your first major operation?"

Doc's reply was typical. "No. Why? I just went in, saw what needed to be done and did it."

He had soon developed a skill equal to any emergency, whether in hospital, wilderness cabin or lumber camp. Fortunately, in addition to medical knowledge commensurate with that of most doctors of his day he possessed boldness, imagination, a vast amount of common sense and keen ingenuity. Henrietta Bigney was not the only nurse who gave vivid descriptions of Doc's techniques in the operating room. He was as independent in surgery as at the bedside. He abhorred the rubber gloves available at that period, heavy and cumbersome. Instead, after scrubbing he would use a hand lotion somewhat resembling shellac. It never slipped off and never tore. Dandy! He often carried it in his pack for emergency operations in the wilds. He never wore a mask but saw to it that there were no germs flying about in the vicinity. Never sneezed, kept his mouth shut. Always kept his cap on. Often, in those days before adjustable tables, being of short stature, he stood on a stool to operate. And his motions were so swift that only the most efficient nurses could keep pace with him. Except for rare exceptions—the incompetent, the slow, the super-sensitive—the nurses who trained or worked under him became staunchly loyal devotees. One of these, Nellie Morrell, when living later in Portland, brought her daughter back to Doc for an appendectomy.

"I just can't have her done down here," she thought. "I must get her back to Dr. Pritham." Much later, when the daughter had her children she was living in Connecticut, where the most skilled medical service was available. But did she take advantage of it? No. It was Doc who delivered her babies.

That backpack of his! I examined it with delight, a wicker basket made locally which Doc could strap on his back. It was fitted with a cardboard tray which he filled with medicines; then on top of that he would throw in whatever he might need, perhaps a spare pair of stockings or mittens or a sweater, strap it on, and away he would go. He carried it on all his trips which involved walking, showshoeing, any type of journey he made without a horse, car, snowmobile, or boat . . . and always on the railroad trains. He could not have managed in those days of limited transportation without the railroads. He rode them as a passenger, jumped them, dropped from them, climbed their iron ladders, pumped their jiggers, helped work their hand-cars.

Once a new brakeman called down from the cupola excitedly to the conductor. "Hey, I just saw someone climbing up over the side of a car. He came running toward us, like a goat, with something on his back!"

The conductor laughed. "So? That's just Doc Pritham carrying his medicine pack and maybe snowshoes. He's likely to come aboard anywhere. Just open the window and let him in."

The train had been going full speed. "How in thunder did he do it?"

"When you can do that," the conductor replied dryly, "you'll be a real train man."

There was no dearth of such anecdotes. They came to me

from a hundred sources—nurses, fellow doctors, people whom Doc had delivered, tourists he had treated, lumbermen, sportsmen with whom he had hunted ducks or deer, ministers in the Methodist Church whose paths he had shoveled and salaries he had paid, letters from patients and friends who lived far from Greenville. It seemed as if everyone I met knew Doc and had some tale to share.

There was the story of his being mistaken for a guide on one of the pleasure boats frequented by sportsmen. "Here, guide," a city fisherman bound for a sporting camp addressed him peremptorily, "please change the water in our pail of live bait."

"Sure," replied Doc agreeably, and did so.

"Thanks," said the sportsman, and handed him a half dollar.

"Thank *you*," replied Doc, slipping the coin in his pocket. When they reached the camp and discovered their mistake, the visitors were chagrined. Not Doc. He felt highly complimented. He was constantly being mistaken by summer visitors for a guide or woodsman. Why not? He was both. Even the unmistakable skepticism with which prospective patients eyed his unprofessional appearance disturbed him not a whit. They usually changed their minds.

For instance, there was the woman who had been summering on the Allagash. Answering a frantic telephone call from the sick woman's husband, Doc met her with his boat at Rockwood halfway up the lake. Having walked across the Carry from Round Pond to Caucomgomook Lake, then ridden in an odorous supply boat to the head of Moosehead, followed by sixty miles in a car over a bumpy road, she must have suffered the torments of hell. Doc made her a bed on the top of the engine box, placing her above the heat of the engine and amidship, then opened the engine just enough to time the rise and fall of the boat with the waves. "How are you riding?" he asked once.

"It's like heaven," she murmured. "At last—warm and comfortable."

At the hospital Doc diagnosed acute appendicitis and advised immediate surgery. The man looked his shock. Entrust his wife to this little backwoods runt in work shirt and sneakers? "We'll take her to Boston," he said abruptly.

About one in the morning Doc received another frantic call. The woman was worse. Would Doc come and operate? Doc would. He removed a gangrenous appendix, also a suppurated gall bladder. The woman made an excellent recovery. When the man bade Doc goodbye, his eyes expressed only the most grateful and profound admiration. It was one instance out of many.

If I was asked once, I was asked ten times, "Have you heard the story about the time Doc's snowmobile went in the lake?" I had at least ten versions of it. Doc's, chronicled in his notebook, was the simplest, and I used it.

He had made himself a snowmobile out of an old Ford car. Fortunately I was able to secure a picture of the strange vehicle. Bringing two sisters, one with appendicitis, to the hospital from Shirley, he had to cross the lake for a mile or so, the road between the Village and the Junction being bare. The girls were having too good a time to take his advice and ride in a taxi to the hospital. The ice was rotting. As Doc neared Mile Island he saw just ahead a smooth strip of ice. Instantly he turned the runners, but there was no traction, and the vehicle ran straight ahead. It had to run on to thin ice.

"Jump!" he snapped. "Open the door and get out—quick!"

But the girls did not obey. The only door was on their side of the cab! The car broke through the ice, settling to lie on an angle in about eight feet of water. Freeing himself from the wheel, Doc doubled up and dove toward the door and, as the girls floated upward, managed to get through it, pulling one of the girls along with him. Towing her behind him he swam quickly to the front of the cab and emerged through the broken ice on top. There was only a foot or so of water above the car. Shoving the girl to the top of the cab and dropping to his knees he looked down over the side. There were the other girl's feet protruding through the doorway. Luck, indeed! He wouldn't have to dive into the cab after her. Somehow, by pulling and prying, he got her out. Expecting to have to give her artificial respiration, he was amazed when she blew out her breath with a gasp and gulped, "O-oh, it's cold!"

At the hospital he wasted no words. "Get these girls to bed and give them something hot to drink. If she hasn't caught cold, I'll be operating on one of them in the morning." When morning came she hadn't, and he did.

There were stories about Doc and his alto horn, which was almost as familiar an accessory to his person as his backpack or medicine bag. He played in every town band. Then at about age sixty-five he became a member of the high school band and loved it. Except for white hair and slight stoop, his lean short agile body blended into the group like one of themselves. Most of the boys outstripped him in height and weight but he could outrun, outblow, outmarch any one of them. For twenty years he attended rehearsals, accompanied them to games, marched in their parades. And when they presented him with an award, it was accorded a place of honor as distinctive as his medical school diploma and framed accreditations.

The church next door was as much a part of his life as his succession of cars, boats, snowmobiles. Though seldom able to attend religious services, he rendered far more sacrificial service than many of its more pious devotees, mowing its lawns, shoveling its paths, sawing wood for its furnace, baking bushels of beans for its suppers, and for more than half a century acting as church treasurer. One former minister, later the Conference treasurer, sent me the following gem from one of Doc's letters.

"We closed the year in the red both for the repair fund and the budget. But I paid all the bills so all they owe is me, and we will hope that as time runs along they will catch up. They have before and I tell them not to worry too much about it."

He saw that the ministers were paid promptly, a service more to his liking in some cases than others. Climbing the seventeen parsonage steps at eight o'clock on Monday morning, he would often say to one young pastor's wife, "Hmm! It's always a pleasure to come up here and pay a preacher who isn't lazy."

He looked after their health. One Sunday morning a young minister who suffered from an allergy saw him charge into the church, seize a bouquet of roses from under the pulpit and bear it away with indignant mutterings. "Here I'm trying to cure this man of hay fever, and some fool comes along and sticks a bunch of roses under his nose."

Oh, yes, there were enough anecdotes to fill far more than my three hundred pages—stories of his incredibly long treks; of his experiences on the lake when he more than once had to swim for shore, when it was so cold the spray froze in his wake, in raging storms, over rotten ice.

There were stories of cases ranging all the way from the tragic to the ridiculous. One was about a woman who had fallen downstairs, striking her head and peeling off a piece of scalp at least three by four inches. It bled copiously. Neighbors flocked in to render both assistance and advice until Doc could arrive by the next train. The area was dusted heavily with flour, one of the favorite woods' remedies for all kinds of wounds. No good. Bleeding continued. Then one friend, blessed with a happy impulse, tipped a jug of molasses over the wound to thicken the flour. Also ineffective. Then an old woodsman fathered the happiest inspiration of all.

"I know how to stop the dad-blamed thing!" he crowed.

Opening the stove door, he shoveled a liberal measure of hot ashes from the ashpan and added it to the other applications. As Doc commented dryly when he arrived, "that really cooked the goose." Attempting to clean and treat the wound, he found a thick layer of molasses candy, reinforced with hair and dried flour paste and clotted blood. And unless he could finish the job in the hour between trains, a fifteen-mile hike would be in prospect! Somehow he managed. Not that the hike would have fazed him, but there were patients waiting for him back home.

Many of the stories came from others than Doc, for he was no publicity hound. It was much to his astonishment and distaste that through the years he found his exploits touted in newspapers from Maine to California. He read the articles with tongue in cheek and dour amusement. "All poppycock!" he spluttered indignantly at an article appearing in a widely read national magazine. "Didn't happen that way at all. Somebody's fool daydream!" He was always a stickler for details, as I was to discover.

Once a reporter came from a national magazine for a scheduled interview, doubtless expecting the subject of his projected article to be waiting in panting but humble eagerness. It was Sadie who answered his ring.

"I've come to talk with a real *man*!" he announced with gusto.

"Sorry," replied Sadie, "but I'm afraid you'll have to talk with a real woman, because the doctor has just gotten a call and he's gone to the head of the lake to be gone for some time. I don't know when he'll be back."

The reporter gasped. This obscure little backwoods medic breaking a date which would reap him national publicity, just because of some ailing country bumpkin?

Sadie was indeed a "real woman," a personality almost as

colorful as Doc. Her roster of services to the community read like a prominent listing in "Who's Who." For almost as many years as Doc had been church treasurer she had been delegate to our Maine Methodist Conference. Anecdotes about her abounded—her mountain climbing; her night in the woods when lost and half the town had turned out to find her; her visit to Panama where their son Howard, a doctor, was employed, during which she caught a ten-pound jack in the Chagres River and hooked a big tarpon; her trip home, not by air or proper ship but, to the horror of her son, by a Japanese freighter carrying a load of coffee and oil. She had always yearned for a long cruise and had a most enjoyable week's trip. In New York there was difficulty in getting cleared, for the captain spoke little English, but he finally got a chance to land. She arrived in Bangor at five-thirty in the morning, with no train to Greenville until evening. But she hadn't come this far to content herself with a twelve-hour wait. She took a train part way and begged a ride to Greenville by the mail truck. At the village she met the connecting truck from the junction, with the postmaster driving.

"Warren, have you got room for me?" she asked.

He grinned. "Well, Sadie! What in tarnation are you doin' here, comin' by parcel post? Sure. Jump in."

As usual she arrived home from the trip unannounced. And as usual there was little sentimental fanfare of greeting. She and Doc looked at each other, discovered that all was well with each of them and nodded with quiet satisfaction.

The book was written and published and in June, 1971, there was an autographing party in the Greenville library. I have had many such parties through the years, most of them poorly attended, but none like this. Of course it was Doc's party, not mine. People came, hundreds of them—friends, patients, people Doc had delivered, treated, operated on, advised, scolded, traveled over lakes and mountains, mud and snow and rain and ice to save. We signed books, Doc and Sadie and son Howard and I, until—welcome plight for an author!—I almost got writer's cramp. There Doc sat all the afternoon, unsmiling, methodical, apparently tireless and unexcited, writing his name over and over, ad infinitum, his pen held with the delicate firmness of a scalpel, his inscription as precise and neat as the incisions which decorated many of our patrons' torsos.

The book did not set the world afire. In fact, except for a

212

paperback published locally, it is now out of print. But it certainly was a bestseller in Maine.

"Oh, I've read your book," I hear over and over, and when I ask which one, they often look surprised. "Why, the one about the old Greenville doctor!" It might well have been the only one I had written.

Doc died not many months later after a painful siege with arthritis and a short confinement in the nursing home which had once been the hospital where he had treated so many others. He had never become fully adjusted to the new hospital next door, though he had studied and approved the plans, turned the sod and participated in its dedication. He had felt more at home in the makeshift old attic of the Y.M.C.A. building than in the gleaming, sterile one-floor complex with all its gadgets. Progress by all means, and that was it! Only a fool would go lumbering with a bucksaw in these days of the colossus that could snip off a two-foot pine trunk like a pair of scissors cutting string. Oh, he had heartily approved of the new hospital. But it did not belong to his world.

Yet what was the extent of Doc's world, big and little? The five thousand miles of Maine wilderness where he labored for sixty-five years? Hardly. Witness the woman wandering through a huge outdoor art show in Buffalo, New York, stopping short before the portrait of a slender, white-haired man, eyes almost fiercely straight and steady, lips quirked in a mere hint of a smile, hands firmly grasping a big black bag, in the background a medley of logs, snow-spray, pine trees, a swirling stream.

"O-o-oh!" She turned to the artist with obvious emotion. "That is Dr. Pritham, isn't it? If it weren't for him, I wouldn't be here."

Witness Doc's son, Howard, another doctor, working in a clinic in Panama, spending a little extra time, hard to spare, in giving personal attention to a poor East Indian with twelve children, because "Dad would have done so."

Witness Howie, Doc's grandson, now in his four-year residency at a big New Hampshire hospital, who decided to be a doctor at age twelve because he admired his grandfather so much he wanted to be like him.

"Grandpa would do this . . . or that," his wife Ellen wrote me that she had often heard him say. Then he might rush back to the hospital after hours to see a patient, or deny himself an extra hour of skiing to play with his small son, or even make an important decision determining their whole future.

And perhaps—who knows?—some other young person who reads the saga of Doc's life may be challenged to leave the world of big city hospitals and specialization and high profits for the opportunities of pioneering and adventure which still exist in vast areas of human need.

10
ROGER ARNETT: 'HANDICAP RACE'

At first it seemed just another of the many letters expressing an interest in Dr. Mary Verghese and a desire to learn more about her continuing life. But there were sentences which not only aroused my curiosity but stimulated my imagination. For it was written by another victim of paraplegia.

"My back was broken in an auto accident in 1931," Roger Arnett wrote in July 1965, "when there was very little hope held out that such a person could live a year. But I was fortunate. After two-and-a-half years of floundering I went back to college, married, adopted and raised three children, worked, and am still going pretty good at fifty-seven years of age. I owe much to my parents, doctors, and above all my good wife, LaVerna."

LaVerna. What was she like, I wondered. What sort of woman would be willing to marry a man paralyzed from the waist down, struggle with him through all the physical and mental difficulties of paraplegia for thirty years? Had there been opposition to her marriage? Had she ever been sorry for what must have been an agonizing decision? And this man himself, what qualities had enabled him to conquer such a handicap? How had he dared to take on the responsibility of a wife and three adopted children? Questions, questions. The letter triggered them in swift succession. Arousing further curiosity was its heading: "THE METHODIST CHURCH, Ministry to the Handicapped, Roger Arnett, Minister."

"You sound as if you might have an interesting story yourself," I wrote back.

"If there's a story," he replied, "it's my wife LaVerna who has it. It's she who has shown the courage, the patience, the steadfast devotion which have made everything possible."

Though my first thought was to write her story, I soon discovered that it was Roger whose experience was the more dramatic and that he must be the central character in any book I might write. He was hard to persuade and agreed only when convinced that such a story might encourage others with similar handicaps and instill in some persons a concern for the ministry to special needs which had become his life purpose. Like Mary he insisted that I reveal all his weaknesses and failures.

"If you 'crawl into our skins,'" he wrote in November, "you will often feel you are in goats' instead of sheep's skins, as Jesus in his parable separated the bad from the good guys. LaVerna has often been embarrassed by my bitterness and frustration."

Questions went off immediately based on letters the two had sent—for Roger and his sister Vivian, for LaVerna and her sister (oddly enough with the same name Vivian), for the three adopted children. As with Dr. Mary, I tried to probe for incidents and traits of character even in early life which were basic to Roger's ultimate triumph.

"What would you say are your most outstanding traits as revealed in childhood? Illustrate with incidents. What did you want to be when you grew up? Were you especially proud of or dependent on physical strength? Did you know any disabled people, and what was your attitude toward them? Looking back, can you see ways in which unwittingly you were preparing to cope with a life of handicap?" and so on, page after page.

Roger, like Paul Brand, was communicative. Fortunately both he and LaVerna had kept diaries of their most critical years and soon tapes were forthcoming. To my delight I found his story even more dramatic than I had at first supposed. Imagine discovering that your paraplegic hero had been a noted collegiate runner with a prospect at the time of his accident of participating in the Olympics!

He was a first year student at Michigan State Normal College when the track coach noted, almost by accident, that he could run and ordered him to go into training. Roger was working his way through by a part-time job in a gas station, which permitted him only about four hours sleep in twenty-four, but he managed to eke out a few hours practice each night before going to work from eleven to seven in the morning. Running was sheer drudgery. He felt like a farm horse threshing grain on a treadmill, with aches and groans in every joint. But it did not occur to him to stop. He was not that kind of person. After two weeks he was entered in an interclass meet, and he came in second to the school's star two-miler.

"Awkward looking guy," commented one of the track squad. "Reminds you of a daddy-long-legs, but he sure can run. Who is he?"

The grueling practice continued, harder even than his summer job as shaker-out in an iron foundry in his hometown of Owosso. At the Handicap Trials of the Amateur Athletic Union in Detroit he made his first appearance on the squad. His track mates dubbed him "Abe," secretly amused by his appearance. No wonder. He felt like a scarecrow among Greek statues, overtopping most of them by half a head, reed thin, gangling, his size eleven track shoes sticking out like a skin-diver's fins. But after the race they stopped smiling: he came in third, close behind the world champion and a runner-up of national reputation.

Handicap race! As soon as I heard the words I knew they *had* to be the title. They were a perfect description of the marathons he would be running through most of his life.

By 1929 his exploits were flashing headlines across the

217

Michigan news media. It was the six-mile cross country in competition with some of the strongest eastern colleges that taxed his powers to the limit. The movement of limbs became but a reflex of his body, along with pounding heart, sweating pores, running eyes, hammering temples, near-to-bursting lungs. Yet somehow he kept going. The red haze dissolved into faces. Hands were clapping him on the shoulders. "You did it, Rajah, old boy! Bravo!" He had won the national championship for Ypsi. And by no means the least of the rewards was the approval of his teammates, which had changed the derisive "Abe" to "Rajah."

He became a college hero and began to date Alice, a senior one of the biggest "wheels"on campus. Already he was being mentioned as a certain candidate for the Olympics, to be held in Los Angeles in 1932. At the very thought the muscles of his legs flexed, his pulses quickened. Yes he wanted to go to the Olympics more than anything in the world—except, of course, to graduate with high marks and without debt, to become a teacher and to marry Alice.

In March 1931 he was entered in a race at Notre Dame. Alice, now his fiancée, was teaching in St. Joseph. Roger planned to drive her and a friend the forty miles from there to South Bend. He drove to St. Joseph on March 6, and the next morning they started, with snow predicted. It soon developed from a few lazy flakes into a snarling blizzard. The road was winding, coated in many places with ice. They crept along for what seemed like hours. A slight curve in the road seemed perfectly clear, with nothing to show that under the drift of snow there was thin ice. The car slued, the girls' screams mingling with those of the tires. Roger reached out, pushed Alice and her friend down and toward the dashboard. Then he was flung back over the seat. The car overturned, its frail top crumbling. His world reeled, exploded, fell on him, crushed him. Then mercifully he lost consciousness.

How do you probe the emotions of a person in the sudden crisis of loss, a Beethoven deaf to melody, a Milton blind to beauty, yes, or a Roger Arnett with his racing limbs forever immobilized? I asked as pertinent questions as I could formulate: "How soon did you know your back was broken? What was your reaction? Did you want to live? Was there temptation to take your own life? Were you resentful, self-pitying?"

In the hospital, after days of near death and periods of only partial consciousness, he suspected that he was partially paralyzed. It was to Norman Hagen, his college roommate, that he voiced his fears.

"Tell me, Norm. Give it to me straight. How bad am I?"

Unlike the nurses and doctors, Norm did not evade. "Bad enough so you're lucky to be alive."

"Lucky? I—I can't move my legs, Norm. Does that mean—?"

"I don't know, Rog. I doubt if the doctors do."

Roger clenched both hands. "If I can't be myself, Norm, I—I don't want to live. There's nothing to live for."

"You'll be yourself," replied Norm quietly. "Whatever happens, feller, you'll be yourself."

He went home, at first hopeful of recovery, not realizing that he had been discharged because there was nothing more the doctors could do. His parents were poor, his father a day laborer in the iron foundry, and these were depression years, but they gladly assumed the burden and expense of his care, lovingly and without complaint. Dependence on others was galling. He became morose and bitter. He blamed God—if there was a God. At first Alice's visits made life worth living. Then when she sent a letter breaking off their engagement he withdrew into darkness, had the shades drawn, refused food and for three days retreated into a netherworld. Surely his was the greatest misfortune that could befall anybody. Why had God let him live? But it wouldn't take long to remedy that. His life wasn't dependent on God. It was in his own hands, no farther away than the razor on his bedside table. Just a neat simple slash in the artery of his leg, and the irony was that he wouldn't even feel it! But, no. After three days he emerged, had the shades raised, ate the food brought him, received visitors. Not that he had experienced any spiritual resurrection; he had merely come to the conclusion that self-pity didn't do him or any others a bit of good, especially those who were sacrificing everything for his welfare.

In July he left his bed for a wheelchair, a big wooden affair bought at cost through a funeral home. It opened a new world—and new problems, functional accidents, pressure sores, need for a ramp. Grimly he determined to live as normal a life as possible, attended church, went camping with the family, even watched the National AAU cross-country run and congratulated Clark Chamberlain, the winner, knowing that this would have been *his* chance, perhaps for the Olympics. In December, ill with pressure sores and infections, he entered University Hospital to remain for six months. The doctors were surprised to find him still alive.

Back home with a Strycker frame bed, he tried with grim desperation to engage in all possible activities—sailing, swimming (nearly drowning himself), conducting the Methodist orchestra, learning to walk with braces (six feet in four minutes plus, just the time he had taken to run a mile!), even going riding with a former girl friend (discovering to his dismay that she had taken him out of pity). But there was no meaning, no planning in his movements. He was like a runner crouched at the starting line all set for a race—life? death?—waiting for a gun that never went off. Until one day...

He was sitting in the yard watching his mother hang clothes. Somehow she had always managed to make poetry out of the commonest things. She did so now, separating a sheet from a tangled mound, mating its corners, fitting it into smoothness and straightness, then, arms stretched high and wide, flinging its whiteness against the blue of the sky, almost like an act of worship. She had planted morning glories at the foot of one set of clothes posts, turning them into a cross of heavenly blue. But it was at the other set of posts that Roger stared, ugly, bare, gaunt, dead wood, like a pair of useless legs. And suddenly he faced facts. No more fooling himself, hoping for a miracle. *He was not going to walk again.* He could be one or the other of the two posts, remain dead wood, or plant something that gave a semblance of life. Not morning glories. Beautiful, but they wouldn't earn a man a living. Perhaps—pole beans?

He determined to go back to college, earn his degree, perhaps even be able to teach! The state Vocational Rehabilitation Department agreed to pay his tuition. The town Rotary Club offered to supply fifty dollars a month toward board, room, and medications.

"We'll never find the right place," worried his mother, almost hopefully. "Ground floor, wide doors, board with room, and—a woman who would be willing to see after you a little."

But they did, a rooming house for men only a block from the college, with a room on the ground floor. He could eat with the family, and, yes, Mrs. Tabor was the sort of person who would treat him almost like a mother. They had a ramp built and brought his hospital bed and Strycker frame. By meticulous planning he performed all necessary procedures without help. Swallowing his pride, he learned to welcome assistance from the other fellows in the house. They pushed him on icy days, saw that he attended sporting events, even carried him up a long flight of stairs to attend a concert. He graduated in late March 1934 with a record for the two final terms of five A's, four B's, and one D (in physical training). Only one thing made the event unusual, a letter from the President of the United States complimenting him on completing his education.

Now—to fulfill his dream of becoming a teacher. He approached the superintendent of schools in Owosso, who suggested that he open an insurance office.

"But I'm trained to teach, not sell insurance."

The superintendent hemmed and hawed. There was no opening this fall for a teacher.

"And there never will be?" probed Roger quietly. "For me, that is."

Well—surely Roger must realize the difficulties.

"You mean because I'm a cripple?"

The superintendent flushed, averted his eyes. Queer, thought Roger, how people tried to avoid mentioning your handicap? They would talk all around it, show they were

221

conscious of it by every word and gesture, yet be shocked if it was mentioned.

So—teaching was out, even though a man didn't teach with his legs. He finally got a job as bookkeeper in the welfare department, only twelve dollars a week, but a job. His father took him to work each day, lifting him in and out of the car, then driving while Roger held the heavy wheelchair on the side, thankful for the strong arm and shoulder muscles developed by work in the foundry. One day he found he could get into the car himself, a tremendous discovery. Another step to independence!

He decided that if he must do office work he must have more training. The head of the high school commercial department was glad to teach him typing and shorthand. And if he wanted bookkeeping she would recommend Miss La-Verna Bowen who was a capable teacher and had a car. His father drove him to the teacher's apartment and she came out and talked with him, agreeing to come to his home two evenings a week.

"Sounded as if she knew her business," remarked his father. "And not a bad looker."

Not a bad looker indeed! She was beautiful. But the picture Roger took back with him was not so much of a daintily slight figure, blond hair, blue eyes, and a warm but shy smile. It was of a game little person walking with an awkward limp, slender shoulders straight, obviously making the best of a long-time handicap. For some reason the sight made him feel tenderly protective. Ironic! Protectiveness? For a girl who walked with a slight limp from a man who couldn't walk at all?

Their tapes kept coming. Bless the diaries and good memories which enabled them to detail events in accurate sequence and the frankness with which they revealed their most intimate emotions! The six typed pages of questions that I sent LaVerna produced even more personal details than I had hoped for: her ordeal with polio at age six; her father's faithfulness in massaging her limbs an hour at a time three times a day, so that walking became possible; schooldays made grim by ridicule of her ungainly movements;

fierce attempts to attain perfection in pursuits not dependent on facility with limbs, croquet, piano playing, scholarship. She was a student at Central Michigan Normal School when her father arranged for her to consult a polio specialist. To her amazement he found one of her legs was two inches shorter than the other.

"But her shoulders are even," protested the family doctor. "How could that be?"

"By will power," answered the specialist with a grim smile.

Operations, excruciatingly painful, stiffened her ankle and inserted a series of wedges in the back of her knee until two inches were added to the limb. When the doctor told her to walk across the room with the cast removed, it did not occur to her to protest, though they were the most agonizing steps she had ever taken.

"LaVerna," he told her, "I have told every one of my patients to do that. You are the first one who ever did it."

In spite of warning that her diffidence and handicap would create impossible problems of discipline she became a proficient mathematics and commercial teacher. On March 9, 1931, when teaching in Owosso, she wrote in her diary, "Roger Arnett, a graduate of 1927, was in an accident yesterday, and his back was broken. He may never walk again." She thought, "I can't remember walking any differently, but here he had been a trackman and known all that glory. How can he take it! Poor boy, hope, ambition all cut short. To be half alive, half dead!"

But when she first saw him the shock of revising this picture left her breathless. Poor boy? He was not a boy at all, but a man, and a very attractive one. Hope, ambition gone? His every word vibrated with them. Half dead? She had never seen anyone more alive. Life glowed in the blue eyes, the dark, curling, wind-blown hair, the ruddy cheeks, above all in the sudden smile which illumined the rugged features like sunlight on crags of granite. And when I first saw him I understood exactly how she had felt, for thirty years later there were the same vivid blue eyes and beaming smile, the same zest for living in every line and fiber of his face.

I went out to Michigan in February 1966 to complete my research. After visiting friends in Michigan and lecturing on Vellore in several churches, I came to the Arnetts' in Belleville.

During the two weeks of Dr. Mary's visit I thought I learned much about the problems of the paraplegic. Now I found I had known almost nothing. Roger's difficulties had been legion: infections, daily struggles with colostomy and cystostomy, pressure sores and ulcers (he almost bled to death from one), the amputation of one leg, innumerable sessions in hospital with their ever-recurring operations, for removals of dead bone, of a kidney with a stone grown around it half as large as a football, of a growth in the bladder, then recently of a decayed hip socket—the most massive of all.

"Guess you'll find it a little hard to operate this time, won't you?" Roger asked his surgeon, Dr. Berry, half jokingly. "There can't be much flesh left."

"You'd be surprised," returned the doctor, but his face was grimmer than usual. "It's lucky we didn't amputate that leg any higher. We'll remove the bone and use the rest of its flesh to bring back over the hip."

"Some of you folks live in spite of us doctors," he remarked later almost wonderingly when Roger not only survived the operation but snapped back into his usual vigor of activity. It was like watching a dynamo recharging.

I had a talk with Dr. Berry who could not even remember how many operations he had performed on Roger, most of them potential killers. But it was he, not I, who asked most of the questions. What kept Roger going? Was it super ego or super *alter ego*? This ministry to the handicapped, was it inspired by religious zeal, a yen for service, pure self-achievement—or what? And this everlasting cheerfulness, was it an act or genuine? What was his source of supply—ego, faith, or just sheer human spunk? I had no answers as yet. But I knew I must find some.

With LaVerna the answers were easier. Motivation for marrying one so severely disabled? For cheerfully enduring through those thirty years the burden of his dependence—

extra washing and ironing, remodeling of clothes to fit the wearer of a brace and an amputee, medication of the frequent infections and pressure sores, cleaning up after accidents; for facing crisis after crisis with despair, hope, relief, then fear of the next one; for bearing a generous share of the family's support often by a full-time job? One had only to see them together to know the answer. The motivation was love, pure and simple.

Their romance was simple and understandable. LaVerna found Roger an eager and apt pupil, and the lessons proceeded with businesslike efficiency.

"At this rate you'll finish a whole semester in a month!" she marveled.

"I like bookkeeping," replied Roger. "Or"—his glance shot out to enfold her in a sudden blue intensity—"maybe it's just because I like my teacher."

She flushed, then felt foolish when the intensity turned into an engaging grin. He was just teasing her. But realizing he must be lonely she began yielding to his request that she stay a while and talk. Their intimacy grew. She found herself sharing with him the little hurts and deprivations of her own handicap which she had never confided to anyone else.

"I know." He was gently sympathetic. "Funny, isn't it, how being handicapped yourself makes you know how every other handicapped person feels."

When he professed his love for her she was disturbed and chagrined but deeply moved and, yes, excited. She asked her doctor, a personal friend, if a girl could be happy married to a paraplegic. "No!" he exploded, then amended, "Let me take that back. I suppose that would depend on the girl." He explained what all the difficulties might be. Following his advice she and Roger went to consult the latter's doctor who assured them that there was no physical reason why a paraplegic should not marry. Friends realizing what was happening urged her to break off the relationship before it was too late. It was her father's violent disapproval which most distressed and confused her. "That cripple! I tell you I won't have it!"

It was when she was visiting a friend in Cleveland, after

she had decided to tell Roger it was all over, that she came into the house and saw a letter from him lying on the table. She did not need to open it. She suddenly knew that she would have no more doubts or misgivings. They belonged together. She could not get back quickly enough to tell him. The shocked reactions of friends ("She can't be that crazy!" ... "Why, she'd have to support him!" ... "That wonderful teacher, turning into a nursemaid—or worse!") had no effect. Family opposition was partially if grudgingly overcome but even that would not have deterred her. Gentle, shy, unassertive she might be but the same will which had conquered the two inches kept her unswerving.

They were married on a Saturday afternoon in LaVerna's apartment. Roger insisted on standing for the ceremony. Once on his feet, he locked his braces, a despised encumbrance. LaVerna, a bare five feet tall, felt strange with his six-foot height towering over her. It was the only time in their lives they would stand side by side.

Though LaVerna slipped easily into her new role, taking his mother's place in performing the necessary services, Roger's dependence on her, both physical and financial, was to him a gnawing frustration. He resolved to minimize it. His first small triumph came in designing and having installed in her car hand controls for clutch, brake, and throttle. When he drove home for the first time, it was a "high day" indeed.

"Boy, does this feel good!" he exulted. "Now I'm really a *man* again!"

But even more galling was his financial dependence. His meager wages were a pittance beside her teacher's salary. And the new house they bought was purchased with money she had saved and inherited. His new knowledge of typing and bookkeeping while enhancing efficiency at the office opened no extra opportunities. A ditchdigger without brains was apparently less expendable than a college graduate without legs. It was finally a very simple act which helped solve the problem.

He answered a magazine advertisement offering twenty small gladiolus bulbs for a dollar. To his surprise and delight every one bloomed. It was while he was in bed recovering from a hospital session that he got the idea of specializing in growing glads. As weeks passed he studied more and more catalogs, bought more and more bulbs, became more and more excited. He remembered the two clothes posts, dead wood at one end, morning glories at the other. Well, he had planted the pole beans, covered up the dead wood with something living. Maybe he could make it blossom into something as beautiful and creative as morning glories.

He could hardly wait for spring to come. On his birthday, May 1, he hired a boy to help plant bulbs. The beds, four feet wide, went the length of the garden, a walk between wide enough for his wheelchair, so he could do his own weeding, hoeing, cutting, cross-pollinating. Near the end of the afternoon LaVerna urged him to stop.

"Not on your life!" he retorted, resolved to plant as many of the nearly five thousand bulbs as possible that day. He was still working, tired, sweaty, begrimed, when guests arrived, invited by LaVerna to celebrate his birthday. It was too genuine a surprise party.

"And I thought I was coming to visit an invalid!" joked one of his friends.

That was the beginning of the profitable business which in time was to bring Roger true financial independence. He needed more land and rented a lot two blocks away. He began crossing plants seriously, developing some rare varieties. People came to the house day and night to buy cut flowers and bouquets LaVerna made.

They adopted a boy. It was doubtful, the doctor told LaVerna, if she could ever carry a child. Dick was a ten-year-old left without a home, a thin little fellow with a generous unsmiling mouth, brown curly hair and a lost look in his big brown eyes. They loved him immediately. He was curious about the missing leg and unable to understand the paralysis. "You mean I could—could kick you in the leg, even stomp on your foot, and—and it wouldn't hurt? Honest to gosh, mister?"

"Honest to gosh," replied Roger. "But you may as well start calling us 'Mom' and 'Dad,' because it looks as if we're going to be your parents."

But LaVerna wanted a *baby*. Adoption agencies would not consider them. Finally the social agency gave them a baby to board. "Oh, no, the mother would never give him up. He will not become adoptable." There followed months of ecstasy and agony for LaVerna until finally Ronnie's mother agreed that she could not care for him and the adoption was finalized. Later they took a third child, Faye, a year younger than Ronnie, sadly abused and bound for an orphanage, a tiny slip of a girl, black eyes as brightly wary as a frightened animal's, black hair surrounding her elfin face like a halo. Of course there were conflicts and problems, especially with Dick, but with love and patience most of them were at least partially solved.

Independence! There were setbacks—a hospital session in which he nearly died, a dry season for glads. When Ronnie came and LaVerna had to give up her teaching, Roger had to get a new job. To his surprise and delight he was hired by the Bendix Aviation Company at good wages. But this was wartime and the job was temporary. They moved to Corunna, three miles away, where he could have more land, and when the plant threatened to close he determined to raise glads as his main occupation. He invested in a tractor and devised ways of getting on and off and driving it himself. He developed a new strain called White Challenge and won an American Home Achievement Award for the best new variety. During 1947 and 1948 he won nine championships.

But even this precious independence was not the end of his goals. His abounding energy flowed into two other channels—church and work with the handicapped. Appointed to the President's Committee on Employment of the Physically Handicapped, he organized groups of disabled people, fought for legislation and made many trips to Washington.

Independence? He was running a treadmill. His driving impulse to assume full support of his family had long since backfired. Watching LaVerna struggle through hours of sorting, packing, marketing, work which was a far greater burden than the teaching he had wanted to spare her, he felt trapped.

In 1948 they bought an old house with much land in Columbus, Indiana, where the growing season would be weeks longer. Here also Roger became involved with helping the handicapped, and it was the impact of such experiences that led him to a strong conviction. He wanted to work with *people.* He still cherished the dream of teaching. Surely attitudes toward the abilities of the disabled had been changing. He wrote to his alma mater, now Eastern Michigan University, and asked them about a teaching position. When the reply came in the spring of 1951, he was transported to the seventh heaven. The university was awarding him an honorary master's degree.

"It's a college job," he exulted. "It must be."

On May 1 there came a telephone call, a telegram from Ypsilanti. "One moment, please." Roger turned from the telephone, smiling from ear to ear. "It's come, darling. Wire from Ypsilanti." It had come, yes, but not the announcement of a teaching job. A stereotyped wish for a "happy birthday." It tore LaVerna's heart to see his face fall. But he did not give up hope. When they went for the award the university outdid itself in paying him honor. The eulogy dripped with honeyed phrases. But he waited in vain for the subject of his future employment to be broached. Finally he said to one of his former teachers, "Well, how about it? Did you find a job for me?"

She looked startled. "A job?" Then, after a pause, "Well, we might be able to find a part-time one some place. How—how much would you expect to be paid?"

Listen, sister, he wanted to say, *it's a job I want, not charity.*

Another daring possibility—he might become a minister. He had done everything in churches except preach. Moving back to Michigan, he was able to secure a well-paying job with the Data Processing Group at the University of Michigan's Research Center. But his dream of the ministry persisted. He took evening classes at Wayne State University in Special Education. He became a local preacher in the Belleville Methodist Church and began conference courses leading to ordination. Then in 1953 he was appointed an assistant at Glenwood Church, Wyandotte, as special minister to the handicapped. In 1957 he completed his course of study and was ordained elder, and also received his master's degree in Special Education at Wayne State. In 1961 he was appointed minister to the handicapped of the Ann Arbor District of the Methodist Church.

I might have accumulated most of these details—and did—from tapes, correspondence, newspaper and magazine articles, letters from Roger's relatives and friends, but only through these weeks of first-hand experience could the years of his ministry come alive. Not even Dr. Mary had given me such sympathetic insights into the world of the handicapped.

"Are you nervous riding with me?" Roger asked as we started on an early expedition.

I looked at his capable hands on the wheel, his super-strong shoulders, remembered how he had swung himself from wheelchair to car seat using only his arms, then folded the chair with one hand and lifted it easily into the back seat space. "No," I replied," not at all."

Still holding a full-time job, as did LaVerna, at the Willow Run Research Center, he spent many evenings and all his weekends in work with the handicapped. In addition to many personal calls he was regularly visiting fifteen nursing homes, plus several wards in Wayne County General Hospital. In three of the homes he conducted church services.

I traveled with him into many of these homes, saw the faces of a long line of idle men light up as Roger swung into view, gave them his broad smile and lifted his hand with a cheery "Hi ya, fellas!"; visited with him in room after room where he would admire patients' handiwork, listen to complaints and problems and promise to help, pass out devotional booklets, administer communion to hopelessly ill bed patients. A wheelchair, he had long since discovered, was an advantage. Entering a room he was immediately one with its occupants, *on their level*. No need to stoop to take their hands, to place an arm about a thin stooped shoulder, to look eye to eye, to speak so they could hear.

Empathy, he made me understand, was a costly business.
230

It meant personal involvement with every one of the hundreds of people to whom he ministered. And loneliness was the major ailment among the residents (he never called them inmates or even patients) in all the homes he visited. Society had outdone itself in concern for the sick, the aged, the handicapped. It had provided everything they needed— except the things they needed most, love and concern as individuals.

I read some of his diaries for the last ten years. Month after month the same names would recur, objects of prolonged concern: Lloyd Hughes, a paraplegic, father of two children and separated from his wife ... Noah, paralyzed from the neck, practicing his frog breathing and balancing on his rocking bed ... Jessie, the piano player in Ward K ... Bob, the paraplegic at Eloise who had to have both legs amputated at the hips.

"August 7. This morning I awoke at 4:30 with a deep concern for the hundreds (perhaps more than a thousand) poor souls in Building N at Eloise. I shudder at their plight. In places they are decked one over another. They go through the motions of living and still have no opportunity to live. There are rows on rows on rows with no chance of privacy. No TLC (Tender Loving Care). There isn't time."

I knew what he meant for I had walked with him through the wards at Eloise. I wished I could have been with him at Christmas time when he delivered hundreds of personal cards and bushels of apples, one to each person in all the homes and hospitals he visited.

I interviewed the many people he had inspired to do volunteer work: Ralph Ridenour, a photographic specialist who helped produce a film on Roger's work; Jim Alward, who provided musical equipment and recordings; Doris Ritter, who gave time as secretary; Barbara Hass, a church school teacher who brought her junior high pupils to one of the homes to help. The experience had wrought amazing changes in the young people. "They really *want* us," marveled one seventh grader. Some overdid their enthusiasm. One overactive participant was discovered pushing an elderly lady at breakneck pace down the hall, shouting "Whee!" The lady was as disappointed as the boy when he had to be toned down.

"He's a cool guy," the same boy said of Roger.

Never again shall I see a church or other public building with unmanageable steps for the handicapped without thinking of Roger. They affected him as the sign FOR WHITES ONLY must have affected blacks. They were a mark of segregation. For years he fought them. One triumph was a carefully designed entrance to a new church in Memphis resulting from his friendship with a Roman Catholic priest. It gave him far more satisfaction than the highest honor he received in that year of 1964, selection by the President's Committee on Employment of the Handicapped as Michigan's "outstanding example of a handicapped American."

Roger took me to visit many of the persons for whom he had opened new doors. There was Vivian Wakeford, victim of a society which with all its social and psychological insights had still not learned to distinguish between the physically and mentally handicapped. It had taken him five years and endless red tape to get her out from behind locked doors in Eloise. There was Stefan Florescu, a quadriplegic for whom Roger, with Ronnie's help, had built a ramp, inspired to get a job, marry and participate in the Paralympics. He proudly showed me plaques, medals, certificates, statuettes, all won in swimming and table tennis competitions in England, France, Spain and Japan. There was Frank Aymer. Roger was in hospital with infection when he heard about Frank, the despairing victim of an accident which broke his back, then in isolation with a staph germ. He insisted on having his bed moved into the young man's room. Frank's mother, entering the room in the special garment required for visitors to isolation patients, was amazed to find a second bed and a smiling, strangely familiar face.

"Mrs. Aymer? I'm Roger Arnett. I hope you don't mind my joining your son."

"Arnett?" Her face lighted. "The gladiolus man! If you could know how I've hoped and prayed to find you!" She had met him at a glad show, been impressed because a paraplegic could do so much, then when her only son had had an accident had tried in vain to locate him.

Roger's assistance was largely friendship and encouragement, for knowledge of paraplegia had developed at an astonishing pace since his own accident. It was enough that when he left the boy could smile, if a bit crookedly, and wave him a game goodbye.

"Hi ya, fella," Roger waved back. "See you at the race track!"

"Yeah. You said it. At the race track."

Returning home the middle of March I started writing furiously for I already had another project in view. Another trip to Michigan in October to finalize the manuscript with the Arnetts, then delivery to the publishers by the first of November. *Handicap Race* was published in October, 1967, and the Belleville church devoted a Sunday morning service to honoring Roger and LaVerna. Friends came from distant places. The aisles were full of wheelchairs. One of my most cherished colored slides shows Roger sitting in his wheelchair in the chancel, face alight with that wonderful beaming smile, framed by two glorious bouquets of gladiolas, symbols of his triumph over physical, mental and spiritual defeat.

At the reception and autographing party after the service many were there whom he had helped to a similar conquest—Clara Kelley, crippled by polio, patient for twelve years in a tuberculosis sanatorium, whose life had been brightened by a Christmas spent with the Arnetts; Vivian Wakeford and her devoted husband Gabe Wellett; the Florescus, Stefan and Carolyn; Frank Aymer, as independent as Roger in his wheelchair, with his wife and five children.

There were other autographing parties. In December the Arnetts and I were scheduled for one at the Cokesbury Bookstore in Pittsburgh. This time I was glad to fly. The weather was bad and the roads snowy and icy after a severe storm. Hardly a pleasant prospect, a three-hundred-mile drive for the Arnetts from Detroit!

"Surely they won't come," assumed the bookstore manager.

He did not know Roger. I recalled the trip he and LaVerna

had taken to California in the spring of 1964 to see Faye's new baby, traveling as many as 750 miles in a day. On the way they visited the Carlsbad Caverns, one of the spots Roger had had a lifelong ambition to see. He was taken down in an elevator in his wheelchair. While spending ten days with Faye and her husband, who was located at Camp Pendleton, Roger traveled all over the area alone, seeing everything possible, even finding a boat into which he could get his wheelchair and go deep-sea fishing. On the trip home they visited the Sequoia National Forest, the Hoover Dam, and the Grand Canyon. Here he insisted on taking one of the airplane rides down into the canyon, but when he came to enter the small plane, he could not be lifted in the door. Persisting, he was finally dragged in over the wing, an operation which raised havoc with his tender skin. But the thrill of cleaving the magnificent cavern was worth it.

"They'll come," I told the manager confidently. And they did.

One of Roger's greatest pleasures in the book derived from the letters we both received from readers, many of them disabled persons who found his life inspiring. Its publication in England and Germany added to the breadth of this correspondence. One reader in South Africa became so interested in the Arnetts that she visited them for three weeks, planning a trip especially for this purpose. Some were from schoolchildren curious to make his acquaintance. Some wanted to use the film on his work. A blind student from India who had listened to the story on Talking Books came to their house to call.

The wheels kept rolling, up and down ramps, through hospital corridors, into room after room in nursing homes.

"Right now," reported Roger's year-end letter in 1971, "I am busy delivering 4,000 Christmas letters and apples to individuals in the 28 nursing homes and hospitals."

He continued his two-fold activities full steam until retirement at age sixty from his position in the Research Laboratories, then for the next five years devoted every ounce of energy available to his ministry. But the wheels were slowing down. The hospital sessions became even more frequent and serious, four of them in one year, each one critical. He had to turn over more and more of his ministry to Ed Hoff, another paraplegic, who with his wife Mary had become his able assistant. At least the work would go on! Then one day I had a telephone call from Val, Dick's wife. Roger had gone.

Handicap Race! He had certainly run it to the end—with time, with death, with human need, with the lack of concern and the indifference of people—a far harder and more demanding race than the Olympics or any other challenge could have offered and with a victory far more satisfying. Coach Olds had defined it for him long ago and he had followed the specifications to the limit. A handicap race—where you just ran and ran until you couldn't possibly go any farther, and then you kept running some more.

11
HILARY POLE:
'HILARY'

She could not see, speak, breathe, swallow or move except for a sixteenth of an inch of mobility in one toe and a much lesser movement in another. She was certainly the most severely disabled person in England, short of total paralysis, perhaps in the world. Yet because of a remarkable electronic device she was leading a life so rich in imagination, enjoyment and actual achievement that she put an able-bodied person like me to shame.

Again it was my English friends Albert and Phyllis Jefcoate who sparked my interest in this new subject. Their son Roger, a specialist in electronics and a consultant for the disabled, had been instrumental in providing young Hilary Pole with the amazing equipment which had changed her life from one of almost complete helplessness to one of incredible blessing to thousands of people. Finding her in the hospital, where she had been incarcerated for seven years, Roger had introduced her to the electronic miracle, Patient Operated Selector Mechanisms, P.O.S.M., aptly dubbed *Possum* from the Latin "I can." The invention of an engineer, Reginald Maling, these devices were revolutionizing life for the severely disabled, making it possible for them to control their environment and operate machines using whatever residual motion they might have—yes, even the sixteenth of an inch movement in one toe!

The Jefcoates, you may remember, were responsible for my writing two other books, *Take My Hands* and *Ten Fingers for God*. So when Jef wrote to me suggesting that Hilary Pole should be next on my list, I knew this project must have priority, especially since he had already persuaded my British publishers that it was a must. I arranged with my American publishers to postpone their deadline on a book I was writing and set off for England again in October, 1971. Already I had started the process of research by learning everything possible about myasthenia gravis, Hilary's rare disease which affects the impulse between the nerves and the voluntary muscles, reading numerous articles about her and sending a barrage of questions to be answered by her and her family and friends.

You should see the itinerary Roger, who was Deputy Director of the P.O.S.M. Research Project, arranged for me! Remembering the whirlwind tour of London he had given me ten years before, mostly on foot and in the rain, I should have been prepared. Since the book must be a story of Possum as well as of Hilary, he wanted me to become thoroughly acquainted with its techniques and ministry to various types of disability. Practically every minute of every day for more than three weeks all accounted for! The second day of our schedule was typical. It read like a ship's log.

"0900 hours to Cyril Kohler, Woking,
1100 hours to Wandsworth,
1145-1230 hours Pamela La Fane,
1300 hours Hodder and Stoughton (publishers),
1500 hours to Kensington
1530 hours Christopher Jones,
    Stay night in Amersham."

Each one of these notations was accompanied by full address, including telephone number and map reference, and, in the case of Possum users, the nature of the disability.

237

Thanks to Roger's remarkable efficiency, the whole schedule for the three weeks was followed almost to the minute. No wonder with that brain and energy he was able to accomplish such scientific miracles for the disabled!

"What!" I thought with some dismay. "See all these people before having any time to interview my biographee? And with the time so short!" But I soon found that it was a wise decision. Jean, Roger's young wife, was my competent chauffeur on many of these journeys, and I was able to see the miracle at work in many forms, besides meeting some of the most courageous and inspiring people I had ever encountered. It was essential preparation for writing the book.

There was David Hyde, chief demonstrator for Possum, one of the first to be saved from depression and frustration after breaking his neck playing rugger, now running typewriters, telephones, conducting all manner of business with his blow-suck equipment, the first method devised by Maling to help the disabled control their environment. . . . Elizabeth Twistington Higgins, daughter of one of England's noted surgeons, a professional dancer until in 1953 polio had left her almost incapacitated, but, outfitted with a voice amplifier which enabled her to teach ballet, constructing sequences and coaching girls in her room, then going with them into the large Chelmsford theater to complete the instruction. . . . Betty Witham, who had spent sixteen hours a day for more than fifteen years in an iron lung, typing, seeing what she wrote, backward, in a mirror over her head. . . . Dick Boydell, perhaps the most remarkable of all, a spastic with a grimly contorted body, useless hands and arms, garbled speech. For thirty years his parents had had no communication with him, had tried to teach him without knowing whether he understood a word. Then he had gotten Possum and a typewriter. After nine days he wrote a letter to his mother. There was not a mistake, in spelling, punctuation, grammar! He proved to be a mathematical genius and became a computer programmer for Ford.

And at last after a dozen such visits I came to Hilary. At

first sight of her I felt a complex of emotions—dismay, sadness, embarrassment, pity. I stared in silence at the hunched figure lying on its side, motionless, eyes closed, skin stretched taut over sharp shoulder blades, a long tube protruding from the throat like a great umbilical cord.

"Oh," I thought, "what a tragedy, and so young! She might be a vegetable, or a statue, or—yes, even a corpse. Surely there is nothing here worthy of the word *life*!"

Then suddenly by no apparent means the room erupted into sound. Music burst on my ears. I heard a swift succession of clicks and clonks and was magnet-drawn to their source, a big typewriter with keys flicking and carrier clacking back and forth as if by magic.

"Hello." I read the last lines on a long sheet of paper. "Ples mak self home. Sit dwn. Is 2 cold 4 u? Wd like wndw closed? So gld u came."

Life? The room was filled with life, all emanating from that motionless, speechless figure on the bed. I looked at it again, noting the smoothly brushed hair, the dainty pink nightgown blending with the deep rose of the coverlet; the beautiful hands with tapering nails polished to blend with both; the jade ring on one slender finger a perfect note of contrast; the graceful feet, nails polished in the same rosy hue. I stared at these in fascination, almost unable to detect the slight toe movement which activated the delicate mechanism fastened to the side of the bed, able to pick up the slightest tremor of the Achilles tendon and setting all this activity in motion. Vegetable? Statue? Corpse? Hardly! It was a woman lying there, fastidious, artistic, imaginative, fiercely determined to use every means left her to live life to the full.

She had been twenty-one, I knew, just graduated from college, when she developed symptoms of myasthenia gravis. Though the disease is not as yet curable, many myasthenics have been able to control it through surgery or drugs or both, so as to lead fairly normal lives. Not so Hilary. Surgery had brought her but temporary relief. Tablets of

239

prostigmine, effective for a time, had had to be superseded by injections until now it was requiring an injection of the drug every four hours to keep even that tiny movement in her toes alive. Every two hours she was fed a multipurpose food called Complan through a nasogastric tube.

"How!" I marveled. How could she even want to live, much less face life with zest? What was there in those twenty-one years, in herself, to make possible such an incredible acceptance and courage? It was my job to find out.

The typewriter being a cumbersome method of communication, even with her clever shorthand (shortfoot?), I soon learned to "talk" with Hilary, as did her family, nurses, friends. "Beginning?" you would say, your fingers held lightly on her ankle, and if the letter she wanted was in the first half of the alphabet, you would feel a slight motion in your fingers. You would start at "a," and another motion would stop you at the correct letter. If it was in the last half, there would be no motion, and you would start with "l." It was amazing how easy conversation became.

Easy, yes, but indescribably slow. I had allowed myself just a week with Hilary. Only a week to plumb the depths of a complex personality, discover all the emotions, achievements, frustrations, likes and dislikes and a hundred other details of more than thirty years of living! But the problem wasn't as insuperable as it sounds. Much work had been done already. The pages and pages of questions I had sent Hilary had borne fruit for she had been long at work click-clonking pages and pages of answers, retyped by her helpers and all clipped together under neat headings: Early Life, Schools, Summary, Me, Nurses, Daily Routine, etc. I had been given a copy of her case history and a delightful journal of her hospital experiences called "Hotel Elizabeth." She had sent out over two hundred letters to friends enclosing another set of questions I had sent, and I found a hundred and more replies, letters and tapes waiting. There were diaries, high school and college notebooks, concert programs, newspaper clippings, magazine articles, her original poems and other writings. The dining table was soon so full of my research materials and typewriter that we had hard work finding room to eat!

The family was super-cooperative. Mona, Hilary's mother, a highly trained and dedicated headmistress of a private school with a fine flair for dramatic detail, wrote many pages of reminiscences and put much material on tapes. Hilary's father, Eric, made invaluable contributions. It was they, of course, who bore the brunt of the burden of Hilary's care with great love, unable to have more than an occasional hour to call their own. Though a volunteer always remained with her, it was Eric and Mona who had to perform the long routine late at night. Then Eric would rise again at six to give the injection of prostigmine and go back to bed to sleep till seven. Certainly it was from him that Hilary had inherited her rare sense of humor. "Hello, darling!" I heard him call that first day when he came home from work, going immediately to Hilary's room to share some humorous incident or story. From her mother came the legacy of a phenomenal mind, a meticulous command of order and detail.

Hilary's sister Wendy, also a teacher, and "Aunty Betty," Mona's younger sister, furnished many anecdotes and acted as interpreters. Later, tapes and letters came from Hilary's brother Ian, an engineer in Brunei. Friends came for interviews. Slowly the child, the student, the young teacher, the invalid, the incredibly courageous and creative battler with adversity sprang into life.

Her childhood fully justified her parents' choice of names, for "Hilary" means "happiness." She lived in a charmed world of birds, animals, flowers, games, mischief, and a younger brother and sister who willingly followed her through mud and treetops, forages on the pantry, original plays (of which she was author, producer, director and principal actor). Superior physical strength, abounding energy, insatiable curiosity—all were "open sesames" to adventure. Even the inevitable tensions roused by an indomitable will were mitigated by unusual family love and unity. Long af-

241

terward, lying motionless in a hospital bed, she strung memories of those years into words. She called the poem "My World."

> "I have a world that's mine alone,
>   A world where no one else can roam,
>   Of books I've read and plays I've seen,
>   An opera, a ballet theme;
>   Of roads I've walked and hills I've climbed,
>   Woods and fields stored in mind.
> So if at night I cannot sleep
> I do not end up counting sheep.
> Instead I think of days gone by,
> Of picnics 'neath a clear blue sky,
> The thrill of watching unawares
> A pair of boxing, mad March hares.
> I roam down Lapal Lane again,
> I find a nest, I see a wren!
>   The fields are full of ripening wheat,
>   The banks are walls with meadow-sweet,
>   And searching closer to the ground,
>   Bashful violets I have found.
>   I squelch along the bridle path,
>   Thus evoking Mother's wrath; I tear my coat, I cut my knee
>   But there's a squirrel's drey to see.
>   The landscape blurs, light fades fast,
>   I smile and fall asleep at last."

She exulted in the sheer joy of *motion*. On the athletic field at King Edward High School in Birmingham or at the beach on holiday she excelled in games, especially cricket. The yen for mischief abated but still reared its head. Teachers whom I interviewed remembered her pranks, like climbing over all the partitions in the "johns" and leaving each door locked behind her. But they remembered also her furious activity in favorite courses—botany, zoology, art, music. At thirteen she heard her first concert—Beethoven's *Emperor Concerto*—and was hooked on music of all kinds.

Museums and concert halls were as favorite locales as the gymnasium and athletic field. Her art notebooks with their accurate drawings were almost as thorough as textbooks. And on the wall of her room hung an original painting of flowers riotous with color.

"Art promising," rated one school report. "Original and courageous, though sometimes a little too free." (*Rebel*, scrawled Hilary beneath it.)

It was not surprising that she chose to specialize at the I.M. Marsh College of Physical Education in Liverpool. Here were all the subjects she loved best: gymnastics, biology, physiology, anatomy, English, music, art—and dance. Yes, she would become a teacher of athletic dancing! Even the joy of one's own creative motion could not compare with the excitement of bringing out the best in others. Only one other activity in her last year equalled its thrill—going to Garston baths to help polio children with swimming. Some could not walk, others were in huge calipers. But in the water a miracle took place. They could move freely, play with joyous abandon. It held all the joy of creation.

It was during this last year that the first signs of the disease appeared. She tired easily. A trip to Wales with a climb of Snowdon, Britain's highest mountain, became a marathon. "Better turn back," urged her roommate. *No!* She had started for the top and she would reach it. She did, crawling sometimes on hands and knees.

During her first months as physical education teacher in a school near her home, symptoms increased. She began seeing double. Speech became blurred. Her eyelids drooped. She dropped things. Sometimes it was hard to swallow. Doctors were reassuring. "Overtiredness. Delayed nervous shock, possibly"—a wise smile. She knew what they meant, for she had undergone emotional strain in breaking off with a boyfriend. Presently they used other words: "nervous hysteria." She was appalled. The kind of person without strength of will to keep from going off the deep end? *No!* It was almost a relief when the trouble was finally diagnosed as myasthenia.

There followed months of treatments, medication, a thymectomy, which brought temporary improvement. Then on December 23, 1960, she went into the hospital for what she thought might be several months of treatment. She stayed ten years.

She not only endured them, this former dynamo of energy and strength. She used them. The hospital room became a second home. Through all the years her mother and father made the ten-mile trip almost every evening to visit her. Nurses, interns, orderlies, visitors, all found the room a jolly place to congregate, the patient a willing listener and sound adviser. She promoted some of their romances. Her mind strove fiercely to atone for the gradual loss of other faculties. She wrote a pithy story of hospital experiences called *Hotel Elizabeth*, illustrated by cartoons and humorous drawings.

"Although I cannot recommend the City of Birmingham as a holiday resort," it began, "I can strongly recommend 'Hotel Elizabeth'—all modern conveniences, personal service ('Just ring if you want us'), breakfast in bed and a wonderful cuisine. . . ."

She called her room "The Ritz." Her Barnet Ventilator was "Jonathan William Barnet," known affectionately as John Willy, soon shorted to "J.W." She called the connection between them a marriage and hoped to get a divorce as soon as possible.

When after three years she became unable to hold a pencil, she communicated by forming letters with her fingers on the sheet. The family was soon expert at deciphering—but not always correct at interpretation! Once Uncle Doug, Aunt Betty's husband, was on the receiving end.

"N-o-o-n-e," he spelled aloud, then hesitated in bewilderment. "What's that? I don't get it. Noonie?"

The bed shook with Hilary's silent laughter. Then one by one the others in the room, including Uncle Doug, caught on. "No one!" There were bursts of hilarious glee. Uncle Doug never lived it down. Henceforth he was known as "Noonie" by the whole family and hospital.

244

After she was unable to write she created poems, some profound, many humorous, imparting the words by the alphabet method through a bell hitched to her toe. I was able to include many of these in the book, such as "The Monster," a potshot at her problems with her "sucker"; "Learner's Lament," an attempt to poke fun at her frightening struggles with new nurses and, a bit bawdy, a piece of doggeral called "Bottoms" which was quoted with glee from one end of the hospital to another.

When the drooping eyelids became immobile, ears became keener, memory more exact. During the first years she was able to plan, through much labor by nurses and family, trips from the hospital—a cricket test match, visits home, the weddings of nurses. When these became impossible, she was often "bridesmaid by proxy," as for the wedding of her sister Wendy to Peter, complete with bouquet and all the finery. I secured full details of this event, with pictures.

"You don't even seem to notice that she is bedridden," said her engineer brother Ian, "her personality so oozes all over the room."

Communication! It was her biggest problem next to survival. Her will to communicate was almost as strong as her will to live. As one method failed, her agile brain would devise another ... pencil ... sheet writing ... bell and alphabet ... the fingers on her ankle. All were increasingly cumbersome and slow, frustrating. And then—the miracle!

She had been in the hospital seven years when Roger Jefcoate found her. Her case was the hardest challenge Possum had ever faced. It required experts of all kinds to make the exceedingly delicate and complicated mechanisms which enabled her to control her environment. But the miracle was performed. She was able to sound a bell and a buzzer, turn a radio off and on, and, wonder of wonders, run a typewriter! Hilary learned its complicated code in two days and was soon click-clonking away like mad. When I visited her she was operating not only two typewriters, but three radio channels, a tape recorder, a talking book. Best of all she was able to go home.

"Operation Homecoming" was completed in August, 1970, and blazoned in headlines through England and across the world. "BRITAIN'S BRAVEST PATIENT GOES HOME..." It was there I found her, mistress of a small apartment built on the back of the house. District nurses came in three times a day to perform her intricate routine, and over thirty volunteer helpers, in addition to her devoted family, were in regular attendance, caring for her physical needs, transcribing her shorthand, attending to her voluminous correspondence, helping to sell thousands of Christmas cards for the Possum Users Association which buys typewriters and other accessories for patients who cannot afford them, working on a huge "Fayre" to raise funds for the same purpose, assembling articles for a copy of *Responaut* which Hilary had agreed to edit.

I interviewed them all, the nurses, the volunteers, college classmates reached by telephone, other disabled persons who came to visit. And Hilary herself? Speechless, almost motionless, still she was the center of it all. Of course there had to be intimate communications between us. I must ask questions which only she could answer. How did it feel to be a super-active person, a dancer, a physical education teacher just starting her career, a sports enthusiast, then to become completely immobile? What gave her the courage to remain creatively alive, with imagination and a wonderful sense of humor, during all these years? Suppose this last means of communication, through the miracle of Possum, failed, what then?

"It's hard to make people understand," was her reply, "that I have no fear. As long as people will still communicate with me as though I were able to answer, it will be all right. Difficult for them, of course, but I will not be any different mentally. As long as they still understand that I am *I* and continue to give me information, some means of communication can be found. Look at my little niece Joanne. She can't read the typewriter, or make toe-talk, yet there is wonderful communication between us. No, I'm not afraid of the future. And meanwhile there is *now*."

"If only Possum could give me a thirty-hour day!" she once wrote Roger.

The week passed. I returned to the Jefcoates with a mountain of material, worked over it there another week, stealing time only for some London shopping, a trip to Windsor and a fascinating visit to Coventry Cathedral. Then I came home to write—madly, for my publishers had decided that if possible the book must come out on November 3, the date of a big concert for benefit of the Possum Users Association in the Royal Albert Hall. The manuscript, warned my British editor, must be finished by the end of March. Reams of onion skin paper flew back and forth across the ocean. Hilary was a perfectionist. Every word, every fact, every mark of punctuation must be just right. Would you believe that she and her mother sent a hundred pages, typewritten, single-spaced, of suggestions and corrections? Most of them were minor, an attempt to transform my Americanisms into good British English—"our" for "or," "ise" for "ize," "round" for "around," and so forth.

Meanwhile my friend Jef, the impresario of the concert, was working equally hard, if not harder. His work had started many months before mine. With the help of the concert manager of the London Philharmonic, the date was arranged with both the hall and the orchestra. He had called the London residence of Gina Bachauer, the noted pianist, who happened to be in the city for just thirty-six hours before leaving for Greece.

"How did you know we were here?" demanded her husband, Alec Sherman, and relayed the request to his wife. She had seen disabled people at one of Jef's Vellore concerts and said immediately, "I must come back for it!" And, yes, she would play Beethoven's *Emperor Concerto*, which was Hilary's favorite. Now if they could only secure the services of Sir Adrian Boult, the noted conductor!

Jef went to see Sir Adrian, but with foreboding for his appearances were now few and carefully chosen. Not only did he agree with alacrity but he would conduct the long and exhausting Schubert G Major Symphony. Besides the concert a reception was planned for the official launching of the book in the London Oriental Club. As a final triumph Prince Philip agreed to be patron of the concert and to attend the reception.

Before departing for England on November 1, I got newspaper headlines: "AUTHOR TO MEET PRINCE." You can write any number of books and the papers take little notice, but if you're going to meet the husband of the Queen of England, that's news. Note how we democratic Americans still bend the knee to royalty!

I found the Jefcoate house in an uproar. Letters had multiplied until Jef's office bulged with 2500 of them. Telephone calls had reached the incredible number of 4000. Boxes containing several hundred books were stacked, waiting to be autographed. On the day of the concert Jef had to take the telephone receiver off the hook long enough to take a bath! Everything demanded his attention, from the confusion of local residents over a coach, to the protocol attending the arrival of Princess Irene of Greece who had flown into London and wanted to hear her friend Gina play.

"When this is over," Phyllis Jefcoate said once, "I never want to hear the words 'Possum' or 'Possum Users Association' again." But of course she didn't mean it.

All during the intervening months Hilary had planned to come to the concert, but up until a few days before it seemed impossible. The doctors refused to give their consent. But they did not know Hilary! The first words I heard on arriving at the airport were, "She's coming!" An ambulance manned by volunteers went up from London and brought her the 120 miles, with her mother and sister acting as nurses. I happened to ride up to the hall just as the ambulance arrived and with my camera followed her through the exciting sequence of preparation.

Some exciting things had been happening to Hilary since I had seen her last. An electronics expert had designed a gadget resembling a wrist watch which she could wear around her right ankle. In its padding was a very sensitive crystal which could pick up the slightest tremor from the

Achilles tendon and send an impulse along a fine flex to an electronic device, which she called a "bleeper," on the head of her bed. Now it was no longer necessary to place one's hand on her ankle in order to "talk." She was able to "bleep" when the correct letter was reached.

This same friend, Bernard, with the help of Hank, who serviced her ventilator, had constructed a mobile bed, a masterpiece, completely self-supporting. Ventilator, batteries, sucking machine—all were built in at its base. There were side flaps letting down to permit passage through an ordinary door. It even contained a cupboard for drugs, linen, and other supplies! Without this bed the trip to London would have been difficult, if not impossible. There was a tense moment when we wondered if it would go through the elevator door, but finally it did—just.

Upstairs in the luxurious red-velvet-curtained box reserved for her Hilary was dressed and made ready to receive all the friends and distinguished visitors who came to see her during the evening, among them the beautiful and gracious Duchess of Kent, patroness of the concert. The evening was almost as exciting for me, sitting in the front row next to the royal box, the first—and doubtless the last—time in my life for enjoying such dubious distinction.

"Well, the P.U.A. concert is over," I wrote in my diary on November 4. "The fluid arpeggios of Gina Bachauer and the majestic harmonies conjured by Sir Adrian Boult's baton are echoes in our memories. We have awakened from dreams of the lovely Duchess of Kent. The offering has been counted, six thousand pounds, which will buy a lot of Possum equipment. Many autographed copies of *Hilary* have been sold. The 180 persons who came in wheelchairs from all over England have returned home. And Hilary Pole, the indomitable, who traveled the hundred-plus miles and back on her bed, arriving home at 4:30 this morning, has added another link to her chain of incredible achievements. 'Fab!' (Short for 'fabulous!') clicked her eloquent toe in summing up the whole adventure."

She came to London again for a reception at the Oriental

Club, thanks to her loyal family and the volunteer ambulance crew who sacrificed more work days to make it possible. Prince Philip arrived per schedule promptly at 6:30 with his equerry. My moment of presentation was swiftly over, a simple handshake and salutation of "Sir" in lieu of the curtsy and "Your Royal Highness" I had feared might be required. He was most kind and gracious, displaying his well-known concern for the problems of the disabled as well as an unusual interest in Hilary and her biography. She wanted to look at his face and since she had limited vision if her eyelid was lifted she was able to do so. One of my most treasured pictures is of the Prince leaning over and looking up at her smiling.

Later we had another exciting experience. "Perhaps tonight," I wrote on November 10, "has been the greatest thrill of all, Hilary's 'At Home,' when many of her friends, well over a hundred, came to the Poles' home for an autographing party. The lines at the long table where I had done so much of the research seemed endless. Hilary herself was able to "autograph," having prepared typewritten slips with her name to be pasted on the fly leaves. She has already sold 300 books and will have orders for many more. She looked like a queen in her flame-colored nightdress, finger and toe-nails varnished to match perfectly, a dark blue coverlet a note of counterpoint."

One of the delightful features of these events was the presence of Hilary's brother Ian and his wife Beth, on leave between assignments in Brunei and Nigeria.

By the time I left England a week or so later I had autographed over 1200 books and Hilary herself had sold over 600. The Jefcoates' town of Amersham was near enough London to make possible several sightseeing trips, one as it happened coinciding with the twenty-fifth anniversary of the Queen's marriage. I shall always regret (more American kowtowing to royalty!) that somehow I missed seeing the Queen in person. But watching the festivities that night on the "telly" I found it hard to connect the dignified figure beside her in the crimson-lined chariot with the delightfully informal guest who had leaned over and smiled up with such charming graciousness into Hilary's face.

Much happened to my heroine after the book's publication in both England and America. Perhaps it was the result of Prince Philip's interest that in June, 1973, she was awarded the M.B.E. (Member of the Most Noble Order of the British Empire) in the Queen's Birthday Honors, for her service to the disabled.

"I was absolutely stunned," confessed Hilary when apprised of the recommendation by the Prime Minister. "Had it been possible I would have gasped"—there was a pause like the deep silence before the thunderous applause breaks at the end of the concert—then life went on.

She celebrated the awarding of the M.B.E. at home with a family party. Her medal and a letter from the Queen came just in time.

"Buckingham Palace.
I greatly regret that I am
unable to give you personally the
award which you have so well earned.
I now send it to you with my
congratulations and my best wishes
for your future happiness.
Elizabeth R.
Miss Hilary Pole, M.B.E."

"I wore the medal that evening," wrote Hilary, "though by rights my ventilator should have been sporting bow tie and tails. There were 127 guests. My room was so full of cards, telegrams and flowers there was hardly room for me. I am really thrilled with my M.B.E. It is an honour for all disabled people and all who help us. I am specially delighted as it shows that at last that mysterious body 'the general public' has started to recognise that disabled people have their part to play in society."

She continued her activities, selling nearly a thousand of the books in all, raising thousands of pounds for the work through her "Fayres," the sale of Christmas cards for which she wrote the poems, a television program which she planned and letters to innumerable companies, foundations and other sources of charity.

Then one day in June, 1975, I received a cable. HILARY DIED WEDNESDAY MORNING. SHE WAS VERY HAPPY. ERIC AND MONA. It was just as she would have wanted to go, under anesthesia for surgery on her tracheotomy with no warning of danger. Hilary—happiness. Her name described her life from beginning to end.

How? Even after all this I still do not have the whole answer. Courage, faith, indomitable will? She had all of them. She was stubborn, too, and demanding. She had to be in order to survive. I know only that lying there motionless hour after hour, day after day, year after year, she was far more alive than most of us who can breathe and swallow and see and move. Perhaps a poem she wrote tells the secret of her triumphant life far better than I was able to do. In fact, she called it "My Answer."

"I'm often asked if I am bored,
 Frustrated, lonely,
 My life abhorred.
 And so I answer,
   'I am not'—
 That now I can accept my lot,
 Remind the sadly shaking head,
 'It is my body, not my mind, in bed.'

"I'm rarely frightened or in pain,
 For this I thank my God again.
 I have many loyal friends,
 My joy in them despair transcends.
   There's music, too,
   Books to read.
 Discontentment cannot breed.

252

"Although I can no longer play
I can listen every day
To football, rugby, tennis, cricket,
Imagination has no limit.
    Add to this
    A sense of humour
Killing that 'depression' rumour.

"Now I have my Possum, too,
A miracle in all men's view.
No longer do I have to wait,
My poems and letters to dictate.
    Just flick my toe
    And type myself.
I have no time to brood on health."

Certainly if immortality is the triumph of spirit over body, something we all hope in the fullness of time to achieve, then Hilary attained it long ago.

12
AFTERTHOUGHTS

It's a fascinating business living other people's lives but not an easy one. Along with the glamor of travel, the lure of exotic scenes and far places, the bazaar treasures which transform your living room into a museum of fond reminders, the thousands of colorful slides, the new friends of many races and cultures, all happy by-products of research, have gone the ubiquitous typewriter, the tape recorder, the hundreds of little three-by-five bits of paper. And often there are no such by-products, only the nine-to-five daily grind in a library, poring over ancient letters with a magnifying glass, snatching a half hour in a cafeteria for lunch, taking materials (when permitted) back to the room at night to read and catalogue.

It's an expensive business: the travel (even by bus), the hotel rooms (even the cheapest possible), the meals (also frugal), the xeroxing and reproducing of pictures and other materials, the percentage of royalties one feels obligated to give the contemporary subjects or their families, to say nothing of the reams of paper, the typewriter ribbons, the postage.

It's a demanding and nerveracking business, requiring the

utmost patience and exacting thoroughness. What questions should you ask in interviewing your subject or other persons? Have you acquired all the material necessary about your subject? Has every quotation been properly annotated, checked and re-checked? Is your delineation of this or that trait of character of your subject accurate, or colored by your personal prejudice or desire to shape it into your own mold of thought? Can you find an intriguing title? (Don't try too hard, for your publisher is almost sure to change it!) If your subject is contemporary, have you explored his or her environment so your every detail will be accurate? If historical, have you become thoroughly immersed in the period you must relive? If belonging to another land and culture, are you sufficiently versed in all the manifold influences which have surrounded and molded the person's life—language, manners, dress, foods, processes of education, family life, travel, communication, politics, national history, religion, flora and fauna, housing and a hundred other subjects?

Then—the writing. There are many types of biography. Which one will you choose? You can merely present known facts as if standing off and looking at your subject, being completely objective, no surmising as to what took place in the thoughts of your hero or heroine, no attempt to dramatize the action. Then there is what might be called novelized biography, in which you try to get inside your character, dramatize incidents in the thought and speech and action of the subject as you think they might have happened according to all the evidence you have accumulated, never falsifying facts, but—yes, using your imagination to make them more credible and interesting to your reader. Being by instinct and practice a dramatist, could I choose any type except the latter?

Some people criticize this form of biographical writing, calling it deception, juggling with the truth. But is it? Catherine Drinker Bowen, one of the finest biographers of our time, says, "No." The reader knows we cannot actually be in the subject's mind, that behind our narrative is historical

255

source. I admit that once or twice I have introduced incidents which, while not contradicting any facts I discovered, are unlikely to have occurred and always I have been sorry for it. I would like to expunge them from the finished product. But for the most part I make no apology for the dramatization of materials and all manuscripts have been read and approved by the subjects themselves wherever possible.

"But *how* do you write? When? Where? How long at a time? Do you use a typewriter? Do you rewrite?" I am asked such questions over and over at lectures, at writers' conferences, in letters, over the telephone, at informal gatherings. If you are one of those who are curious about the mechanics and discipline of one author's writing, I invite you to come into my study.

I am sitting there now at the typewriter which I always use whether in first draft or finished product or even personal correspondence. At the moment my machine is "Old Faithful," a big standard model purchased second-hand sometime in the thirties, doing yeoman service while my new electric model, only a year old, is undergoing repairs. I am indulging in a habit which my husband decries as niggardly, writing the first draft of this book on the back side of an old discarded copy of a manuscript. Others share his amusement.

"What in the world are those pages written on both sides, completely unrelated?" queried the curator of the special collections in the library of the University of Maine where my papers are being slowly deposited including, she had urged, the first drafts of manuscripts. When I explained she smiled politely but, I fear, with certain reservations as to my mentality. But—why not? I find waste abhorrent, whether of paper or of food leftovers in this hungry world where millions could easily be fed from our garbage pails.

Through the windows at my side above the desk I look out into a sun-dappled woodland of pines, cedars, hemlocks, the earth still wearing its beggar-tatters of snow, for though it is April spring comes late in this north country. We are lucky that this fast-growing university town has not yet encroached on this beautiful woodland behind our house, unpopulated except for squirrels, an occasional rabbit, a few birds—very few since we stopped feeding them, believing hungry people more important—and the neighbors' children who like to visit our old beagle Midget, age 105 as dogs count time, who roams the area behind the garage on her chain.

Facing me as I sit at the typewriter are two bookcases and an old wooden file, bought nearly forty years ago from the estate of a beloved fellow minister, its six big drawers containing correspondence and personal records. Stored in its five small drawers at the top, plus four more card files, are all those little three-by-five cards and bits of paper, the labels bearing the names of almost all the books I have written. And in two modern steel files in my husband's study where there is more room is the more bulky residue of xeroxed papers, pamphlets, pictures and other materials acquired through my dozen lives, two full drawers on India, another on the Blackwells, still others filled with innumerable manila folders bearing such labels as Egypt, Palestine, England, Rehabilitation, American Indians, Women's Rights. I pity the poor curator who will eventually have to sort, refile and consign most of it to oblivion!

The bookcases, a tiny fraction of the dozen and more scattered through the house, are reminiscent more of the past than the present, for three of their five shelves contain much of my biblical resource library. An indication perhaps that I cherish a bit of nostalgia for that original chamber of my writing shell, and a subconscious suspicion that I may some day return to it? Another of the five shelves contains writing helps, such as *The Writer's Handbook*, *Writer's Market*, a *Word Finder*, a *World Almanac*, a dictionary and most essential of all a two-volume *Roget's Thesaurus*. A crutch for lame thinking, an insecure author's Linus blanket—call it what you will. I would hate to do without it. I even have another copy at our wilderness camp where I do much of my writing in the summer.

The fifth shelf is shifting in contents, depending on the

biographical subject, at one time filled with books about India; at another on Elizabeth Blackwell and medicine and women's rights; again with volumes on the American Indian, or rehabilitation, or on insanity and mental health. At present it is a pot-pourri of catch-alls, for the materials of my twelfth life, hopefully involving India and another doctor, are still on tapes and bulging a huge plastic bag in a corner of my study.

"When do you write?" I am constantly being asked and "In the morning" I always reply. During periods of actual writing instead of research I try to get to the typewriter at nine and keep going until twelve when it is time to start lunch. Afternoons when not assigned to church work, club meetings or other personal or community activities are devoted to necessary housecleaning, cooking, and other household chores, for in recent years I have had no hired help. (In fact, I just interrupted the last sentence to remove a load of clothes from the washer—and this one to answer the telephone for a conference about Church Women United, of which I am a local co-president.) Fortunately I have a helpful and efficient husband who in addition to his treasurer's work for church organizations assists with the cooking and dishwashing, keeps our freezer filled with garden products and our fireplace with wood.

"Why don't you write us another biblical novel or perhaps a novel about India?" my present editor recently asked me. Partly because I feel an inadequacy at this stage of life to create characters and incidents but chiefly because I have found real life more exciting and challenging than fiction. Moreover, remembering the hundreds of letters in my files from people who have been inspired by the faith and courage of Dr. Mary and Hilary and Roger Arnett, or stimulated to Christian service by the examples of Dr. Paul Brand and Granny and Dr. Ida Scudder, or stirred to a fresh appraisal of some vital social problem by the experiences of Dr. Elizabeth Blackwell or Bright Eyes or Dorothea Dix, even the possibility of a best-selling novel might not tempt me. Yet those three shelves of biblical books are there before my
258

eyes, and somewhere in my files are the beginnings of research on various subjects—Jeremiah, Hosea, Abraham, Jerusalem—as well as a few preliminary chapters on a biblical subject. Who knows? I may yet crawl back into that beloved first chamber of the shell.

Meanwhile there are those tapes and the bulging bag of materials waiting for me, with the story of a man so dedicated to the service of Christ that he has brought physical and spiritual sight to myriads of blind eyes. He will be, I hope, my twelfth biography, a fitting addition to a succession of caring disciples.

I first saw his work one day in India when I was invited to attend an "eye camp," an attempt to carry the benefits of the Eye Hospital to the thousands of villagers who needed its services but could not make the long journey to Vellore. With a team of ophthalmic surgeons, nurses and other workers I traveled seventy miles to where the camp was to be held in the compound of a rice mill warehouse. A "teller of good news" had previously gone through surrounding villages advertising that all with the *poo padera* (cataract) or other eye ailments could come to this place on this day for examinations and if need be operations. When we drove into the mill compound I stared in amazement. In the small bare rectangle were crowded at least three hundred people!

I saw the team examine patients way into the night by the light of gasoline lanterns and flashlights. Many were either totally blind or with serious eye disorders. They ranged in age from great-grandfathers to babes in arms. Late in the evening I sat with the workers on grass mats eating rice and curry from big plantain leaves, shared in the prayers that the work of the following day be blessed. The next morning I watched the surgeons operate on cataract patients in the shed under strips of clean canvas to shield the tables from the rusty and badly cracked corrugated ceiling, saw the patients, sixty or more, placed in rows on the earthen floor, a pillow of straw under each head. When night came the team was still at work. Leaving competent helpers in charge—a cook, a pharmacist and four orderlies—I drove back to

Vellore with the weary team, exhausted after twelve continuous hours of intensely skilled application at the end of their hard week's work. Later I went with them when they returned to remove stitches, make fittings for glasses; witnessed the excitement as the patients, bandages removed, found that they could see dim objects; shared the crowning moments when glasses were adjusted to pair after pair of recently sightless eyes; saw the light of joyous discovery dawn in a dozen faces. *Whereas I was blind, now I can see!*

Do you wonder that all these years I have wanted to write the story of Dr. Victor Rambo, the man responsible for thousands of such mobile eye clinics which have brought sight to hundreds of thousands of India's curable blind?

"What are some memorable moments in your writing career?" appeared recently in a questionnaire from a public school class which was much impressed by the story of Hilary. Almost as difficult to answer as another in the same questionnaire: "What book do you consider to be your greatest achievement from your own values?" How do you pick out the mountain-top experiences and from what categories? The few literary successes, the spiritual high points, the meetings with great human beings, the little personal satisfactions?

It was thrilling of course when my novel about Moses, *Prince of Egypt*, won the Westminster Award for Religious Fiction; when my alma mater gave me an honorary doctor's degree; when, just a few days ago, I learned that the University of Maine at Augusta was conferring on me a Distinguished Achievement Award for "an outstanding job" in my particular field. But equally satisfying, perhaps more so, was a recognition received in 1975 from my denomination— the New England Methodist Award for Excellence in Social Justice Actions. For this has been the purpose and goal of all my writings, to share my deep Christian concern for social justice and human betterment.

There have been many memorable moments connected with my writings. Standing on that hilltop above Nazareth where the Boy once stood and stretched his arms high and wide ... meeting Nehru, one of my heroes of non-violence and having lunch at his home ... standing with Dr. Ida on a rooftop overlooking the vast complex of healing which her indefatigable energy and faith had brought into being ... seeing Dr. Mary in her wheelchair helping others gain new strength and mobility because she herself will never walk again ... watching Dr. Paul recreate a human hand and give new life and dignity to a hopeless outcast ... sharing Hilary's delight in the presence and concern of Prince Philip ... and, perhaps most memorable of all in a personal spiritual sense, mounting above the clouds on my first flight to India and struggling to express in words an ecstasy of communion with the Infinite:

"So this is how You saw it—wrapped in white magic!
Glittering blades of mountains, sheaves of forests;
Thin ribbons, bright blue shafts of rivers, lakes, and
    seas!
No wonder that You looked—and called it good!

"Tell me, are the clouds Your playthings?
Do You laugh as You shape and mold and fling them into
    being,
Delighted as a child with his snow images,
Forever breaking them apart and making new? ...
Do You, like me, stare spellbound at Your handiwork,
I hour after hour, You eon after eon? ...

"The plane roars through the night,
The friendly sky becomes a treacherous thing,
Making our strength seem weakness, our greatness
    indescribably small.
Lightning flashes about us. Thunder roars,
Louder even than this roaring of man's making.
Is it possible that in his superb audacity
Mankind has climbed too far, invaded realms
Too vast for his control, harnessed with knowledge

261

Powers he has not with wisdom learned to tame?
No matter. It is past, the storm behind,
And for the present man has won...

"It is day again, and we mount up with wings like an
    eagle
Into the clear full sunlight,
Sunlight on silver wings, bright as a dazzling
    sword-thrust,
Sunlight enmeshed in motion, whirling, throbbing,
    blinding,
Caught and imprisoned in a shaft of rainbow fire...

"We lie on the ground, earth-bound, rain beating like
    stones upon us.
I am afraid. My spirit too is earth-bound.
But the signal is given. We roll relentlessly forward.
Up—up we rise, heavily, climbing, climbing.
Black clouds enfold us, drag us down, but we escape.
Up, always up, till suddenly
We break into the light, breathless, glorious,
Where the stars and a full moon are shining!
The storm is beneath us, its bright tongues darting
    harmlessly,
Flinging their barbs like idle, foolish chatter.
I am no longer afraid. Like the plane
Winging its way proudly, confidently, through the
    night,
My spirit too is free.

"Dear God, help me to remember.
When again I am earth-bound and the storm clouds are
    about me,
Help me to remember that once, up here, I met You
    face to face."

Since then there have been many trips across the ocean,
most of them by much swifter jets, but none has ever

brought the spiritual ecstasy of that first one. Such mountain-top experiences can seldom be repeated. Yet on every journey of discovery, whether to foreign or homeland, into past or present, there has been the consciousness of divine commission, an assurance that "this is what God wants me to do."

A dozen lives. Will there be more? I hope so. As long as God gives life and strength I hope I will still be trying to relive the experiences of creative pioneers who have helped transform human society into something more nearly approaching the Kingdom of God.